# THE DEATH
# OF AFFIRMATIVE
# ACTION?

# Sociology of Diversity series

*Series Editor:* **David G. Embrick**,
University of Connecticut, US

---

The Sociology of Diversity monograph series brings together the highest
quality sociological and interdisciplinary research specific to ethnic, racial,
gender and sexualities diversity.

## Forthcoming in the series:

*Brewing Up Race*
*On the Whiteness of Beer*
**Nathaniel Chapman** and **David Brunsma**, October 2020

*Racial Diversity in Contemporary France*
*Rethinking the French Model*
**Marie Neiges Léonard**, December 2020

*Craft Food Diversity*
**Kaitland Byrd**, June 2021

*Disproportionate Minority Contact*
**Paul Ketchum** and **B. Mitchell Peck**, September 2021

## Find out more at
bristoluniversitypress.co.uk

# THE DEATH OF AFFIRMATIVE ACTION?

## Racialized Framing and the Fight Against Racial Preference in College Admissions

J. Scott Carter and Cameron D. Lippard

BRISTOL
UNIVERSITY
PRESS

First published in Great Britain in 2021 by

Bristol University Press
University of Bristol
1-9 Old Park Hill
Bristol
BS2 8BB
UK
t: +44 (0)117 954 5940
e: bup-info@bristol.ac.uk

Details of international sales and distribution partners are available at bristoluniversitypress.co.uk

© Bristol University Press 2021

British Library Cataloguing in Publication Data
A catalogue record for this book is available from the British Library

ISBN 978-1-5292-0112-3 paperback
ISBN 978-1-5292-0111-6 hardcover
ISBN 978-1-5292-0114-7 ePub
ISBN 978-1-5292-0113-0 ePdf

The right of J. Scott Carter and Cameron D. Lippard to be identified as authors of this work
has been asserted by them in accordance with the Copyright, Designs and Patents Act 1988

Cover design: blu inc, Bristol
Front cover image: Getty

# Contents

List of Figures and Tables     vii
Series Editor Preface     ix

1    Introduction     1

2    Affirmative Action and Higher Education     19

3    Race, the Affirmative Action Debate, Education,     41
and Past Court Cases

4    Who is Fighting the Fight?     67

5    Case Study 1: The *Gratz/Grutter* Supreme Court Cases     115
against the University of Michigan

6    Case Study 2: The *Fisher* Supreme Court Cases against     155
the University of Texas at Austin

7    Conclusions     189

References     203
Index     215

# List of Figures and Tables

## Figures

| | | |
|---|---|---|
| 2.1 | Percentage support for affirmative action-type intervention | 35 |
| 2.2 | Percentage support for aid and affirmative action | 36 |
| 2.3 | Percentage support for racial equality | 37 |
| 5.1 | Identified themes in supporter briefs for *Grutter* and *Gratz* | 127 |
| 5.2 | Venn diagram of color-blind themes among briefs opposing affirmative action | 137 |
| 5.3 | Venn diagram of threat frames identified in supporter briefs | 142 |
| 5.4 | Venn diagram of threat frames in opponent briefs | 151 |
| 5.5 | Thematic connections between color-blind rhetoric and group threats among opponent briefs for *Grutter* and *Gratz* | 152 |
| 6.1 | Venn diagram of color-blind themes in support briefs for the *Fisher* cases | 167 |
| 6.2 | Venn diagram of color-blind themes in opponent briefs for the *Fisher* cases | 173 |
| 6.3 | Venn diagram of threat frames in support briefs for the *Fisher* cases | 177 |
| 6.4 | Venn diagram of threat frames in opponent briefs in the *Fisher* cases | 179 |
| 6.5 | Thematic connections between color-blind rhetoric and group threats among opponent briefs for the *Fisher* cases | 185 |

## Tables

| | | |
|---|---|---|
| 4.1 | Amicus briefs of advocacy groups in support of affirmative action submitted to the Supreme Court cases | 81 |
| 4.2 | Amicus briefs of "various entities" in support of affirmative action submitted to the Supreme Court cases | 86 |

| 4.3 | Advocacy groups (amicus briefs) in opposition to affirmative action submitted to the Supreme Court cases | 99 |
| 4.4 | "Various entities" (amicus briefs) in opposition to affirmative action submitted to the Supreme Court cases | 102 |
| 5.1 | Color-blind themes and concepts for amicus briefs submitted by supporters for *Grutter v Bollinger et al* (02-241) and *Gratz v Bollinger et al* (02-516) | 125 |
| 5.2 | Color-blind themes and concepts for amicus briefs submitted by opponents for *Grutter v Bollinger et al* (02-241) and *Gratz v Bollinger et al* (02-516) | 128 |
| 5.3 | Group threat themes and concepts for amicus briefs among supporters for *Grutter v Bollinger et al* (02-241) and *Gratz v Bollinger et al* (02-516) | 139 |
| 5.4 | Group threat themes and concepts for amicus briefs among opponents for *Grutter v Bollinger et al* (02-241) and *Gratz v Bollinger et al* (02-516) | 143 |
| 6.1 | Color-blind themes and concepts for amicus briefs submitted by supporters for *Fisher v University of Texas at Austin* | 162 |
| 6.2 | Color-blind themes and concepts for amicus briefs submitted by opponents for *Fisher v University of Texas at Austin* | 168 |
| 6.3 | Threat themes and concepts for support briefs | 176 |
| 6.4 | Veiled threat themes and concepts for opponent briefs | 178 |

# Series Editor Preface

In the dawn of 21st-century US society we are fixated, many would claim, with the words "diversity" and "inclusion." These ubiquitous terms saturate many of our institutions—business, military, legal, government, media, all levels of education, etc—and our everyday lives. We are told, and led to believe, that diversity and inclusion are foundational, necessary, and the hallmarks of equity and equality. When not dangled in front of us across a variety of forums, we witness these words become center stage as they are used in reaction to racial, gender, or other fissures of inequality that hold our attention in a world we believe to be beyond such social ills. For instance, universities and colleges are quick to proclaim their mission and obligation to diversity and inclusion, particularly when confronted with issues of inequality on their campuses. They claim they are advocates for diversity and will not tolerate any individuals whose actions promote divisiveness, hate, or intolerance. Yet, for all its feel-good aura or "happy talk,"[1] diversity and inclusion are mostly empty rhetoric. Diversity ideology (see Embrick, 2011; Mayorga-Gallo, 2019) promotes ambiguity; it allows for individuals and institutions to proclaim a progressive agenda centered on equity and equality, while in reality promoting the status quo.

The aim of the *Sociology of Diversity* series is to interrogate the contradictions of diversity and inclusion as they are currently manifested in our social institutions and everyday lives. That is, it is my hope that research in this series will allow for peeks into everyday racism, sexism, classism, ableism, or other persistent inequalities that plague our society, yet are often swept under the rug by diversity and/or diversity ideology. By peeking behind closed doors, as the famous social scientist W.I. Thomas once described sociology, or peeking behind the curtain, to use a metaphor from the classic story of *The Wizard of Oz*, we can get a better sense of the world around us. In doing so, we can better understand how, despite our best efforts, nothing really changes—or worse, existing inequalities actually seem to get worse.

Professors J. Scott Carter and Cameron Lippard's book, *The Death of Affirmative Action? Racialized Framing and the Fight Against Racial Preference in College Admissions*, is the first published book in the *Sociology of Diversity* series. In this book, the authors fully flesh out and analyze debates, legal precedents, and policies that led to what they (and other scholars) claim to be the death of affirmative action. The movement against affirmative action does not exist in a vacuum; counter movements by students, educators, and civil rights advocates create a complex web of intersecting and opposing arguments that have the outside appearance of being a complicated issue, and one that has time and time again—certainly since the Reagan era—been difficult for all parties involved. The basic premise is often aligned with the idea that in a post-racial society (read: in an era remarkably different from slavery), we no longer need affirmative action, and that this policy may be anti-white, anti-meritocratic, and/or constitute reverse racism. However, this white logic only works if one truly believes we are a post-racial society. The death of affirmative action does not do much more than help maintain the current racialized social system that is the US. And here is where this book shines. Carter and Lippard do the extremely detailed work in examining the public debates that have (and continue to) surround affirmative action cases, arguing that diversity ideology (or the language of diversity) has weakened the case for affirmative action—in a way it has become a rallying call for conservatives to further maintain the status quo, a call back to the so-called days of glory when we actually believed in the US Constitution and American ideals of meritocracy and democracy. In this vein, and as we have seen in during the whitelash in the Reagan era and are currently witnessing during the Trumpism years, affirmative action is argued to be unAmerican, anti-white, and racist, in and of itself.

**Note**

[1] This term is coined by Joyce M. Bell and Douglas Hartmann in their 2007 *American Sociological Review* article and refers to the many contradictions in the term "diversity"—one that evokes feelings of happiness, yet is ambiguous at best.

David G. Embrick<br>University of Connecticut

# Introduction

On June 29, 2016, a young white woman named Abigail Noel Fisher lost her long-fought case against the University of Texas at Austin (*Fisher v University of Texas at Austin*, 539 US 306):

> It [the 2016 *Fisher* Supreme Court Case ruling] was really disappointing, honestly, but it's a long battle and if this case doesn't end affirmative action, then another case will. (Abigail Fisher, quoted in Edwards, 2016)

In the case and in the media surrounding it, she claimed the university's race-conscious undergraduate admissions policy had discriminated against her and others based on race. The university disagreed and viewed the policy as necessary to ensure a diverse campus. The Supreme Court sided with the university. The 4–3 ruling in support of the university's use of affirmative action in admissions came after almost eight years of challenges by Fisher and her legal representatives. The case was, in fact, argued in front of the Supreme Court not just once, but twice. Before ultimately ruling in favor of the university in 2016 (*Fisher II*), the Court remanded the case back to a lower court in 2013 (*Fisher I*).

The *Fisher* case became a lightning rod for debates in the US surrounding affirmative action, higher education, and race relations. With a conservative-leaning Supreme Court and lagging support among whites, many political pundits predicted that the end of affirmative action in higher education had arrived. However, the sudden death of Justice Antonin Scalia, who came out publicly against affirmative action, and the recusal of Justice Elena Kagan, who served as US Solicitor General and authored an amicus brief[1] in support of affirmative action in the *Fisher* case when it was pending in the US Court of Appeals, created uncertainty leading up to the 2016 ruling. Nonetheless, a shorthanded court that continued to lean to the Right surprised many and upheld the controversial policy. Affirmative action, as implemented in higher education, would receive a stay of execution at least until the next high-profile case came along:

> Sooner or later, affirmative action will die a natural death. Its achievements have been stupendous, but if we look at the premises that underlie it, we find assumptions and priorities that look increasingly shopworn. (R. Roosevelt Thomas, Jr, 1990)

Although Fisher held center stage in the media and legal coverage of the case, she did not pursue the case independently, and, in fact, was barely mentioned in connection to the case itself during the hearings. Rather, the claim arose primarily through the efforts of an advocacy group, the Project on Fair Representation (POFR). The POFR is a conservative legal defense foundation created by Edward Blum to challenge the use of racial preference in government decisions, including the use of affirmative action in higher education. This challenge was not Blum's first foray into the affirmative action legal milieu; Blum has initiated dozens of lawsuits challenging affirmative action and other race-based cases in recent years. For instance, Blum was instrumental in the 2013 Supreme Court case (*Shelby County v Holder*, 570 US 2) that successfully contested a provision of the Voting Rights Act of 1965. Blum also founded Students for Fair Admissions (SFFA), an offshoot of the POFR, which has been instrumental in recruiting well-credentialed students who feel they have been discriminated against based on their race, for the very purpose of filing lawsuits. Indeed, the SFFA is leading the charge in the current lawsuit against the use of affirmative action by Harvard University, a case many experts predict will eventually make its way to the Supreme Court in the next few years. Roger Clegg from the advocay group Center for Equal Opportunity stated:

> The court's decision [on the 2016 *Fisher* Supreme Court Case ruling] leaves plenty of room for future challenges to racial preference policies at other schools… The struggle goes on. (as quoted in Liptak, 2016)

While the fight in the *Fisher* case was quite heated, it was not without precedent. In the past the Supreme Court has upheld decisions supporting affirmative action in college admissions policies such that a university can use affirmative action so long as it is *narrowly tailored* to meet challenges faced by universities to recruit racial diversity because it remains a *compelling interest* of the state. Thus, affirmative action in admissions is a constitutionally acceptable mechanism that universities can use to ensure diversity in higher education. To many, the *Fisher II* decision was a win for affirmative action advocates. *The New York Times* proclaimed that the decision handed supporters of affirmative action a major victory (Liptak, 2016). It also stated that supporters considered this ruling a "landmark" decision in favor of racial equality. While suffering a loss in this instance, however, it is without doubt that the POFR and other advocacy groups have had and will continue to play a significant role in the viability (or lack thereof) of affirmative action as a mechanism to remedy inequality in the future.

Rather than simply one legal case exploring the boundaries of civil rights initiatives, we argue that the *Fisher* case represents a cultural marker of sorts, one that reveals broader patterns in contemporary US politics of race relations in which conservative elites and advocacy groups actively contest the existence of racial inequality and methods for responding to such perceived inequalities. At the most basic level, this book speaks to this marker. Lee Cokorinos, author of *The Assault on Diversity* (2003), posed that a color-blind and neoliberal conservative movement to eliminate civil rights or social justice initiatives began in the 1970s, and appears to be only gaining momentum as we move into the 21st century. This movement has not risen unchallenged. Counter movements led by students, educators, universities, and other civil rights supporters have vigorously fought against these pursuits. Accordingly, as this battle plays out in the US (particularly in legal, media, educational, and political institutions) today and in the future, Americans who support and oppose affirmative action and other civil rights policies will seek to define both the status of race and racial inequality in the nation and the role and breadth of government intervention into such matters.

Throughout this book, we focus on such oppositional dynamics as an opportunity to make sense of race relations in contemporary US society. Specifically, we offer a case study of how debates over affirmative action play out at the level of the Supreme Court among supporters and opponents who pour millions of hours and dollars into their causes to either build up the policy or tear it down. To this end, we look at legal documents produced by supporters and opponents in reaction to the four latest Supreme Court cases on affirmative action in higher education: *Gratz v Bollinger* (539 US 244, 2003), *Grutter v Bollinger* (539 US 306, 2003), and *Fisher v University of Texas at Austin I* (539 US 306, 2013) and *II* (579 US__, 2016). We contend that an examination of public debates surrounding these cases will not only shine a light on the status of affirmative action in the coming years, but also give us insights into the state of race and race relations in the US today.

Accordingly, the purpose of this book is quite simple. First, we take a close look at who participates in such an important debate at such a high level that may lead to the end of affirmative action in higher education. That is, we compare supporters and opponents of affirmative action who have the financial resources to lobby the Supreme Court through legal briefs (discussed further below). Who are these influential people and groups who attempt to act as social authorities and sway court decisions and ultimately public opinion? Are they elite individuals, common citizens with interests, civic groups, or organized advocacy groups? Since advocacy groups (special interest groups, think tanks, and legal foundations) are an emerging force in politics and the fight on civil rights issues (Moore, 2018), we further ask if these groups play a more significant role among supporters or opponents. Maybe these groups will be equally represented among supporters and opponents, or perhaps they will not. With these questions in mind, we move past the analysis and explore what these dynamics mean for the state of affirmative action in the US today and in the future.

Second, we turn to the messages created by supporters and opponents. While portraying themselves as social authorities, how do the authors of these legal documents make sense of race, racism, and persistent institutional discrimination? How do they handle continuing and deleterious racial disparities found in the US today, and what do they see as the role of the government in remedying these issues that have such insidious racial overtones? How do they frame racial minorities and their arguments for the Supreme Court? Furthermore, do they use multiple discursive frames to make their cases to the Court? If so, how do these frames work together to strengthen their arguments for and against the policy?

Throughout this book, we return to these questions and more as we synthesize and consider arguments in support and opposition to the most prominent Supreme Court cases on affirmative action in the 21st century. It is the goal of the book not to treat these cases as isolated events; instead, we hope to place them and the arguments accompanying them into a socio-historical context that will provide readers with a more thorough and, hopefully, satisfying understanding of why they are created. Anti-affirmative action arguments, while championed by some and dismissed and rebuked by others, have the type of message and weight behind them that can ultimately lead to the death of affirmative action in today's America.

# External forces, color-blind racism, and the framing of social life

Throughout this book, we draw on existing social scientific theory and research concerning the development and activation of racial attitudes in the US. Herbert Blumer (1958) noted long ago that much of what people think of as very personal attitudes and beliefs are actually impersonal and located outside of the individual. That is to say, people develop attitudes and beliefs about subjects (race or otherwise) from their exposure to ideas, feelings, and truths promoted by outside entities in society, particularly those entities that have access to valued resources that allow them to get their message to the masses. Attitudes and beliefs are thus not reflective of some intra-personal pathology or deficiency or even personal experience for that matter; instead, they are social constructs that are constantly being created and recreated outside of themselves. Lawrence Bobo and Mia Tuan (2006) demonstrated that social authorities often play an influential role in how people define and react to other groups and toward policies related to race.

Accordingly, we take on the call made by Blumer and Bobo and Tuan that to truly understand intra-personal racial attitudes and views toward racial policies, we must focus on how prominent social authorities (that is, elites, leaders, advocacy groups, media, etc) contribute to the production and reproduction of meanings and narratives directed at an out-group. This assertion stands at the heart of this book as we take seriously the idea that those with access to resources (eg, economic, political, and social) have the ability set the "lines of discussion" (Blumer, 1958) around an issue (racial or otherwise) for an audience. We look particularly at this endeavor within a broader affirmative action debate occurring in society and at the level of the Supreme Court. For various reasons that we will discuss in more detail throughout this book, it is not surprising that the next big fight over civil rights will occur in the courtroom rather than in the streets. It is also not surprising that the conflict will revolve around affirmative action, a policy that is highly racialized and as contested as any policy implemented by the government.

As prominent sociologist Erving Goffman (1974) noted in an examination of the social organization of ideas, beliefs, knowledge, and truths, one manner for examining the construction of "other" groups and policies by social authorities involves ascertaining how these prominent groups "frame" or "define" out-group members or issues. Building on this observation, social movement scholars (see, for example, Snow and Benford, 1988; Entman, 1997; Richardson and Lancendorfer, 2004) have demonstrated a multitude of ways individuals and groups—both formally and informally—define issues for each other, for the public, and to achieve specific goals. Further, researchers have noted that frames that work and that have the greatest impact generally resonate with a given population emotionally (Schrock et al, 2004) and culturally (Snow and Benford, 1988).

Robert Entman, Jörg Matthes, and Lynn Pellicano (2009, p 177) defined a discursive frame for what it does: it "repeatedly invokes the same object and traits, using identical or synonymous words and symbols in a series of similar communications that are concentrated in time." In more extensive rhetorical strategies, framing distinguishes itself from persuasive communication by being repeated over time through words and symbols, maintaining cultural resonance, and reminding the audience of information presented to them in the past. James Druckman (2001) described two basic types of frames: frames of communication (also termed media frames) and frames of thought. Frames of communication refer primarily to how individuals or advocacy groups with access to the media portray social issues publicly, while frames of thought refer to the ways individuals judge various social issues. Frames of communication produced by social authorities have been shown to significantly affect frames of thought, which are ways in which individuals make sense of the social world around them. This book focuses mainly on frames of communication.

Recent work demonstrates that the framing efforts of social authorities play a powerful role in people's understanding of race, racism, and racial inequality (Feagin, 2010a; Carter and Lippard, 2015; Embrick and Henricks, 2015; Sumerau and Grollman, 2018; Carter et al, 2019). David Embrick and Kasey Henricks (2015, pp 166–7) posed that frame analysis can be a useful mechanism to explore how "micro-level understandings of social action can converge with macro-level interpretations of structure"—especially for race. Specifically, such research shows how social authorities define racial minorities in specific—often negative— ways to facilitate ongoing patterns of racism and white supremacy in the US today. This scholarship, as well as countless others in the race-related literature, demonstrates that whites often use individualistic and non-racial frames to explain the world around them while ignoring or minimizing structural determinants of disadvantage faced by non-whites (Doane, 2006). Indeed, researchers consistently show this color-blind ideology in discourse ranging from humor (Pérez, 2017) to political speeches (Bonilla-Silva and Dietrich, 2011) to defining what is racism (Doane, 2006) to commentary on Hurricane Katrina (Shelton and Coleman, 2009). Ashley Doane (2017) argues that while this research has done much to advance scholarship, it primarily focuses on "frames of thought" rather than the ways institutional practices produce and reproduce inequality and ideology.

A demonstration of the importance of this type of work comes from sociologist Eduardo Bonilla-Silva (2018), whose work looks at how individuals use subtle, non-explicitly-racial, and color-blind frames in their everyday activities. Based on interviews, Bonilla-Silva identified four discursive frames commonly used in US discussions today to oppose and devalue progressive racial policies and attempts to lessen contemporary racial disparities. These frames include abstract liberalism, cultural racism, naturalization, and minimization of racism (further defined in Chapters 5 and 6). He argued that these frames ultimately enable whites (and some non-whites) to minimize the realities of racism and racial discrimination despite an abundance of research demonstrating their persistence. Such tactics, as also noted by Doane (2017), create a new racism that is much more subtle and harder to diagnose and challenge than more traditional forms of racism that directly espouse beliefs in biological inferiority and persistent discrimination. Jason Sumerau and Eric Grollman (2018) further posed that such implicit frames justifying existing racial disparities also find a voice among other minority communities and their persistent issues of discrimination, thus, expanding across various social identities of race, class, gender, and sexualities.

Considering the widespread use of color-blind narratives and the deceptive impact they have on views toward racial issues, recent scholarship points to the importance of ascertaining the communication tactics and framing endeavors of social authorities, both conservative and progressive. Put simply, since both racists and non-racists can ultimately reproduce systems of social inequality that benefit whites at the expense of non-whites, it is essential to interrogate any usage of racialized frames regardless of who or what group is delivering them. This is because of efforts to frame things in ways that "obscure oppression" and persistent inequality and discrimination can lead people to view a system of racial discrimination as neutral or even benign (Sumerau and Grollman, 2018, p 322). Such minimization tactics, even if they are portrayed amicably ("lite racism") by those who seem racially progressive, act to produce and reproduce inequality experienced by marginalized individuals. Accordingly, we draw on these ideas throughout this book to examine how frames produced by social authorities—even those seemingly in support of the policy—can shape views on race and racism and the contours of debate on race-related issues such as affirmative action in higher education.

In so doing, we draw on past research that has examined frames of communication related to affirmative action debates since the 1980s (see, for example, Entman, 1997; Clawson et al, 2003; Richardson and Lancendorfer, 2004). These studies show that media of varied types typically describe affirmative action in terms of injustice or unfairness. However, in this case, the policy is framed as potentially unjust and unfair to *whites*, often painting them as the victim of unnecessary government overreach and cultural wars against innocent whites due to things that happened in the past. Such frames resonate with whites as they raise concerns that affirmative action will grant preferential treatment to other less deserving racial groups while they, who are more deserving, are left to suffer. Jennifer Pierce (2012), for example, argued that these injustice frames paint whites as innocent in historical and current patterns of racial disparity in the US, and even as current victims of policies seeking to correct such discrepancies (reverse discrimination). Although this has been the most common framing of affirmative action, the policy has also been framed in other ways, each of which calls for the end of the policy. Affirmative action has been framed, by some, as a policy harmful to minorities because it perpetuates stereotypes and exposes unprepared minorities to rigorous universities where they may fail (Wise, 2005; Sander and Taylor Jr, 2012). This paternalistic perspective allows the authors to characterize themselves in a positive and even benevolent light while avoiding negative labels such as "racist." From this perspective, a call to end such prominent civil rights policies is simply an attempt to protect minorities from themselves while also promoting justice and fairness.

While color-blind framing tactics are common among opponents of racial-related policies, there is evidence that threat plays an influential role in debates about race in general and race-related policies in particular. Scholars maintain that threat frames work because they operate at the emotional level with an audience. Concerning a racialized policy such as affirmative action, whites, in particular, are affected because they are afraid of losing the privilege and resources they feel are due to them in a white-dominated society. Indeed, many whites often view any policy designed to shift the balance of resources and opportunities as a threat (Bobo and Tuan, 2006). Fear of loss has been associated with negative attitudes toward affirmative action (see, for example, Bobo, 1998, 2000; Renfro et al, 2006; Sweeney and González, 2008; González and Sweeney, 2010), busing to ensure racial integration in schools (Bobo, 1983), residential integration (Schuman and Bobo, 1988; Bobo and Zubrinsky, 1996; Zubrinsky and Bobo, 1996), black activism (Bobo, 1988), and opposition to treaty rights for Native Americans (Bobo and Tuan, 2006). Research has also shown social authorities often use threat frames in arguments against affirmative action in media outlets (Entman, 1997) and legal documents (Carter et al, 2019). Entman (1997, p 40) found the most prominent media frame to be one of competition, where affirmative action is consistently described as a "zero-sum conflict of interest between whites and blacks in which only one group could win, and one must lose."

Tapping into fear by using threat frames is a common technique when framing other prominent issues in recent US political and legal history as well. Threat and fear were used in the framing of the US and Iraq War (Luther and Miller, 2005), immigration reform (Brader et al, 2008; Carter and Lippard, 2015), and terrorism (Norris et al 2003). As such, it is not surprising that social authorities often utilize notions of threat—and fear tied to them—in their arguments. Threat was used to bring emotion into the conversation and to create and maintain animosity between groups that would experience a given social policy in different ways, ultimately allowing one group to either keep or gain an advantage in the political contestation.

Concerning this project, among opponents of affirmative action in particular, we fully expect frames of threat to be prevalent and play a significant role in the arguments. However, we pose that arguments will be more complicated than simply wrangling up fear to produce an outcome. We expect authors will use a nuanced multi-framing technique where they embed threat frames within more general abstract liberalism arguments that attempt to minimize race and racism. To this end, threat frames will be used to "activate race" within broader arguments that attempt to explain why race no longer matters and why the policy is no longer needed or harmful for society. We label this multi-framing tactic *Racialized Framing*, a process where dual frames are used to both *minimize* race through color-blind rhetoric while also *activating* race using threatening arguments in the same abstract liberal argument. Drawing on the work of Blumer (1958), we see activating race as a type of framing technique wherein social authorities—and especially whites—utilize discourse that will produce racial animosity or prejudice toward an out-group using emotion-laden language. However, in a so-called post-race world where overt racism is often rebuked and punished, the authors of these briefs will attempt to conjoin threat frames with more benign and race-neutral color-blind frames to make their arguments more palatable and subtle to the general audience.

In so doing, our work draws from and extends long-standing efforts within Symbolic Interactionist and Critical Race Studies. In the former case, Blumer (1958) long ago started a wave of Interactionist work focused on the ways race and racial relations depend on social identification. He argued that racial prejudice is fundamentally about group identification and how groups come to define themselves relative to out-group members over time. A long history of unequal relations spanning slavery and Jim Crow (even today) has produced certain feelings of superiority and control among the dominant group not found in minority groups. In the latter case, Critical Race scholars have outlined the ways people's beliefs and values related to white supremacy and racial discrimination also find a voice—intentionally or otherwise—in historical and contemporary unequal race relations (see Omi and Winant, 2015). In both cases, such scholarship demonstrates how ongoing patterns of interaction, interpretation, and reflection facilitate the development, maintenance, and adjustment of racial meanings over time. Accordingly, the positional arrangement of different groups impacts the way they define (or frame) the other over time and provides the foundation for ongoing racial relations and reactions to efforts to improve such patterns.

As a result of these dynamics, people develop expectations for how other groups experience social life and how they are supposed to experience society themselves (Blumer, 1958; Ray, 2017). In such cases, propositions to change these dynamics in small or more significant ways—such as affirmative action policies—among minorities or out-group members can trigger a sense of threat to the way people believe the system was supposed to operate and the resources that groups see as valuable. At the same time, social authorities can utilize emotional appeals of threat and fear to encourage people to see policy interventions in this manner (as a zero-sum competition), and in so doing, mobilize support for their efforts to oppose any given policy concerning a specific social group. As Blumer (1958) noted long ago, central to these efforts is the ability of social authorities to define some groups as threatening to other groups in ways that facilitate adverse reactions to such perceived threat.

Throughout this book, we outline the ways these processes occur in affirmative action debates at the level of the Supreme Court by showing how social authorities active in these debates utilize color-blind and threatening rhetoric to produce the terms of the discussion. In so doing, we demonstrate how such efforts activate racial anxieties and fears among whites while at the same time doing so in a color-blind, seemingly neutral and benign, manner. As such, our work here blends Symbolic Interactionist and Critical Race Studies to demonstrate how color-blind strategies (racial deactivation) combine with group differentiation processes (race activation) in the case of affirmative action and broader race-related policy debates in contemporary US society.

## The study

It is essential to note that affirmative action as an ameliorative policy has and continues to occupy a complicated position in the annals of the US.

It is not an overstatement to say that the relationship between most whites (and some non-whites) and affirmative action is highly strained, which will most likely result in the death of this policy in the not so distant future. However, the relationship between whites and affirmative action has never been simple, and one characterized by overarching support. This will be made clearer as we look at public opinion over time in Chapter 2.

Speaking to this, we utilize the case of affirmative action for our analysis for a few reasons. One, affirmative action presently inspires much heated debate, legal maneuvering, and passionate reactions in the US like no other policy. The policy has indeed become a lightning rod for hostility, particularly among whites. Two, affirmative action is also highly aligned with the Civil Rights Movement and other ameliorative racial policies where race and racial inequality are automatically part of the debate. Finally, affirmative action also offers a case study where a race-related topic or policy is heavily influenced and impacted by the arrangement of groups occupying different social locations within a racialized system. That is to say, when implemented, affirmative action is a policy that redistributes resources valued by all groups, including the dominant group. And the group that currently stakes a claim to a higher proportion of the valued resources in question will see the loss of resources and react accordingly.

Throughout this book, we thus use in-depth analyses of 21st-century affirmative action legal battles as case studies in racialized political tactics in the post-race era. We focus on two fundamental elements. First, we look at who supports and opposes affirmative action at the level of the Supreme Court. Second, we explore what arguments these entities are making and assess the ways they may activate race to influence political activity, even when utilizing color-blind rhetoric to minimize race and also the need for the policy. To this end, we examine contemporary arguments for and against affirmative action in higher education. We use higher education because it is the site of many high-profile debates about racial representation and inequality historically and at present, and because access to this institution is often framed as a pathway to greater social mobility. As such, we examine the narratives created and mobilized by social authorities surrounding the four most prominent Supreme Court cases in the 21st century related to affirmative action in higher education. Following research by others examining political discourse among social authorities (Rohlinger, 2015), we use these cases as a snapshot of the ways racial relations play out in response to specific race-related policy debates.

For this analysis, we focus on the following four Supreme Court cases dealing with affirmative action in higher education admissions: *Gratz v Bollinger*, *Grutter v Bollinger*, and two iterations of *Fisher v University of Texas at Austin* (*Fisher I* and *Fisher II*). Since each of these cases set precedents and standards for affirmative action in higher education and received substantial media attention, we utilize them to analyze and compare the ways race, affirmative action, and framing play out in a concrete context where a debate over affirmative action is occurring. For this reason, we looked at archival data to answer the following questions: (1) who is participating in the debate for and against affirmative action and (2) what they are saying.

In terms of who is participating in the debate, we look at their characteristics. Are they individuals, civic groups, or organized advocacy groups? We know that advocacy groups (special interest groups and think tanks) are an emerging force in the fight on civil rights issues in general and affirmative action in particular (Moore, 2018). Indeed, these groups were instrumental in bringing forth the *Gratz/Grutter* and *Fisher* cases to the Supreme Court as well as other prominent cases dealing with affirmative action and other racial policies. Do advocacy groups play a bigger role for supporters or opponents, or are they equally represented in these opposing factions? Regardless of the answer to this question, what does the answer mean for the state of affirmative action in the US today? Scholars have tracked the growth of advocacy groups over the past century and argued that conservative advocacy groups have outpaced their more liberal counterparts since the 1980s. Accordingly, we can assess whether this plays out in a contemporary debate over affirmative action found in the Supreme Court. In looking at what they are saying, we also look at how they are making their arguments. Are these social authorities, whether they support or oppose the policy, using multi-framing techniques to make their arguments stronger for the Court and for the public? If so, we attempt to shine a light on these techniques.

While we draw on data collected from personal websites to understand the types of groups and organizations participating in the debate, the primary data source we use throughout the book is archived legal documents submitted to the Supreme Court related to the four cases. We collected and analyzed amicus curiae briefs (amicus briefs, hereafter) filed by supporters and opponents of affirmative action in each Court case.[2]

The most apparent manifest function of amicus briefs is simple: to provide new and useful information on a case to the justices. In this vein, as "friends of the court," amicus briefs serve as expert testimony on issues the justices may not know much about within the current case presented. The inclusion of briefs in the legal process is supposed to keep the Court informed or updated on current scientific standings. As such, they can be considered friends of the Court because they provide much-needed information that allows judges or justices to make informed decisions. However, these briefs, arguing against or for individual standings, are often socially and politically motivated. Tying arguments to politics changes the general purpose of briefs and makes funding for lobbying efforts much more critical. Thus, while attempting to inform the justices, a latent function of these briefs is to lobby the Court into handing down a particular decision in a given case that conforms to a specific ideology or stance. Although many commentators question the impact of amicus briefs, research shows that these efforts can have a direct effect on Court decisions that have significant social consequences.

Amicus briefs also serve other latent functions that are not readily considered. One of these is their ability to influence and find a voice in the media. Because the media generally plays a dominant role in framing any social issue (Caldeira and Wright, 1990), the content produced by brief authors can make its way into media outlets and impact political debates and public perception. Historically, the briefs in high-profile cases have been used to garner mass attention through the media. The Supreme Court has been quite wary of briefs and how their authors use the Court to promote arguments over time. Justice Felix Frankfurter, in 1949, stated that, "I do not like to have the Court exploited as a soapbox or as advertising medium, or as the target, not of arguments but of mere assertion that this or that group has this or that interest in a question to be decided" (as cited in Caldeira and Wright, 1990, p 784). The justices frowned on the use of amicus briefs in this manner, the primary reason the Court limited the submission of briefs for many years. Another latent function of amicus briefs is quite simple: to demonstrate to the justices the power of a position by displaying what the public wants or will tolerate at a given time in the evolution of Constitutional Law. One indicator of importance is in the overall number of briefs submitted by various entities in either support or opposition to a case. We feel that total numbers will be telling in these cases as well.

Throughout this book, we share insights drawn from this data and discuss how they relate to broader debates about the state of race and race relations in America today. In so doing, we utilized systematic analysis of the ways supporters and opponents frame the discussion around affirmative action in higher education. Put simply, each amicus brief is treated as an individual unit for analyses, and we created a count of how many of these representations made a given argument about affirmative action utilizing a specific frame. We then created counts of the volume of particular frames within and between each observation. We use this quantitative data to provide context and outline the most and least common arguments made by social authorities in these cases.

With this context in place, we then examined the qualitative themes and sub-themes throughout the data. To do this, we drew on conventional approaches in qualitative social sciences to explore what people said about this or that aspect of affirmative action; as Bonilla-Silva (2018) puts it, "in situ" or situated within a concrete record of social life (see also Charmaz, 2006). To accomplish this, we openly approached the representations, and went through each one multiple times, establishing themes and patterns within the discussions. This analysis continued over various rounds in an iterative process to induce what the most common elements of the representations were and to pull out illustrative examples of such patterns for use in the book. In so doing, we captured a snapshot of the ways authors constructed and expressed specific frames or definitions of what is happening in the case of affirmative action in higher education admissions in the US.

## Theoretical framework: A synthesis

As described above, we argue that, through *Racialized Framing* social authorities will attempt to make sense of race, racial inequality, and the role of government for the audience. In this respect, we are more interested in how frames of communication are used by social authorities to impact the debate on affirmative action in higher education than we are in frames of thought (how individuals make sense of the world around them and about their own lives). Because issues of race are sensitive and readers may rebuke any incoherent or overtly racist statements, authors will use slippery framing techniques to both *minimize race* and *activate race* in the same breath. It is through this multi-frame tactic that we understand the place race holds in US politics in particular and society in general.

As such, we pose a theoretical synthesis of Bonilla-Silva's color-blind framework with Blumer's group positioning framework (see also Bobo, 2000) to explain how frames of communication are readily used by outside entities to simultaneously minimize the role of race and racism while at the same time invoking animosity through the use of threat. We believe the synthesis of these well-respected racial theories will provide a useful framework for understanding the material underpinnings (threat to valued resources) associated with color-blind rhetoric that attempts to remove affirmative action as an effective ameliorative policy in higher education. That is to say, we argue that veiled threats will be strategically placed within color-blind frames to more effectively and efficiently remove affirmative action from the national agenda. While supporters may slip such discourse into arguments as well, we pose that such rhetoric will be most notable and pernicious in opponent arguments. Opponents will actively attempt to use this multi-frame approach to avoid being rebuked in the courts and the court of public opinion. In conclusion, we pose that this book will provide not only insights into court battles over affirmative action, but also the state of race and racism in contemporary American society. We will return to this theoretical framework as we move forward with the analyses in the coming chapters.

## Organization of the book

As suggested in this Introduction, the issues surrounding both contemporary race relations and affirmative action in the US are incredibly complicated. As a result, we utilize the structure of this book to introduce readers to aspects of this complexity while also analyzing the ways such issues play out in concrete settings and legal cases. To this end, the structure of the book itself is designed as a mechanism for better understanding the state of race relations in the US today, the importance of tension surrounding debates about affirmative action in higher education, and, more broadly, the ways the past and present collide in contemporary racial, legal, media, and political encounters related to this topic and others in America today.

Before discussing the findings of this research, it is vital to first understand the history of affirmative action in general and in higher education in particular. We feel that to better understand the debate it is also important to understand the state of public opinion on affirmative action policies historically and at present. Providing historical context is the primary purpose of Chapter 2. The narratives produced by supporters and opponents have long historical roots that play out today. Thus, the primary findings of this book will be better explained and contextualized with an understanding of affirmative action and its history.

Chapter 3 provides a better understanding of where we are today in terms of racial inequality. Do we still need affirmative action or is a relic of days gone by? If race no longer predicts economic, social, and political outcomes for most Americans, is it really a problem in need of a solution, especially a solution that most whites and some non-whites find very controversial? Chapter 3 also provides an insight into the impact of higher education and affirmative action for African Americans today. While education is important for African Americans, has affirmative action helped? Furthermore, once affirmative action has been banned in individual states, do African Americans feel the effects? If the answer to these questions is "no," it is hard to provide a convincing argument to support the continuation of the policy. Chapter 3 ends by providing a synopsis of the prominent cases related to affirmative action in higher education to demonstrate how we got to the *Fisher II* case today and describes the precedents set by past cases.

In Chapter 4 we turn to our analyses. After setting up the context of both contemporary US race relations and affirmative action itself, we discuss the conflicts related to the policy in higher education. In so doing, we discuss who supports and who opposes the policy via amicus briefs as well as the ways their social location within systems of racial stratification may influence the stance a given person is more likely to take on this issue. Finally, we dive in and take a closer and more nuanced look at the prominent organizations that have chosen to fight the fight for and against affirmative action at the level of the Supreme Court. Who are their leaders and what do their organizations look like? Moreover, we ask whether the type of organizations differ by whether they support affirmative action or not.

We then turn to the first half of our discursive analyses of arguments made in prominent Supreme Court cases in Chapter 5. Specifically, we analyze the University of Michigan cases (*Gratz* and *Grutter*) with an eye toward the ways each case was framed by supporters and opponents of affirmative action. We outline the common frames utilized on each side of the debate while discussing how these frames activate race in the service of public responses to the issues in question, particularly among opponents. Throughout this chapter, we note the ways such framing defines affirmative action, the specific cases, and race itself in ways that suggest certain legal decisions would necessarily be the right ones.

We build on the analyses in Chapter 5 by focusing our attention on the more recent cases in our study. In Chapter 6, we thus turn our attention to both iterations of the *Fisher* cases, and the arguments produced by both sides of the debate. In so doing, we demonstrate the similarities and differences in racialized frames used over time from *Gratz/Grutter* to *Fisher*. We also demonstrate the ways such efforts speak to ongoing racial tensions and conflicts in the US. Further, we investigate the ways commentators on both sides came to see the *Fisher* case as both a victory for affirmative action and a potential signal of the impending death of affirmation action in the future. As such, we outline what these recent cases say about the continued evolution of race relations, higher education, and the Supreme Court in US society.

Finally, we draw on insights and discussions from the book to return to the concept of *Racialized Framing* in the final chapter. In Chapter 7, we thus outline the ways that these social authorities attempted to activate race within broader arguments that simultaneously attempted to minimize race and claim that affirmative action was no longer needed or even unjust. In this chapter we try to make sense of debates concerning race relations, race-related policies, and other aspects of contemporary American legal and political conflicts. We also look forward to pending cases that could make their way to the Supreme Court and eventually end affirmative action in higher education. In closing, we also suggest ways that this type of attention could speak to the future of affirmative action and other policies while theorizing about what the future might hold as the patterns throughout this book continue to play out in the US today.

## Notes

[1] Amicus briefs are formal legal documents used by social authorities (eg, interested individuals, advocacy groups, corporations, states, schools, presidents, state governors, etc) that have a stake in the case and the financial capability to lobby the Supreme Court justices in cases before the Court.

[2] We focus our analysis on the primary or first authors of amicus briefs submitted to the *Gratz/Grutter* and *Fisher* Supreme Court cases. While other individuals and groups may have joined the petition, we look solely at those individuals and groups that claim primary authorship over the arguments.

2

# Affirmative Action and Higher Education

## Introduction

We begin our discussion by outlining the contours of the debate surrounding affirmative action in the US. To this end, we provide a brief historical account of the policy in general and then some details about the use of it in higher education in particular. Understanding the socio-historical context of affirmative action will provide a better understanding of why some arguments gain traction in the debate while others do not. Further, we address proposals suggesting diversity as the only constitutionally valid rationale for implementing affirmative action in higher education. We then discuss the complexities of diversity as it relates to affirmative action in higher education, and why this idea may not necessarily be popular among conservatives or liberals.

In this chapter, we also provide an insight into the ideological divides in politics, litigation, and public perception that drive the debate around affirmative action. We demonstrate how these dynamics influence public opinion on the policy. In general, public opinion polls regularly find that whites hold quite negative attitudes and beliefs (that is, frames of thought) toward affirmative action. As such, we note here how such negative impressions develop and find a voice via the operations of outside entities with the ability to shape public debate on such issues. While we return to this idea at the end of this chapter, we begin with a discussion of the emergence of affirmative action in the socio-political debate on the national stage.

## The beginnings of affirmative action

Unequal relations and pernicious treatment of minorities have left an indelible mark on the current landscape of the US since its inception. From slavery to Jim Crow, the history of the US is inextricably connected with the oppression of African Americans and people of color. It was W.E.B. Du Bois ([1935] 2017, p 5) who poignantly stated in *Black Reconstruction* that "Black labor became the foundation stone not only of the Southern social structure but of Northern manufacture and commerce, of the English factory system, of European commerce, of buying and selling on a world-wide scale…" Thus, no region was exempt from the oppression of black bodies despite stereotypes of Southern intolerance and racism, which often paints whites in other regions of the country as innocent. Gunnar Myrdal (1944) famously surmised that the most urgent dilemma in America is that of race and racial inequality. Layers of published research reports provide evidence that this problem persists and continues to shape the lived experiences of non-whites today.

After the Reconstruction era (1865–77), the federal government largely ignored the plight of African Americans (Myrdal, 1944). If anything, the government was complicit in the re-segregation and oppression of African Americans. For example, in *Plessy v Ferguson* (163 US 537, 1896), the Supreme Court ruled racial segregation laws to be constitutional as long as the public facilities where the law was implemented were equal in quality. This decision became known infamously as the "separate but equal" doctrine despite clear evidence that facilities serving different races were anything but equal. Such an orientation to public facilities and race relations re-established invidious racial segregation that was shunned during the Reconstruction era and once again distanced African Americans from whites socially and economically.

The lack of recognition of inequality and persistent discrimination was primarily fueled by legislature antipathy, especially among conservative Southern Democrats who outwardly supported a re-segregationist policy. However, in the 1930s and 1940s, things began to change and federal government attempted to alleviate persistent discrimination based on race through policy (Kellough, 2006). Both the Hatch Act of 1939 and the Classification Act of 1940 included provisions that prevented discrimination based on race, creed, or color (Kellough, 2006). However, these policies were quite ineffective as they relied almost exclusively on victims of discrimination coming forward and because, again, many conservative and Southern politicians were staunch opponents of any policies seeking to enforce integration of the races (Kellough, 2006). For example, in response to President Harry Truman's sweeping civil rights initiatives that called for an end to the segregation of all public spaces, discrimination, and the establishment of a civil rights commission, Strom Thurmond left the Democratic Party and established the Dixiecrats Party (or the States' Rights Democratic Party). In his first address to the party, he stated, "[T]here's not enough troops in the Army to force the Southern people to break down segregation and admit the n***r race into our theatres, into our swimming pools, into our homes, and into our churches" (as cited in Smith, 2012). Thus, while the government at least acknowledged the problem faced by African Americans during this time, these policies did not seriously challenge the racial status quo, and went mostly unenforced and ineffective at best.

It was not until the 1960s that the federal government took a more forceful stance to eliminate persistent racism and discrimination (Kellough, 2006). Shortly after being elected into office in 1961, President John F. Kennedy announced that he supported equal opportunity of employment for minorities, and accordingly restructured federal efforts to improve the conditions of groups historically disadvantaged. His Executive Order 10925 of 1961 required federal contractors to take "affirmative action to ensure that applicants are treated equally" without regards to race, creed, color, or nationality. This 1961 Order was the first instance that mentioned the concept of affirmative action.

As opposed to earlier attempts to address racism and inequality, President Kennedy envisioned a more proactive federal program that required employers to take specific actions to oppose further discrimination against marginalized groups and promote greater opportunities for employment (Kellough, 2006). Federal government agencies and private businesses that received federal money were encouraged to recruit minority persons, particularly recent college graduates and those graduating from high schools made up mostly of minorities. Furthermore, these agencies were asked to reconsider their policies and procedures to ensure that they did not intentionally or unintentionally block the hiring of minority candidates through faulty practices. While not often associated with affirmative action, such efforts to reach out to minorities were a big part of the policy from the beginning. As upper division jobs remained elusive to minorities, this more aggressive approach led to positive outcomes for underrepresented minorities. Under Kennedy's presidency, the representation of African Americans rose significantly (Kellough, 2006).

Considered by some the hallmark governmental effort to end discrimination, the federal government passed the Civil Rights Act of 1964. More than symbolic, this order brought significant change to the national equal employment policy by establishing provisions preventing discrimination by public businesses that received federal funds (Title VI) and by private companies (Title VII). Title VII established a permanent governmental agency (the Equal Employment Opportunity Commission) to actively fight discrimination by supervising the development of anti-discrimination policies, investigating any violations, and providing resolutions to those violations (Kellough, 2006). Title VI could combat discrimination in both the private and public sectors, whether the business received federal funds or not. After the Civil Rights Act of 1964 was signed into law, President Lyndon Johnson issued Executive Order 11246, which replaced Kennedy's executive order and affirmed the role of the government in these matters by requiring all government contractors and subcontractors to take affirmative action to improve the opportunities of minorities. Johnson later amended this order by issuing Executive Order 11375 that added sex as a protected group not to be discriminated against within various institutions.

Affirmative action, practically speaking, was an attempt to provide procedures and guidelines that assist in remedying long-standing discrimination against groups often marginalized, including women, minorities, and more recently, transgender people, sexual minorities, and those with disabilities. In so doing, this policy attempted to assure well-qualified marginalized group members the equal opportunity and access to various social benefits viewed as necessary for broader social mobility, including, but not limited to, admissions to higher education, employment, governmental contracts, and housing. Affirmative action is and never was a policy meant to give underqualified minorities opportunities at the expense of qualified others. It was abundantly clear to some legislators, civil rights activists, and supporters that these groups were not given the same opportunities despite being qualified as were whites due to racism and persistent discrimination characteristic of the US at the time. Accordingly, exceptional attention to these matters by the government was needed to dismantle structural, racial, and other forms of inequality and persistent discrimination that blocked the success of many.

## Why focus on higher education?

Almost immediately after the passage of the Civil Rights Act of 1964, conservative elites began searching for ways to dismantle the ameliorative programs of the 1960s, including affirmative action (Cokorinos, 2003). Just over a decade after the passage of the Civil Rights Act, the Supreme Court agreed to hear the first significant case in higher education dealing with affirmative action (*Regents of the University of California v Bakke*, 1978). Despite a politically splintered Court, the *Bakke* case went a long way in establishing the legal rationale of diversity and set the stage for current lawsuits against affirmative action. Some scholars pose that the fight against ameliorative policies focusing on higher education admissions among conservatives did not occur by chance. Education, as a social institution, was a central location to wage the fight against affirmative action for particular reasons. With that in mind, we situate this case study on the debate surrounding affirmative action in higher education admissions for the following reasons.

First, many Americans view higher education as the preeminent institution that assists both in maintaining socioeconomic status and, more importantly, improving social mobility (Haveman and Smeeding, 2006; Zamani-Gallaher et al, 2009). Access to education allows most members of society a mechanism to better themselves and their families. A recent Gallup poll found that 70 percent of Americans view a college education as "very" or "somewhat" important (Jones, 2016) to social and economic success. Historically, this has generally been the case. From non-landowning siblings during colonial times to freed slaves post-Civil War to women seeking independence, education has and continues to be viewed by many as a way to improve career opportunities and as a symbol for social and economic prosperity. However, relative to the dominant group, non-white citizens have not always had the same access to education in general and higher education in particular, hence the need for affirmative action policies.

Because education is seen as a valued resource, it is clear why marginalized groups and the dominant group clash over the use of affirmative action in this venue. Enrollment and subsequent graduation from elite state universities can have a significant impact on a person's career trajectory (Pierce, 2012). Any increase or decrease in admission seats can lead to non-trivial consequences for all parties involved, particularly in relation to seats at highly selective elite universities. Taking California as a case study, the removal of affirmative action via Proposition 209 in 1996 witnessed not only a drastic decrease in the number of African Americans in higher education but also a restructuring of sorts. Minority students who did go to college were ushered into non-elite universities at a higher rate than their white counterparts (Pierce, 2012). Accordingly, at least on the surface, it is clear why the white majority may view such policies that deal with the redistribution of resources negatively and as a threat to their continued social and economic successes. Many whites believe that they deserve better options based on merit and that they have a priority claim to valued resources, including education, above all others.

Second, another reason we focus on affirmative action in education is at the heart of the debate: some view the idea of preferential treatment or any use of race as being inconsistent and even at odds with notions of social and economic justice where merit should be the defining characteristic of success in the US. Research has generally shown that when affirmative action is framed as preferential treatment, support generally collapses (Kinder and Sanders, 1996). Ideologically, the use of affirmative action in higher education in particular is often labeled by some as an affront to the American Creed of rugged individualism and the American value of a strong work ethic. Any attempt to circumvent the established mechanism (eg, studying hard and a strong work ethic) for entering into higher education is often viewed as simply unfair and unjust, particularly by whites (Glazer, 1987; Thernstrom and Thernstrom, 1997; Sowell, 2003; Alon and Tienda, 2007). This very individualistic perspective focuses on the harm felt by innocent whites who are trying to build careers and severely ignores the harms felt by marginalized groups. That is, whites often ignore past and present societal injuries felt by race, class, sexual, and gender minorities and women of various social locations when thinking of affirmative action. Nonetheless, this concern seems to be sharpened when considering the use of race in higher education enrollment.

## Affirmative action and education

Since the 1960s, to comply with affirmative action mandates set forth by federal government, universities and colleges began re-working their admissions process to increase the number of minorities, women, and other marginalized groups enrolled. However, the use of affirmative action in state universities and colleges is almost universally voluntary, and has actually been banned in eight states. In the remaining states, the purpose and use of this policy has been to increase access to higher education for groups historically marginalized and omitted from participation, yet how they recruit minority students differs. Not all schools make use of affirmative action-type policies when making admissions decisions, and when they do, it is often minimally invasive. The determination to use affirmative action is usually made by schools that maintain a more elite status due to the selectivity of the admissions process, that struggle with the admission of minorities, and that have strong histories of racial segregation. Thus, rules to increase diversity are needed for these universities.

When implemented, affirmative action in higher education takes different forms that have changed over time. The most common way is the direct recruitment of minorities (eg, recruiting at high schools) who may be overlooked in the admissions process. While recruitment is not often labeled affirmative action, it is a primary mechanism used by schools to increase minority enrollment. Interestingly, states that have *banned* the use of affirmative action often invest more in minority recruitment at high school level. Recruitment can use tools such as scholarships to increase minority enrollment. For instance, the State University of New York (SUNY) actively identifies and recruits candidates to increase diversity on campus. One way SUNY attracts a diverse body is by offering scholarships to both undergraduate and graduate students. The state of New York has a program, termed the "Empire State Diversity Honors Scholarship Program," that seeks to attract minorities and "contribute to the diversity of the student body" on university campuses. In 2015–16, this program awarded 917 scholarships worth approximately $1,662 per person to attend 43 institutions (Office of Diversity, Equity, and Inclusion at SUNY, 2016, website). Such affirmative action-type mechanisms are rarely discussed in the media and social and political debates. Instead, affirmative action decisions that consider race in their admissions policy get most of the headlines and backlash. Interestingly, research looking at attitudes toward policies that promote "equality of opportunity" fare much better than public policies that promote "equality of outcome" (Bobo and Kluegel, 1993).

In the past, schools have chosen to set aside a select number of seats for underrepresented minorities. While this tactic seems to be a very effective and direct way of ensuring diversity and representation of marginalized groups, it has been the most controversial. This type of policy has been labeled a "quota" system by some, and stood at the center of the *Bakke* Supreme Court case against affirmative action. In *Bakke*, the medical school reserved 16 of 100 seats of incoming students for African Americans and other minority groups. However, the Supreme Court ruled this to be unconstitutional, making the use of quotas illegal in higher education admissions. Post *Bakke*, schools have chosen two other affirmative action techniques to improve enrollment for minorities students. One, schools have decided to allot points based on racial status to increase enrollment for minority students. This was the case for the undergraduate admissions process at the University of Michigan in the 1990s that led to the *Gratz* case. The Supreme Court ultimately ruled the use of affirmative action in such a manner to be unconstitutional. That is to say, the use of such points was not *narrowly tailored* to the university and was thus deemed to be unconstitutional. Second, schools have chosen to use race as *one* factor, not *the* deciding factor, in a *holistic approach* to making admissions decisions. Other factors, such as state residency and economic status, are considered along with race when using a holistic approach. The use of race as one factor has been described by some as quite minimal at best given the history of racism and institutional discrimination and the current state of inequality found in the US. This approach is quite common among elite universities and colleges across the country yet has also come under high scrutiny and even been the subject of prominent court cases (Walsh, 2004). The one-factor approach has gained traction based on the ruling in the *Grutter* Supreme Court case that held such a plan to be *narrowly tailored* and thus, constitutional. This approach was implemented at the University of Texas at Austin and was found to be lawful in the 2016 *Fisher* Supreme Court case (*Fisher II*) as well.

We would also like to note that the Supreme Court rebuked the use of affirmative action to atone for past discrimination. Justice Lewis Powell stated succinctly in his opinion in *Hernandez v Texas* (347 US 475, 1954) that affirmative action is not to be used to counter "the effects of societal discrimination." He further added his rationale of why past discrimination cannot be used as the standard for supporting affirmative action, by stating,

> The concepts of 'majority' and 'minority' necessarily reflect temporary arrangements and political judgments. As observed above, the white 'majority' itself is composed of various minority groups, most of which can lay claim to a history of prior discrimination at the hands of the state and private individuals... There is no principled basis for deciding which groups would merit 'heightened judicial solicitude' and which would not.

Most interesting in this quote from Justice Powell is that he quickly erases the history of oppression felt by African Americans and attempts to place the experiences of discrimination felt by other groups on a par with those felt by African Americans. As such, the notion that affirmative action cannot be used to remedy past harms shook the foundation of affirmative action debates and has set the stage for the current fight against the policy. Supporters have expressed grave concern as they believe discrimination continues to be a major issue plaguing the US, particularly in higher education.

## Affirmative action: The ideological divide

It is also essential to understand the ever-evolving division among politicians, the courts, and in the broader public discourse surrounding racial inequality and affirmative action. A recent 2018 internal document produced by the Civil Rights Division of the Department of Justice leaked to the public announced a call for applicants who would litigate "intentional race-based discrimination" in college admission decisions, mainly focusing on institutions that discriminated against white applicants (Savage, 2017). Moreover, President Donald Trump recently announced that he would abandon policies of the Obama administration that supported the use of race as a factor in higher education admissions and support more color-blind standards (Green et al, 2018). This hiring initiative and ideological stance against the use of race reflects broader signs of the divide separating the political parties in general as well as the state of mind of the current Republican administration.

This divide is not confined to, nor did it originate with, the current Trump administration and present political leaders. While white backlash has been associated with civil rights gains since the 1960s, former research director of the Institute for Democracy Studies Lee Cokorinos (2003) argued that the current opposition to affirmative action and the movement to dismantle civil rights legislature is rooted in moves made by previous Republican administrations. President Ronald Reagan enlisted several young conservatives in his administration that maintained strong anti-civil rights agendas and also nominated conservative federal judges who were more likely to hold anti-affirmative action views. For instance, Supreme Court Justice Clarence Thomas was vetted to play a role in the administration for this very reason. Thomas was ultimately nominated by President George H. Bush to replace civil rights stalwart Justice Thurgood Marshall, further substantiating a conservative anti-civil rights agenda on the Supreme Court. This pattern was reinforced by the election of President George W. Bush, who included a new generation of anti-affirmative action conservatives in his administration. Responding to the 2003 University of Michigan *Gratz* and *Grutter* Supreme Court cases, Bush himself came out in opposition to affirmative action, claiming that quotas had no place in higher education. While President Barack Obama, a Democrat, expressed lukewarm support for the *Fisher II* ruling and affirmative action in general (Bonilla-Silva and Dietrich, 2011), this support seems glowing in the shadow of the election of Trump in 2016, who expressed disdain for such a policy and is attempting to undo all of former President Obama's endorsed policies.

Similar to the political world, the divide over affirmative action seems to be only growing in the courts. The division over civil rights initiatives, such as affirmative action, in the Supreme Court, is palpable, with a small majority maintaining more conservative views (Jayakumar et al, 2015). However, the election of President Trump may only increase this divide. Trump successfully nominated Neil Gorsuch in 2017 and Brett Kavanaugh in 2018, two justices who have been associated with conservative opinions. Justice Neil Gorsuch has been described as having an ideological perspective similar to that of deceased Justice Antonin Scalia (who he replaced on the Court), and a history of conservative opinions while serving on the 10th Circuit Court of Appeals (de Vogue, 2017). Indeed, Justice Gorsuch will serve as the tiebreaker on prominent social issues, including future affirmative action cases. The successful nomination of Justice Gorsuch is a particularly bitter pill to swallow for Democrats given that many feel the seat should have been filled by Judge Merrick Garland, a more centrist judge nominated by President Obama after the passing of Justice Scalia who was considered one of the most conservative members of the Court. The nomination of Garland was seen as a possible watershed moment that could have changed the leanings of the Court to the Left but was ultimately blocked by Senate-controlled Republicans who declined to hold a vote for his nomination until after the election. When President Trump won a surprising election in 2016 by receiving less votes than Hillary Clinton (the Democratic nominee), the fortunes of the Court swung back to the Right and possibly away from civil rights policies such as affirmative action.

We would also be remiss in not discussing the retirement of Justice Anthony Kennedy in 2018. This position was filled by Brett Kavanaugh, despite accusations of sexual assault. Kavanaugh brings the Supreme Court a history of conservative opinions on a wide array of social issues, including abortion and gun rights (Foran and Biskupic, 2018). This confirmation assures that the Court will only become more conservative, especially on the notion of affirmative action in higher education. This successful nomination is more worrisome because of the role Justice Kennedy played in past affirmative action cases. Despite being considered a conservative justice who was appointed by President Reagan in 1987, he sided with the University of Texas at Austin and the continued use of affirmative action back in 2016. This pro-affirmative action vote will most likely be absent with the new justices when the Supreme Court hears the next affirmative action case, which may be sooner rather than later (see our discussion in Chapter 1).

Legislatively, eight states have already outlawed affirmative action and the use of race in admissions at public colleges and universities, including California (1996), Washington (1998), Florida (1999), Michigan (2006), Nebraska (2008), Arizona (2010), New Hampshire (2011) and Oklahoma (2012). The state of Colorado attempted to pass a similar ban, but the initiative to amend the constitution failed. In California, the electorate voted in 1996 to ban affirmative action at state institutions via the passage of Proposition 209. Interestingly, this public backlash against affirmative action was preceded by a vote of the University of California Regents to eliminate the policy in the University of California system in 1995. Quite recently, a bill was vetoed by then Governor Jerry Brown in 2011 that would have allowed schools in California the ability to once again consider race in higher education admissions. In 1998, the state of Washington followed California's lead and voted to ban the use of affirmative action in higher education (Initiative 200). Because Ward Connerly partly wrote Proposition 209 and Initiative 200, a high-profile and outspoken critic of affirmative action and author of an amicus brief in the *Gratz/Grutter* cases, the language in the initiatives was quite similar (Blume and Long, 2014). In 1999, Florida became the third state to ban affirmative action in public institutions. Termed "One Florida," Executive Order 99-281, which prevented the use of racial or gender preferences in higher education, was signed by then Florida Governor, Jeb Bush.

While these states actively banned the use of affirmative action in higher education admissions, some passed and implemented policies they viewed as a color-blind alternative to increase minority enrollment and improve diversity. For instance, labeled the "Talented Twenty" program, Florida students were guaranteed admissions when applicants had graduated in the top 20 percent of their class, completed specific academic required courses, and taken the SAT or ACT. In 2001, the state of California implemented a color-blind admissions policy similar to that of Florida, termed "Eligibility in the Local Context," to increase minority enrollment in 2001. This policy provided access to one of the state's universities and colleges to applicants who graduated in the top 4 percent of their class. However, unlike California and Florida, the state of Washington never passed a percentage plan to bolster minority enrollment in higher education institutions. On a related note, responding to the *Hopwood* decision in 1996, Texas moved to a system in 1997 where the top 10 percent of students ("Top 10% Rule") in a graduating class would gain acceptance to any public college or university. Like other states, its ban on the use of race was lauded as a race-neutral alternative that reintegrated justice and fairness into the admissions decision process (Blume and Long, 2014).

Concerning the public perception of affirmative action, the ideological divide might be as great or more significant. There tends to be two ideological camps of thought. On the one hand, we have those who feel that civil rights policies, such as affirmative action, are needed due to the history of unequal treatment and discrimination of minorities, women, and other marginalized groups. Or, at the very least, affirmative action is needed to improve diversity in higher education. This ideological position holds that a color-blind approach that ignores harms felt by minorities in the US historically and today is detrimental to all involved. Individuals who espouse this position are more likely to support the use of affirmative action in higher education admissions where race and ethnicity are given preferential treatment and used as a factor in student selection to address unequal opportunities. As described above, one of those supporters was former President Obama, who stated that the *Fisher II* ruling assured an "equal shot" for all applicants in college admissions (de Vogue, 2017). However, President Obama supported the use of affirmative action to ensure diversity but did not mention the history of racial inequality and persistent discrimination in the US today. Indeed, he implied that affirmative action would be more appropriate to consider economic disadvantage.

Thus, many of those in support of affirmative action view the *Fisher II* case as a practical and even moral victory for affirmative action. By upholding the use of affirmative action, the Court is fulfilling an obligation to uphold the values set forth by the US Constitution to pursue ways to provide equal opportunity for marginalized groups and to ensure a diverse student body at colleges and universities throughout the nation. This notion of diversity is viewed as one mechanism to improve the experiences for all students, including white students. For minority students, they are admitted to historically white elite universities that might better their chances of economic success and social mobility. Diversity also provides minorities with "like" others to interact with and provide support during their years in university, eventually improving the campus climate for marginalized groups. This perspective also proposes that such policies help white students benefit from exposure to divergent views, which will not only help them in social relations but also when they eventually enter a diverse workforce.

The diversity rationale has been celebrated and championed by many observers while decried by others. In response to the *Fisher II* decision, the National Association for the Advancement of Colored People (NAACP) Legal Defense and Educational Fund stated, "Universities all over the country are breathing a sigh of relief ... the court very compellingly reaffirmed the importance of diversity" (quoted in Liptak, 2016). Lawrence H. Tribe, the Carl M. Loeb University Professor and Professor of Constitutional Law at Harvard, stated, "No decision since *Brown v Board of Education* has been as important as *Fisher* will prove to be in the long history of racial inclusion and educational diversity" (quoted in Liptak, 2016). The importance of diversity was echoed by Supreme Court Justice Kennedy, who was in the majority for the 2016 decision:

> A university is in large part defined by those intangible qualities which are incapable of objective measurement but which make for greatness... Considerable deference is owed to a university

in defining those intangible characteristics, like student body diversity, that are central to its identity and educational mission. But still … it remains an enduring challenge to our nation's education system to reconcile the pursuit of diversity with the constitutional promise of equal treatment and dignity. (Liptak, 2016)

However, the diversity rationale is not necessarily viewed in a positive light by all supporters of affirmative action (Collins, 2011a, b; Moore, 2018). Wendy Moore (2018, p 54) argues that the diversity rationale espoused by Justice Powell in the 1978 *Bakke* (438 US 265) Supreme Court case turned affirmative action into the "metaphorical equivalent of using a band-aid to stop the bleeding from an enormous, gaping wound." The metaphor of a "gaping wound" refers to persistent systemic racism and discrimination found in the US. Moore (2018) argued that the diversity rationale might actually bring more harm to minorities than good because it further establishes a color-blind ideology that ignores past and contemporary discrimination and inequality in the US that continues to have a significant impact today.

Opponents of affirmative action, on the other hand, view racial policies, such as affirmative action meant to alleviate inequality, very differently. They view affirmative action in general and the *Fisher II* ruling in particular as institutional support for reverse discrimination against whites, a problem they view as afflicting them since the Civil Rights Movement. This paints a picture of affirmative action as a policy that is inherently unfair and unjust to whites because their race is being used to discriminate against them, a call that turns racial prejudice on its head and portrays whites as the victims of racial discrimination. Many opponents even referred to the policy as merely unneeded. In reflecting on the decision against her, Abigail Fisher stated: "I am disappointed that the Supreme Court has ruled that students applying to the University of Texas can be treated differently because of their race or ethnicity… I hope that the nation will one day move beyond affirmative action" (quoted in Watkins, 2016).

Furthermore, opponents also viewed this ruling as a strike against staunch individualism, a traditional value cherished by many Americans. The individualism critique is not new and posits that the use of affirmative action in university admissions allows individuals to be admitted without merit while others who are working hard and playing by the rules are left out and even punished. Texas Attorney General Ken Paxton stated, "the opportunities [University of Texas at Austin] offers should be available to all students based on their merit, not the color of their skin" (quoted in Watkins, 2016). In this light, many opponents suggest that any admissions policy should be color-blind and if not, would be unfair and unjust to whites by significantly reducing the chances of hard-working Americans to be admitted into colleges and universities of their choice. Edward Blum, the architect of many anti-affirmative action battles, added succinctly, "Today's decision is a sad step backward for the original, colorblind principles to our civil rights laws" (quoted in Watkins, 2016).

As stated above, these color-blind, *neoliberal* appeals turn the work of civil rights pioneers on its head by now stating policies that assist minorities are being used to discriminate against other groups (whites in this case) as Jim Crow-type laws did to African Americans in the past. Neoliberalism refers to the use of political and economic explanations to explain away racial issues. A neoliberal argument ties anti-affirmative action sentiment to support of the free market and concern over economic justice and fairness while minimizing concern over any prior racial injustices felt by African Americans and other marginalized groups (Pierce, 2012). Opponents also oppose the diversity rationale first legitimized by *Bakke*. They view it as arbitrary, inefficient, and even a discriminatory mechanism to deal with persistent inequality in society and higher education. What this means, is that many conservatives not only oppose efforts to increase diversity, but they also oppose the rationale behind increasing diversity in colleges and universities.

These arguments are not new as most debates around affirmative action, since its inception, borrow from these ideas. Cokorinos (2003) posed that such opposition links back to unwanted government intrusion related to forced desegregation in the 1960s. Interestingly, both supporters and opponents of affirmative action base their arguments on the abstract ideas of fairness, justice, and equality (Kellough, 2006). For supporters, fairness revolves around righting past harms experienced by African Americans, women, and other marginalized groups. The arguments of opponents similarly revolve around the notion of justice and fairness as well, but include merit. What differentiates these two perspectives is that opponents argue that justice and fairness should be color-blind. Any policy that gives preference based on race, regardless of how small that preference may be and the notion that whites have historically benefited from such advantages, violates meritocratic principles and is inherently unjust, unfair, and frankly un-American. Given the nature of affirmative action as a mechanism to redirect resources based on group affiliation, these types of arguments are not surprising.

Other arguments have also gained currency among opponents in the fight against affirmative action. For instance, the late Justice Scalia and other opponents of affirmative action have questioned whether policies that use race are detrimental to those it should supposedly help: racial and ethnic minority students. Parroting ideas from "mismatch theory" (Sander and Taylor Jr, 2012), Justice Scalia argued that African American students who were admitted to colleges based on affirmative action in Texas were coming from substandard public schools and were therefore not prepared for the rigor of top-tier college courses. The "mismatch" perspective holds that these students would suffer in the end, either by dropping out or struggling to graduate with adequate grades. Such struggles would lead to minority students not being competitive when applying to graduate school or when entering the workforce. Justice Scalia commented that,

> There are those who contend that it does not benefit African Americans to get them into the University of Texas, where they do not do well, as opposed to having them go to a less-advanced school, a slower-track school where they do well. One of the briefs pointed out that most of the black scientists in this country don't come from schools like the University of Texas. They come from lesser schools where they do not feel that they're being pushed ahead in classes that are too fast for them. (quoted in Mencimer, 2015)

The comments led to an outcry from African American students from the University of Texas and spurred the creation of the Twitter hashtag #StayMadAbby, that included pictures of African Americans in graduation regalia as they graduated from the University of Texas at Austin (UT Austin) (see Visser, 2015, for examples).

Students who took these pictures suggested that this showed "Abby" Fisher, Justice Scalia, and other opponents that African Americans could be successful at UT Austin and earn a degree. However, as reiterated by impassioned minority dissent, Justice Samuel Alito, in the 2016 decision, argued that UT Austin wanted to continue the use of affirmative action in admissions because it wanted to "admit rich minorities" (quoted in Watkins, 2016):

> UT's assumptions appear to be based on the pernicious stereotype that the African-Americans and Hispanics admitted through the Top Ten Percent Plan only got in because they did not have to compete against very many whites and Asian-Americans… When affirmative action was first adopted, it was for the purpose of helping the disadvantaged… Now we are told that a program that tends to admit poor and disadvantaged minority students is inadequate because it does not work to the

advantage of those who are more fortunate. This is affirmative action gone wild. (cited in Watkins, 2016)

As such, many who disagree with the diversity rationale and with affirmative action in general argue that their position is based on fairness, justice, and morality; that is, they see their dissent as a moral obligation to uphold principles of strict individualism and equal treatment for all, regardless of race.

## Affirmative action and public opinion polls

While debate persists in politics and the courts, there appears to be a consensus among white Americans: they do not support affirmative action. While there is sub-group variation among whites, public opinion polls reveal that whites feel very uncomfortable expressing support over ameliorative policies that promote racial equality despite supporting equality in principal. A poll conducted by Gallup in 2016 touched on affirmative action in higher education (Newport, 2016). Gallup found that the majority of white Americans (76%) believe college admissions should be based on merit alone, and only a small percentage of Americans feel that race or ethnic background should be taken into consideration (22%). Interestingly, only 30 percent of white Americans approved of the *Fisher II* Supreme Court decision while 66 percent disapproved. Thus, not only do whites oppose affirmative action to ensure great diversity, but they also believe institutions (of higher education, in this case) should be operating in a color-blind meritocratic manner.

Other national polls reveal similar trends in affirmative action viewpoints among whites as well, including the General Social Survey (GSS) and the American National Election Studies (ANES). These surveys are quite popular among social scientists because they allow for more complicated statistical modeling and often ask questions on various social issues over an extended time period. This is the case with affirmative action as both surveys have sampled public opinion on this controversial issue since the 1970s. Unlike Gallup, questions included in these surveys do not touch particularly on affirmative action in higher education admissions. However, they do tap into general attitudes toward affirmative action and provide a look into attitudinal trends. The numbers (and a plethora of research in the social sciences, for that matter) provided in the figures below do reveal a notable and consistent negative view toward affirmative action-type interventions among whites comparable to the Gallup poll (Schuman et al, 1997).

Before we move on, however, we would like to note that some research shows not all affirmative action-type policies are unpopular among whites. Affirmative action policies that emphasize "equality of opportunity" tend to garner more white support than those focused on "equality of outcomes" (Bobo and Kluegel, 1993). This finding provides some evidence that affirmative action attitudes are more nuanced that what is generally reported. Nonetheless, below, we offer some observations on public opinion among whites regarding affirmative action. Figure 2.1 provides a percentage of white respondents who support assisting African Americans on a variety of questions taken from the GSS. The GSS is a highly respected data source used by scholars of all social science disciplines. It is popular because it asks questions covering a host of social issues ranging from sexism to racial attitudes to a nationally representative sample of the US adult population. Over the years, it has asked several questions of respondents regarding their level of support for policies that promote the *implementation of equal treatment* from busing to hiring preference.

From 1972 to 1996, respondents were asked about their support for busing from one school district to another. While not affirmative action as typically conceptualized, busing in and outside of school districts to reduce inequality for marginalized students has been as divisive an issue as any affirmative action hiring or admissions policy. As can be seen in Figure 2.1, support among whites never increased much above 35 percent, even in the mid to late 1990s when the question was removed from the survey. It is clear that white respondents struggled with the idea of busing initiatives meant to desegregate schools.

Respondents have also been asked about their level of support for hiring preference and promotion ("Hiring preference"), and whether

**Figure 2.1:** Percentage support for affirmative action-type intervention

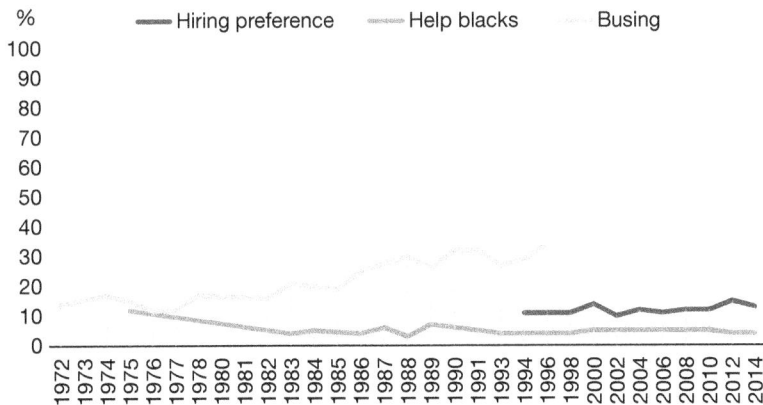

35

the government should have a role in improving the standard of living for blacks considering past discrimination ("Help blacks"). These latter two questions align more neatly with the common understanding of affirmative action. Support for either notion has been minimal at best since inclusion in the survey. As can be seen in Figure 2.1, the percentage of white respondents who support government intervention in assuring a standard of living is only above 10 percent in the initial year (1975) and likewise, support for hiring and promotion preference hovers only slightly above 10 percent for the duration of the survey. These percentages of support (or lack thereof) remain stable over time, even into the most current years 2010, 2012, and 2014.

Another prominent data source used by social scientists is the ANES. Like the GSS, the ANES is very popular among social scientists for studying social issues such as racial attitudes because questions are plentiful, and the sample reflects broader society in terms of the many demographics. Also like the GSS, the ANES is popular because it includes data on these issues over an extended time period, which allows for important trend analysis. Again, this pattern of little support among whites for implementation of policy found in the GSS is also found in the ANES. The ANES asked white respondents about their attitudes toward affirmative action for over four decades, beginning in 1970 and ending in 2012 (see Figure 2.2).

White respondents were asked whether "Washington should make every possible effort to improve the social and economic position of blacks (Aid for blacks)." This question has been asked consistently since the 1970s. As can be seen from Figure 2.2, the majority of whites feel that blacks should help themselves and that the government should not help them. The percentage who support government assistance never increased

**Figure 2.2:** Percentage support for aid and affirmative action

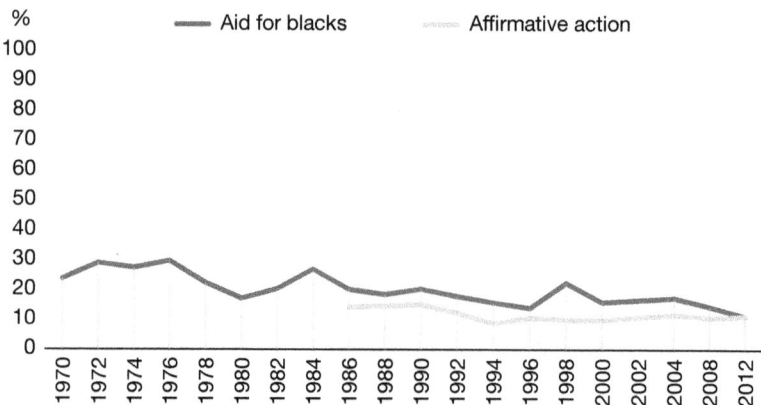

36

over 30 percent, and appeared to decrease from the mid–1980s until 2012. A similar lack of support was also observed for the affirmative action question. This asked respondents to give their opinion (for or against) the following statement: "Some people say that because of past discrimination, blacks should be given preference in hiring and promotion. Others say that such preference in hiring and promotion of blacks is wrong because it gives blacks advantages they haven't earned." Overall, the percentage of whites who support this is even lower than the "Aid for blacks" question, with it peaking in support in 1990 at 15.1 percent. Consistent with the GSS, the ANES questions on affirmative action confirm a lack of support by whites toward affirmative action initiatives.

The lack of support for affirmative action becomes more apparent when considering the increase in support for broader principles of racial equality expressed by whites in public opinion polls (Schuman et al, 1997). Looking again at the GSS, white Americans generally support the notion that equality in principle should be available for all Americans, including minorities and women, in most areas of social life (see Figure 2.3).

Likely appropriate considering the election of Barack Obama to the Presidency of the US in 2008, whites are shown to be more and more supportive of a black president (that is, "racpres"). By 2010, the support among whites reached almost 100 percent, which is quite different from the mid–70 percent of respondents who were unwilling to vote for a black president in the early 1970s. This national survey also shows whites to be less supportive of self-selected neighborhood segregation (that is, "racseg"). While over 10 percent continued to be okay with self-selection, almost 90 percent were not. This finding contrasts starkly with views from the early 1970s. Similarly, a question assessing open housing laws (that

**Figure 2.3:** Percentage support for racial equality

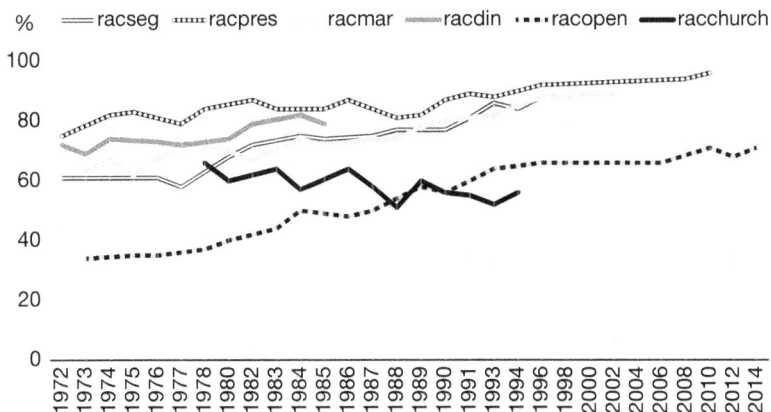

is, "racopen") also reflected the notion that attitudes of whites toward forced segregation are more progressive than ever. While only 70 percent of whites view the restriction of selling houses to African Americans as discrimination, this is quite high, considering that only around 35 percent maintained such beliefs in the early 1970s.

Figure 2.3 also shows that whites are more supportive of other relevant social issues today than before. For instance, whites support interracial marriage more now than at any other point in the history of the US ("racmar"). In 2002, the last year this was a question included in the survey, almost 90 percent of respondents supported interracial marriage. This finding stands in stark contrast to the 60 percent in the early 1970s. Similar upward progressions can be seen for dinner (that is, "racdin") and church (that is, "racchurch") questions, which asked respondents whether they would be okay with eating dinner or going to church with someone who is black.

This general acceptance of racial equality has been a common theme in social science research for over 50 years. A series of social science studies beginning in the 1950s was published in *Scientific American* expressing a very optimistic view of the future of racial attitudes in America (Hyman and Sheatsley, 1956, 1964; Greeley and Sheatsley, 1971; Taylor et al, 1978). The studies provided some positive signs that the clear prejudicial views of the segregationist Jim Crow era were in decline. Citing the GSS, the ANES, and other national surveys, more contemporary work also supports the idea that whites in America are growing more and more racially progressive (Steeh and Schuman, 1992; Schuman et al, 1997). However, this gradual positive shift is most pronounced in questions that tap into principles of racial equality. While these have been greatly criticized in the social sciences for tapping into very shallow-level feelings toward racial issues, it has been argued that they do provide some broader insights into the normative beliefs that whites in the US must adopt to avoid societal alienation.

The positive trend in questions that tap into principles of racial equality also serves as a marker of sorts for measuring viewpoints surrounding other racial issues. When this is compared to the lack of support whites express toward implementation policies such as affirmative action, these comparisons become quite glaring. This principle–implementation divide in public opinion has led to an enormous body of research trying to understand why these questions elicit such stark differences in response patterns. While divergent opinions alone would be worrisome, the fact that such divergence occurs without resulting dissolution of inequalities faced by African Americans is even more troubling (Jones et al, 2018). Public opinion and political stances are now flooded with views that seemingly ignore abject racial inequality and support agendas promoting color-blind perspectives. These viewpoints inexorably place the blame for economic disparities squarely at the feet of the victims, African Americans.

## Conclusion

While intra-individual socio-psychological reactions are indeed crucial for practical reasons (eg, voting and candidate preference), this case study is more interested in how social authorities (eg, elite individuals and advocacy groups) frame affirmative action in debates presented to the Supreme Court. In line with the arguments of Herbert Blumer (1958), we pose that the attitudes of the masses can be significantly impacted by dominant group members or groups that have the ability and resources to shape the narrative surrounding race and racial issues. Blumer argued that to truly understand how attitudes are fostered, one must shine a light on prominent external forces that can reach the masses and define an issue or a group. Sociologist Eduardo Bonilla-Silva (2018) added that such individuals and groups have the greatest impact because they ultimately speak the loudest. Thus, how we come to understand an out-group and ameliorative policies is significantly impacted by external entities that have interests in maintaining the status quo.

In this chapter, we provided a brief discussion about the history of affirmative action in the US. We discussed the shift in the role of government on ensuring equality of treatment for marginalized groups, and how this was met with a backlash from more conservative politicians who struggled with changing norms that accepted racial equality. We then focused in on affirmative action in higher education. We provided insight into why we chose this institute to serve as the case study for this book. In the most general sense, we chose higher education because it is seen as the primary vehicle for social mobility, and success in higher education is often attached to hard work and merit by many. In this chapter, we also discussed what affirmative action in higher education looks like. While the landscape has changed and certain policies (that is, "racial quotas") are viewed as not acceptable today, affirmative action is still viewed by many as a viable policy to increase diversity and assist in social mobility for marginalized groups. In that vein, we also briefly discussed the change in perspective regarding affirmative action from a policy that rights old wrongs to one that ensures institutional diversity. We will discuss this surprisingly controversial change in the next chapter. Finally, we concluded the chapter by discussing the broader ideological divide found in the US at all levels. Politically and legally, the fight for and against affirmative action rages on and serves as the foundation for this book.

Before we get to the analyses in the book, the next chapter asks whether race still matters. Common sense would have it that if race is no longer a predictor of social and economic outcomes, there is no real need to seek out or support particular policies or programs created and maintained by government that attempts to alleviate inequality. In such a case, policies such as affirmative action would become obsolete and should be relegated to history. As will be seen, however, race still matters in the US. Racial systems continue to benefit whites more than any other group, and the difference is not even close. Race is not something that can be wiped away as a thing of the past, but rather, it occupies a central location in contemporary social relations. In Chapter 3, we explore these patterns while also directing attention to the current state of affirmative action and the move to the diversity rationale, a perspective that changed the landscape of affirmative action forever. As we will see, the diversity rationale is surprisingly controversial among both opponents and supporters.

3

# Race, the Affirmative Action Debate, Education, and Past Court Cases

## Introduction

Why is affirmative action still a thing? Haven't we finally moved past race in American society? Why do we still have to reflect on the past, notably Jim Crow segregation and slavery? Many Americans have said, "I'm not a racist, so why am I getting punished?" They also lament that the US has atoned for their racist past and should now focus on merit and rewarding hard work rather than on a person's race. While such questions seem elementary to some, particularly social scientists who study race, inequality, and civil rights policies, these questions reverberate throughout modern debates over the continued implementation and even consideration of affirmative action in higher education.

As discussed in the last chapter, affirmative action was and continues to be a regulatory mechanism that formalizes rules *against* policies and social institutions that exclude and discriminate against *qualified* minorities. *Qualified* is the crucial component of this idea. Affirmative action was never meant to redistribute valued resources away from qualified individuals to unqualified minorities, which is a common misconception. Rather, affirmative action was intended to provide qualified individuals who have historically been excluded from participation due to systematic issues with opportunities not afforded to them based on their race. In this vein, affirmative action policies attempt to increase the chances of social and economic mobility for disenfranchised minorities who may struggle given no affirmative action policy.

This chapter provides insights into the state of racial inequality in the US today. In terms of income, wealth, jobs, and education, does race continue to predict life outcomes? If it does not, there really is no need to consider race when making policy at national and state levels or in higher education. The discussions over affirmative action and how it should be implemented would be moot. This chapter also provides an examination of the impact of education in general and in particular, for minorities. We look at how the elimination of affirmative action at state level has affected the enrollment of minorities in higher education. We then provide a look at the history of affirmative action related to higher education in the courts. As such, we offer a detailed synopsis of past court cases that have set the stage for how affirmative action is viewed and used in higher education today. In this light, we discuss the ever-present and surprisingly controversial notion of diversity and how it shapes the affirmative action landscape. We end the chapter by discussing our methodological and analytical strategies for the remaining portion of the book.

## Race matters... Still?

Before discussing the state of racial inequality today, we would like to highlight that we take the position that *race*, in and of itself, is not an appropriate explanatory variable for inferential statistical analysis, and is often misinterpreted when it is included in such analysis (Zuberi, 2001; Bonilla-Silva and Zuberi, 2008). As such, race is often essentialized and produces more harm than good even when presented in a seemingly positive light because it reinforces the notion that race and any race differences are real (Zuberi, 2001). Race is a social construction that does not have any basis in biology. However, the color of one's skin does appear to be consequential because it is associated with other factors (inequality in a stratified hierarchy) that create the false notion that somehow race is real and causally linked to various social and economic outcomes. When we say the impact of race, what we are saying is the impact of the *lived experiences* felt by racial minorities in a racialized social system that benefits a dominant group at the expense of marginalized groups. Thus, caution is necessary when interpreting statistics that include race. While we do not want to fall into this trap, we do see the importance of sharing statistics along racial lines to highlight the continued struggles of racial and ethnic minority groups. For the sake of argument and discussion, we compare African Americans and whites on a host of social and economic indicators to shine a light on the persistence of inequality in the US today. We also make these comparisons because affirmative action arguments for and against have continually focused on white and black access, unfortunately leaving out most other non-white groups.

With that being said, does race continue to matter today in the lived experiences of Americans? Does race continue to be associated with social and economic disparate outcomes despite seemingly great strides toward ending racism and discrimination in the US over the past half-century? Unfortunately, despite many gains, race continues to matter, as African Americans tend to lag behind their white counterparts on several key social and economic indicators that significantly affect their lived experiences in the US. By no means a comprehensive list, here are some of the most pressing concerns facing the US today:

- *Wealth disparities:* In 2016, African Americans maintained only 10.2 percent of the total wealth held by the median white family, which was only exacerbated by the Great Depression of 2007 when the labor, housing, and stock markets collapsed (Williams et al, 2010; Farley, 2011; Jones et al, 2018).
- *Income disparities:* In terms of dollars, in 2016, the typical African American worker made around 82 cents of every dollar earned by an average white worker. The typical African American household made only 61 percent of the annual income of the average white household (Jones et al, 2018).
- *Poverty levels:* African Americans maintain poverty levels two to three times higher than that of whites (Williams et al, 2010; Jones et al, 2018). In 2015, 24.1 percent of African Americans fell below the poverty line as compared to only 11.6 percent of whites (National Center for Health Statistics, 2017, Table 2).
- *Employment disparities:* African Americans are also less likely to be employed at all levels of jobs relative to whites (Farley, 2012). In 2016, unemployment was up to 7.5 percent from 6.7 percent in 1968, and African Americans were still twice as likely to be unemployed as their white counterparts (Jones et al, 2018). When attempting to get jobs, African Americans were even less likely to be called back for an interview than their white counterparts (Bertrand and Mullainathan, 2004).
- *Home ownership disparities:* African Americans are much less likely to own their own home. In 2016, they were 30 percent less likely to own their own home than their white counterparts (Jones et al, 2018).
- *Incarceration disparities:* The share of African Americans incarcerated tripled from 1968 to 2016, with the incarceration rates six times higher for African Americans than for whites (Jones et al, 2018).

Overall, the amalgamation of these statistics means, as sociologist Thomas Shapiro (2004) argued, that African American families have less homeownership, less wealth, less success in the workforce and higher education, and thus, less social mobility in comparison to whites in the 21st century.

The perverse level of inequality felt by African Americans unsurprisingly also affects health outcomes. For instance,

- *Life expectancy disparities:* The National Center for Health Statistics (2017, Table 15) reported a notable disparity in life expectancy for African Americans and whites of 2.8 years for females and 4.4 for males.
- *Death rate disparities:* In 2015, the age-adjusted death rates were 851.9 per 100,000 for African Americans and 735.0 per 100,000 whites (Cunningham et al, 2017).
- *Age difference disparities:* Morgan Levine and Eileen Crimmins (2014) found that at a specified chronological age, African Americans were approximately three years older biologically than whites. They go on to say that this difference in biological age is accounted for by higher rates of cardiovascular and cancer mortality among African Americans.
- *Infant mortality rate disparities:* The National Center for Health Statistics (2017, Table 10) found infant mortality rates for African Americans more than double that for whites (10.9 per 1,000 live births and 4.9 per 1,000 live births respectively).

Such statistics reflect not only significant health disparities, but also overall divergent lived experiences felt by African Americans and whites, a problem that has haunted and continues to haunt the US today.

While some may argue that racism and discrimination is a thing of the past and does not significantly impact life outcomes (see d'Souza 1991), research in the social sciences continues to show a society where race still matters more than 65 years after the Civil Rights Movement (see Omi and Winant, 2015; Bonilla-Silva, 2018). The lack of equality described above and research demonstrating the persistence of racism and discrimination are the very reasons why many social scientists and educators support ameliorative policies such as affirmative action in higher education and elsewhere. Indeed, social scientists and educators have authored amicus briefs submitted to the Supreme Court in the cases against affirmative action in higher education. In these briefs, they lay out strong empirically based arguments demonstrating the persistence of racial discrimination and accompanying inequality in the US today as well as the need for diversity in higher education.

In theory, these policies (eg, affirmative action) provide minorities with greater opportunities in higher education and the workforce otherwise not offered to them without such safety provisions, ultimately setting the stage for economic success and greater social mobility in the future. Research in states that have eliminated such policies, for example, shows minority representation in elite schools to be already in decline (Pierce, 2012). Even when states attempt to recruit students through other avenues (eg, the "Top 10% Rule" in Texas and high school recruitment), enrollment of minorities continues to suffer. Despite the growing support for diversity and all that it brings, inherent in the support for affirmative action is the acknowledgment that persistent racism and discrimination are still salient in the US, and stand at the root of struggles felt by racial and ethnic minority groups (Bonilla-Silva, 2018). Eduardo Bonilla-Silva argues that to suggest race and racism do not matter today, one must ignore thousands of research reports and published findings, as well as documented hardships faced by non-whites.

Some scholars, including Eduardo Bonilla-Silva (2018), Joe Feagin (2010b), and Michael Omi and Howard Winant (2015), argue that the racial system that existed before and during Jim Crow remains almost entirely intact into the 21st century. However, they pose that while the result is the same (persistent inequality and discrimination), the ideological underpinnings have significantly changed to hide these macro-aggressions towards people of color. Today's dominant ideology encompasses the denial of the existence of race and racism while relying heavily on discourse that suggests fairness and meritocracy should be the real concern rather than residual issues of racism (that is, neoliberalism). This new ideology also relies on arguments that attack the cultural inferiority of non-white minority groups rather than the biological inferiority that characterized the Jim Crow era. Further, researchers show how policies enacted to deal with racism have been met with continual resistance and white backlash (Omi and Winant, 2015). Despite efforts toward change and examples of non-white minority success (that is, Oprah Winfrey, LeBron James, and Barack Obama), it is clear by looking at empirical data that racial inequality remains a persistent issue in contemporary America.

## Inequality in higher education

Despite apparent and persistent debilitating racial inequality, the debate over affirmative action continues to be heated in both the court of public opinion and the judicial system. Concerning public sentiment, as suggested in Chapter 1, supporters and non-supporters alike lay claim to the high moral ground (Bobo, 2000). Supporters of affirmative action see themselves as champions of racial justice, and demand that affirmative action is imperative to move the US to a state where diversity and acceptance prevail. Advocates point to the history of racism and discrimination and to current social and economic indicators such as those listed above as sufficient justifications to warrant race-conscious policies and continued government intervention.

Persistent inequality and research on racism make it unlikely that there are no "special" barriers to academic and economic achievement for marginalized groups. African American students are still less likely than white students to earn their high school diploma and even attend traditional colleges and universities despite a general increase in enrollment overall (Williams et al, 2010; Farley, 2012; Carnevale and Strohl, 2013). These disparities have an overall impact on student success when racial minorities do attend. In 2016, for example, African Americans were 54.2 percent as likely to earn a college degree as whites (Jones et al, 2018).

African American students are also more likely to attend two- or four-year open-access higher education institutions than white students (Carnevale and Strohl, 2013). Since 1995, Anthony Carnevale and Jeff Strohl (2013) found that where 82 percent of the enrollment of whites have gone to the most selective universities, enrollment for African Americans (68 percent) and Hispanics (72 percent) tended to be in open-access colleges and universities lacking accreditation or reputation. While education is seen as an important component of social mobility for many, reliance on such open-access schools exposes African Americans and other marginalized groups to higher levels of debt on completion, which then leads to higher default rates (Cellinni and Chaudhary, 2014).

Given the reality of higher education and inequality in the workplace after graduation, some have argued that placing marginalized groups into direct competition in the job market is unfair without considering structural barriers and persistent discrimination. Specifically, such efforts are likely to reproduce inequality and the status hierarchy that already exists in the US. President Lyndon Johnson stated tersely back in a 1965 commencement address to Howard University that:

> You do not take a person who, for years, has been hobbled by chains and liberate him, bring him up to the starting line and a race and then say, 'You are free to compete with all the others,' and still justly believe that you have been completely fair.

That is to say, if adequate consideration of historical conditions of inequality and persistent discrimination is *not* taken into account, the chances of success for marginalized groups are doomed from the outset.

On the other hand, opponents of affirmative action also see themselves as protectors of justice. While supporters argue that policies are still needed because of the persistent racism and discrimination plaguing the US, opponents pose that forcing equality through race-conscious government intervention is immoral, foolhardy, and likely to do more harm than good. Justice and fairness, from this perspective, would be eliminating policies that use race as a mechanism to discriminate against other races (particularly whites themselves) rather than implementing race-conscious policies. Many opponents even argue that we are at a place where race no longer significantly matters, and that we can rely on a genuinely color-blind society for justice. By using a color-blind approach, they suggest merit and free market processes can be the ultimate determinant of social, economic, and political success (Bobo, 2000). Those who work hard regardless of race and ethnicity will succeed while those who do not commit to working hard will fail.

This color-blind argument relies on a few assumptions: (1) racism has greatly diminished and no longer predicts social and economic outcomes for individuals; and (2) hard work and merit are the primary causes of success. Since research demonstrates that neither of these assumptions are factual, opponents rely on faulty beliefs and social attitudes to overcome existing empirical data. One central tenet of this argument is the idea that whites are now the victims of potential discrimination (that is, reverse discrimination), and most interestingly, this discrimination is placed on a par with that experienced by racial minorities. Following this logic, ameliorative policies are seen as examples of how whites are the new victims of race-based discrimination and that the government can be seen as the primary perpetrator of discrimination (Moore, 2018).

Conservative elites have launched coordinated assaults on affirmative action using this rationale (Moore, 2018). Specifically, they mischaracterize affirmative action as a "quota" policy where groups are systematically hired or admitted into college even though such concrete policies are rarely, if ever, used. They further argue that affirmative action allows minorities who are not qualified to be hired or admitted into college over qualified whites. In opposition to affirmative action (*Gratz* and *Grutter*), for example, George W. Bush (2003) stated,

> I strongly support a diversity of all kinds, including racial diversity, in higher education, but the method used by the University of Michigan to achieve this important goal is fundamentally flawed. At their core, the Michigan policies amount to a quota system that unfairly rewards or penalizes prospective students based solely on their race.

Within this definitional framework (Goffman, 1974), utilizing race as a characteristic to base a policy on is defined as oppositional to the efforts of the Civil Rights Movement that attempted to prevent discrimination based on race.

Given the history of unequal relations among whites and African Americans, however, this neoliberal argument utilizes existing tensions to create conflict. First, it does so by turning the notion of justice on its head and raising concerns among whites about potential discrimination they could face (Moore and Bell, 2011). Second, it limits affirmative action to a zero-sum game where one group must lose if the other is to accomplish anything. Such a stance sparks strong emotion, particularly among whites, and paints them as victims of policies like affirmative action that do not benefit them, and directs resources to groups that do not deserve them (Moore and Bell, 2011). In so doing, arguments that frame affirmative action in such a fashion render the Equal Protection Clause (that promises all citizens equal protection under the law) of the 14th Amendment color-blind by ignoring the unequal racial past and present felt by racial minority groups.

## The impact of higher education

The heated debate and hostile fights over affirmative action imply that education is a good thing, that it has some tangible and positive impact on social and economic outcomes. While education is viewed as the primary mechanism to gain social mobility and improve life chances in the US, does it really help? If not, one could surmise that the fight to gain control over admissions to higher education would not be as bitter or long-fought. Indeed, research demonstrates that education does seem to have various positive social and economic benefits post-graduation. More education has been shown to increase wages, help job options, improve health outcomes, and increase family stability (for a full discussion, see Hout et al, 2011). Individuals with a college degree also report less time being unemployed (Hout et al, 2011), and experience quicker recovery after economic downturns than non-college graduates (Gangl, 2006). Research has also shown an interesting positive association between education and prospects of marrying, getting divorced, and getting married again (Western et al, 2008). The impact of education is especially profound for racial minorities graduating from college. African Americans have benefited more from their education than other racial and ethnic groups, with higher rates of college attendance (Hout et al, 2011). In short, a preponderance of evidence suggests that education is a good thing and improves life chances across marginalized populations.

Education also provides other latent effects for citizens. Scholars have noted that education is an essential institution because it promotes civility, acceptance, and toleration. Universities are theoretically places where information can be exchanged to promote more accepting viewpoints toward others of different social and cultural backgrounds. While some debate in the literature exists (for a discussion, see Jackman, 1994), research generally supports the notion that individuals who attend college have typically more liberal and accepting attitudes toward perceived differences, and exhibit greater support for policies meant to improve the standards of marginalized groups (Schuman et al, 1997; Carter, 2005; Carter and Carter, 2014; Carter et al, 2005, 2014). Universities promote acceptance because they are spaces where individuals of different social and ethnic backgrounds can come into contact under a similar standing, a necessary condition to reduce prejudicial views (Allport, 1954). Indeed, many universities today have some programs focused on diversity and inclusion that emphasize the importance of diversity in creating a quality higher education experience for all students. Some have argued that the type of contact found on college and university campuses allows groups to interact, leading to an understanding of differences that dispels fears and produces respect as individuals from differing backgrounds come together under a similar social status (van Laar et al, 2004; Pierce, 2012).

Given the overall positive social and economic returns of education, it becomes apparent why using affirmative action within admissions policies is a controversial issue that has resulted in a quite contentious debate. Education is a valuable resource being divided and distributed by the government. Such division of resources has been labeled quite pejoratively as "redistributive policies" and produced quite negative views among whites in the US. Michael Hout et al (2011), for example, noted that whites have begun seeing affirmative action as a zero–sum game that they are losing. Whites then connect their failings and loss with perceived entitlements given to other less qualified groups simply based on their race (Hout et al, 2011). Indeed, this frame of argumentation has been standard in court cases and in public disputes against affirmative action in higher education.

With the concern over redistribution in mind, what impact has affirmative action had on college and university admissions for groups that have been underrepresented and underserved in the past? In states that have banned the use of affirmative action, the lack of such a policy has worked to the detriment of African American enrollment (Brown and Hirschman, 2006). Using nationally representative data, Grant Blume and

Mark Long (2014) found enrollment of minorities dropped considerably at elite selective universities in states where affirmative action was banned. Such a drop was not observed in states that maintained the use of affirmative action in higher education, particularly for elite universities.

David Colburn, Charles Young, and Victor Yellen (2008, p 6) described the impact losing affirmative action has had on African-American freshmen enrollment as "devastating." For instance, in two elite California universities, enrollment for African Americans dropped in half, with the most significant impact of the affirmative action ban being felt by the two flagship University of California campuses, Berkeley and Los Angeles (Brown and Hirschman, 2006; Arnwine, 2007). While color-blind initiatives enlisted by the states of Texas ("Top 10% Rule") and Florida ("One Florida") buffered the impact of banning affirmative action on African Americans to a degree, it was not enough as enrollments dropped at their flagship universities. For instance, enrollment dropped at the University of Texas at Austin and Texas A&M and at the University of Florida (Arnwine, 2007). These drops in enrollment were not isolated events as other states that banned affirmative action, Georgia and Michigan, also witnessed similar outcomes (Brown and Hirschman 2006). Looking at the bigger picture, the drop in enrollment was related to a more insidious result than just overall participation. Ben Backes (2012) found that the ban of affirmative action in California re-routed minority students from *more* selective to *less* selective institutions. Such a shift greatly impacts the future economic and social efforts of African Americans. By not receiving a degree from an elite university, the earning potential of students is greatly reduced.

## Past court cases: How did we get here?

One may look at the discussion above, and wonder, how did we get here? Given the state of racial disparities, how did remedial actions such as affirmative action become antiquated, shunned, and even despised in the eyes of many Americans, politicians, and the courts? While there have been only four cases against affirmative action in higher education to reach and be ruled on by the Supreme Court in the past 40 years, three of these have come in the last 15 years. Scholar Gary Orfield posed that this trend is partly due to the inroads made by Reagan/Bush conservative court appointments (Orfield, 2001). Lee Cokorinos (2003) further added that the current-day challenge to civil rights initiatives in general are also associated with the inclusion of key conservative actors in the political and legal system that gained power in the Reagan administration as well as the proliferation of advocacy organizations related to these same individuals. This conservative movement, as described by Cokorinos, is one reason many were surprised that affirmative action received a temporary reprieve in the *Fisher II* case. While this is, indeed, a win, the fight against affirmative action is far from over.

Before we discuss and deconstruct the contemporary cases being analyzed in the next few chapters, we provide a brief history of affirmative action in the courts, both the Supreme Court and lower courts. While there have been many legal challenges to affirmative action admissions policies that have shaped the landscape of this policy in education, only a relative few have made it to prominence and received public attention. These cases have made significant contributions to the narrative of affirmative action, and set the legal precedence leading up to the latest court cases against affirmative action.

## DeFunis v Odegaard

We begin with the 1974 *DeFunis v Odegaard* (416 US 312) case. The *DeFunis* case set the stage for the *Bakke* opinion that illuminated the constitutional importance of diversity while ruling against the use of past discrimination as a constitutional rationale to support affirmative action in higher education. In the early 1970s, just four years before the historic *Bakke* ruling, the Supreme Court heard a case in which a white male, Marco DeFunis, sued the University of Washington Law School (UWLS) because he thought he was being discriminated against based on his race (for a discussion, see Kellough, 2006). DeFunis and his lawyers asked whether affirmative action as implemented by the university violated his basic civil rights.

For the most part, DeFunis was a decent student, earning a 3.6 GPA while completing a degree in political science at the University of Washington in Seattle. During his undergraduate education, DeFunis worked at the local Parks and Recreation Department and taught religion to young children. In the 1970–71 academic school year, DeFunis applied to six law schools. Because of high demand for seats, he was accepted into only two schools, both of which were private law schools. He was rejected by UWLS, which was his primary school of interest. He decided against attending private law school to stay near family in Washington State. To better his application and chances, DeFunis retook the LSAT (Law School Admission Test) where he received higher scores and reapplied to UWLS the following academic year. On being rejected again, DeFunis felt he was being passed over for less qualified minority candidates due to the admissions policy of UWLS, which treated these students differently than white students. On hearing of DeFunis's situation, a local lawyer, Josef Diamond, who had an interest in civil rights cases, asked the university to reconsider his admission. When the university denied the request, DeFunis filed a civil suit against the university, arguing his civil rights under the 14th Amendment had been violated.

Indeed, the admissions policy of UWLS did take into consideration a candidate's race by incorporating approximately 15–20 percent of minorities in its admitting class (Kellough, 2006). In the 1971–72 academic year, UWLS admitted about 44 minority students (or 30% of the class), many of whom scored lower than DeFunis on standardized testing. However, standardized scores were not the only factor considered in the admissions process by the university, and did not necessarily guarantee admissions even when high. DeFunis also scored higher than other groups, including veterans and non-minorities, who eventually *were* admitted to the law school. Moreover, DeFunis received standardized test scores lower than 29 white applicants who also did not get into UWLS. Regardless, DeFunis decided to sue, claiming that he had been discriminated against based on race in violation of the Equal Protection Clause of the 14th Amendment.

Judge Lloyd Shorett of the Superior Court of King County, Washington, ruled that the 14th Amendment could not be used to benefit one race at the expense of another. Thus, Judge Shorett ruled in favor of DeFunis, and the university was forced to admit him. In 1973, the university successfully appealed this ruling to the Washington Supreme Court. Such a decision placed DeFunis's law school seat in jeopardy, so DeFunis appealed the decision to the Supreme Court. A "stay of action" was ordered by the Court, which allowed DeFunis to complete his law degree. Given the fact that DeFunis had completed school and earned his degree by the time the case came up in the Supreme Court in 1974, the Justices decided to render the decision "moot" and not rule on the case. Some posed that such a decision amounted to a sidestep of the issue by the Court (Kellough, 2006). Nonetheless, just three short years later, affirmative action would again take center stage in the highest court in the land.

## Regents of the University of California v Bakke

Shortly after *DeFunis* and just over a decade after the Civil Rights Act of 1964 was implemented by President Johnson, higher education again faced another significant challenge to affirmative action by a white student who felt wrongly treated by the policy: *Regents of the University of California v Bakke* (438 US 265, 1978). Before the *Bakke* case, any challenges to the state of education regarding race were handled by the lower courts, and only *DeFunis* ever got consideration in the highest court of the land. However, this changed with *Bakke*. In 1977, the Supreme Court granted certiorari[1] and placed the affirmative action case on its docket. While the ruling of *Bakke* upheld the use of race in admissions processes, it also changed the landscape of this policy in higher education, and still plays a dominant role in contemporary cases dealing with affirmative action.

In the early 1970s, Allan Paul Bakke, a 35-year-old white male, applied to 12 medical schools, including the University of California-Davis (hereafter UC-Davis), where he applied twice. He was denied entry by all 12 programs, including UC-Davis, which he later sued. While not perfect by any standard, Bakke was a good student with a formidable academic record. He was a graduate of the University of Minnesota where he earned a GPA of over 3.5 and completed two engineering degrees. He also achieved respectable scores on the MCAT (Medical College Admission Test). His non-academic achievements were also noteworthy. He was considered a non-traditional student because he deferred college to serve in the Marine Corps, where he served one tour of duty in Vietnam. By the end of his military career in 1967, he was released with an honorable discharge and had achieved the rank of Captain. He also worked at NASA where he developed much of his interest in medicine (for a full discussion, see Sedler, 1977).

At the same time, because of concern over the lack of diversity in the student body and the general medical profession, UC-Davis implemented two admissions processes: one for standard applicants and one for minority and economically challenged applicants (Sedler, 1977). White applicants were considered under the general admissions, which rejected applicants with a GPA of less than 2.5. The special admissions policies had no GPA limit and focused almost exclusively on minority and economically challenged applicants. In 1973 the university reserved 16 of 100 seats for just these students. Accordingly, applicants who were admitted under the unique admissions process did not have to meet the same standards as students who were admitted through the standard admissions process. On the surface, the purpose of the special admissions program seemed honorable and appropriate considering the history of race in the US. The special program was created to (1) increase the number of minorities who have faced discrimination by medical schools and the profession in the past, (2) oppose persistent institutional discrimination, (3) increase the number of medical professionals in underserved communities, and (4) improve the experience of all students through diversity (Sedler, 1977).

After being rejected for the second time in 1974, Bakke took umbrage with the special admissions process, an affirmative action program he argued violated the Equal Protection Clause of the 14th Amendment and Title VI of the Civil Rights Act of 1964. In line with the Equal Protection Clause, Section 601 of Title VI states, "No person in the United States shall, on the ground of race, color or national origin be excluded from participation in, be denied the benefits of or be subjected to discrimination under any program or activity receiving Federal financial assistance." Accordingly, Bakke posed that such a policy violated these laws by discriminating against him based on his race. Given that UC-Davis obtained funding from the federal government, its policy was argued to be unconstitutional and could be sued accordingly.

The use of the Equal Protection Clause for the fight against affirmative action in *DeFunis* and *Bakke* was a bit ironic given the history of racial exclusion and discrimination in this country. Historically, it was written to protect, at least minimally, racial and ethnic minority groups from discrimination and to provide them every opportunity for social mobility. With *Bakke*, Robert Sedler (1977, p 333) stated, "the *equal protection clause* came full circle to invalidate a very limited preference for racial minorities that was designed to overcome the cumulative effects of societal discrimination against them." By using this argument, *Bakke*, in essence, called for the Equal Protection Clause to be color-blind in theory and in practice. That is, affirmative action and other like policies should treat everyone equally and not consider race, regardless of history and personal context. This argument poses that the extensive history of racism and discrimination felt by African Americans, including over 200 years of slavery, should simply be forgotten and that reverse racism against whites should be viewed in a similar fashion as racism felt by other groups.

In 1974, after being rejected for the second time, and with encouragement from ex-administration at the university, Bakke filed a lawsuit against the university in the Superior Court of California, one of several trial courts in California. The medical school at UC-Davis countered this claim by arguing that using affirmative action as such did not violate his constitutional rights and that Bakke was actually not granted admission to the university due to his scores and not his race. Relative to other applicants that year, his grades were considered insufficient. The university argued that while Bakke was a good student, he would not have been admitted even if no affirmative action policy was in place. Regardless, the Superior Court of California ruled in favor of Bakke, and stated that the special program was discriminatory and violated his constitutional rights. The university immediately appealed the ruling to the State Supreme Court of California. In 1976, by a 6–1 margin, the State Supreme Court of California upheld the lower court's decision, arguing that the use of race as such was discriminatory and unconstitutional. In writing the majority opinion, Justice Stanley Mosk opined that no applicant could be rejected based on race with regards to the standards applied by the medical university.

In late 1976, UC-Davis petitioned the Supreme Court to review the case and, in early 1977, they agreed and placed the case on the docket for later that same year. In the summer of 1978, the Court handed down a 5–4 greatly divided ruling in favor of Bakke. Six different opinions were handed down by the justices. The Court was so divided that Justice Thurgood Marshall even referred to Justice Lewis Powell's opinion as racist (Epstein and Knight, 2001). Regardless, the splintered ruling of the Court held that the system used by the medical school of UC-Davis was effectively a quota system and violated the Equal Protection Clause of the US Constitution. Thus, the school must admit Bakke. This Court's ruling posed that policies that include specific set-asides or quotas for minorities amounted to reverse discrimination against whites based on race.

However, the Court did not entirely rule out the use of race. Justice Powell, while noting that such quota-style policies were inappropriate, added that race continued to be a compelling interest of the state and could be considered as one factor of many when considering admissions. The Court viewed diversity as a compelling interest of the university and the state. Interestingly, this ruling, in essence, allowed diversity to be used as a soft response to past and present discrimination by colleges and universities. In his opinion, Justice Powell wrote, "The file of a particular African American applicant may be examined for his potential contribution to diversity without the factor of race being decisive when compared, for example with that of an applicant identified as an Italian American if the latter is thought to exhibit qualities more likely to promote beneficial educational pluralism" (438 US at 317 [Powell, J.]).

With this ruling, the landscape of affirmative action in admissions to higher education was changed forever. Bakke went on to graduate from UC-Davis in 1982, and practiced as an anesthesiologist after that. While Bakke carried on with his career, affirmative action as an ameliorative policy was in turmoil and under fire. The notion that organizations receiving federal funding could use set-aside or quota policies ended in one ruling. In turn, the idea of diversity became the rationale of choice and by law. Any future attacks on affirmative action policies would need to focus on the role of diversity in higher education and its role in training students for future employment in a diverse society. As parlayed by Justice Powell, "The diversity that furthers a compelling state interest encompasses a far broader array of qualifications and characteristics of which racial or ethnic origin is but a single though important element" (438 US at 318 [Powell, J.]). Conversely, future support for affirmative action needs to take seriously the role diversity plays in higher education, for the university and all students involved in the educational process.

Both opponents and supporters of affirmative action were stung by the ruling. On the one hand, opponents celebrated the end of what they viewed as discriminatory practices of quota programs, where one group was guaranteed and received resources based not on merit but on the color of their skin. Opponents, however, frowned on the notion that race could still be used and continued to be seen as a compelling interest of the university and state (Synnott, 2004). The reason for the concern among opponents was that a large majority of schools would not need to change their procedures at all, and would thus continue to consider race when admitting applicants. On the other hand, supporters of affirmative action were more upset with the ruling. The notion of diversity was seen by many as a color-blind initiative that minimized the steep history of racial inequality and injustices of the past (Moore and Bell, 2011). In many ways, this elevation of diversity would reduce the bite of affirmative action. Now other "types" of diversity could become part of the conversation, an argument that further minimizes the unique experiences of African Americans in the US.

## Hopwood v University of Texas Law School

Since the *Bakke* ruling, several court cases have dealt with affirmative action in different areas yet have contributed greatly to the affirmative action debate (see *Fullilove v Klutznick, City of Richmond v J.A. Croson Co, Wygant v Jackson Board of Education, United States v Paradise, Adarand Constructors, Inc v Peña*, to name but a few). One of the most important of these cases focused on admissions in higher education is *Hopwood v University of Texas Law School* (78 F3d 932, Fifth Circuit, 1996). While ultimately this case did not reach the Supreme Court, its impact on the landscape of higher education for racial and ethnic minority groups is undeniable and comparable to *Bakke*. Up until this time the *Bakke* ruling had not been significantly challenged. However, in this case, it became clear that the Reagan/Bush court appointments were finally making conservative waves in the legal system by restructuring the courts in opposition to racial issues and policies such as affirmative action (Orfield, 2001). The Fifth US Circuit Court of Appeals ruling in *Hopwood* invalidated the *Bakke* ruling that race and diversity could be used as a factor or rationale when making admissions decisions. Instead, the appeals courts ruled that the university and state no longer had a compelling justification for using race in any fashion in the admissions process, even if its stated purpose was to correct a racial imbalance in enrollment. This ruling, to a certain extent, signified the beginning of the contemporary fight to end affirmative action in higher education.

Similar to *DeFunis* and *Bakke*, the *Hopwood* case began with a disgruntled white petitioner who felt discriminated against by a university based on their race. After being denied entrance into the University of Texas Law School (hereafter UT Law) in 1992, Cheryl Hopwood, a white woman, sued the university and state claiming that the racial preference admissions policy used by the school was unconstitutional and amounted to reverse discrimination (for a full discussion, see Scanlan, 1996). Another plaintiff, Stephanie C. Haynes, was summarily dropped from the lawsuit in early 1993 while three others (all white males) were added later, including Douglas Carvell, Kenneth Elliot, and David Rogers. Cheryl Hopwood was, in many ways a perfect candidate to be the face of this anti-affirmative action fight. She was a former Princeton University student who had to drop out of school due to the cost, and ultimately put herself through college and graduated with a high GPA from California State University in Sacramento. Moreover, her test scores were in line with many of the other top candidates of that class. She was also very active in the community and participated in the Big Brothers/Big Sisters program in her community. Hopwood was an unusually sympathetic candidate because she sought to attend college and better herself while raising a daughter who suffered from a rare muscular disease (Scanlan, 1996).

On being rejected, Hopwood was notified that her test scores were lower than some applicants' scores but higher than some minority candidates who did get into UT Law. Hopwood ultimately brought a lawsuit against UT Law for this very reason, claiming that the school had violated her 14th Amendment right to equal protection under the law. She sought a change in the admissions policy as well as punitive damages. Initially, the US District Court for the Western District of Texas ruled in favor of UT Law, denying Hopwood's lawsuit, and affirming that the university's use of race was appropriate when determining admissions. This court upheld the *Bakke* decision that held diversity to be a compelling interest of the university and state (Scanlan, 1996). However, Hopwood appealed the ruling to the Fifth US Circuit Court of Appeals where it reversed the judgment of the lower court. Reversal of the decision meant that UT Law admissions policy was ruled unconstitutional, and that having a diverse student body was not a compelling interest of the university and state. The university could no longer use race as one factor of many for making admissions decisions that would assist them in assuring a diverse student body. This ruling rejected the diversity argument made by Justice Powell in the *Bakke* case, and made affirmative action in admissions more difficult. It also placed all higher education on notice that even such a minimally invasive use of race as *one* factor (not *the* factor) to assist in bringing about diversity would be challenged.

The university eventually appealed the lower courts' ruling to the Supreme Court. While Justice Ruth Bader Ginsburg highlighted the merits of the issue, the fact that UT Law no longer used the policy in their admissions process prevented the case from moving forward. While the Hopwood decision only held for the Fifth Circuit, Laura Scanlan (1996, pp 1582–3) suggested that the decision "stands at odds with Supreme Court precedent and therefore unjustifiably weakens the already embattled status of affirmative action in higher education." The defiant and almost dismissive stance made by this court against using race in such a minimal fashion makes this case quite infamous in terms of the history of the fight for civil rights, and placed affirmative action in the crosshairs of future cases.

## Other less prominent affirmative action cases

While earlier cases of *Bakke* and *Hopwood* have garnered most of the national headlines and scholarly attention, other more recent cases dealing with race and admissions have also been brought to litigation. The rulings from these cases have only confused and muddled the narrative surrounding affirmative action. These conflicting rulings have also brought into question the legal standing and future of affirmative action in general. To a certain extent, these cases have not been consistent with *Bakke*, where Justice Powell spelled out the notion that diversity *is* a compelling interest of the schools and the state, and that admissions policies seeking to increase diversity are constitutional. The fact that these cases did not make it to the Supreme Court may go a long way in explaining why they have not garnered prominent media attention. However, we feel they need to be considered when discussing the recent history of this policy as they provide more insight into the continued fight over affirmative action waged by opponents and proponents alike.

In 2001, three cases dealing with affirmative action in admissions to higher education institutions were ruled on by the lower courts (for a full discussion of each case, see Kellough, 2006). In 1997, for example, several white students, including Katuria Smith, Angela Rock, and Michael Pyle, brought a lawsuit against the University of Washington Law School

(UWLS), arguing that they faced illegal discrimination because of their race: *Smith v the University of Washington* (392 F3d 367, Ninth Circuit, 2004). They collectively claimed that the university applied different standards for white students than they did for minority students. Despite being born into poverty, having an alcoholic father, and dropping out of high school as a teenager, Smith maintained competitive grades (3.65 GPA and 165 LSAT), which increased expectations that she would be accepted into the university's law school. Similarly, Rock and Pyle also maintained competitive scores and expected to be a part of UWLS. However, this would not be the case as each of the three plaintiffs were rejected by the university over three years (1994, 1995, and 1996). Interestingly, they each successfully applied to and attended other law schools after being rejected by UWLS (save for Pyle, who reapplied and was accepted to UWLS in 1999). During this period, the university maintained a race preference policy program to increase minority participation.

In 2000, the Ninth Circuit Court of Appeals ruled against Smith, Rock, and Pyle, and affirmed the district court's ruling that diversity was a compelling interest of the state and university, thus upholding Justice Powell's opinion in *Bakke* that admissions policies can be race-sensitive, and ignoring *Hopwood*'s dismissive tone toward diversity. During this period, 1998 to be exact, the Washington initiative, "Initiative 200" ("I-200"), was approved by 58 percent of the state's voters. This was similar to Proposition 209 in California and Proposition 2 later in Michigan that ruled the use of affirmative action to be illegal. After it was passed in 1998, the university agreed to suspend the use of race in admissions policies, which weakened the need to rule in favor of the plaintiffs at the state level. Even with this I-200 in place, Smith and the remaining plaintiffs appealed the case to the Supreme Court where a *writ of certiorari* was not granted, at least in part for this very reason. This ruling ignored the growing unrest surrounding diversity highlighted by *Hopwood* in particular, and upheld Justice Powell's argument in the *Bakke* case.

While the *Smith* case upheld the use of affirmative action, *Johnson v Board of Regents of the University of Georgia* (106 F Supp, 2d 1362, Southern District of Georgia, 2000), again made admissions more confusing in higher education by ruling against affirmative action. In this case, three white female applicants (Jennifer Johnson's individually filed complaint was consolidated with a claim made by Aimee Bogrow and Molly Ann Beckenhaur) were rejected by the University of Georgia. Like in the *Smith* case, the students maintained good grades and expected that they would be admitted into the University of Georgia. The US District Court for the Southern District of Georgia initially ruled that diversity was not a compelling interest of the state and university, and that very little research supported the notion that educational experience was substantially shaped and positively impacted by diversity. However, on appeal, the Eleventh US Circuit Court of Appeals declined to consider the notion of diversity yet upheld the ruling against affirmative action. This court's opinion was that the admissions policy implemented by the university was not narrowly tailored to the interests of those involved, and was thus unconstitutional.

At about the same time, in 1995, Rob Farmer, a white male, was rejected by the University of Maryland School of Medicine (UMSM). He subsequently brought a lawsuit against the university and state (*Farmer v Ramsay*, 41 F Supp. 2d 587, District of Maryland, 1999), claiming that he had been discriminated against by the university because they maintained a racial quota system that admitted minorities who held lower grades and standardized test scores than many white applicants. The UMSM countered by asserting that Farmer had not been rejected based on his race. Instead, he had been denied based on less than stellar science scores, unspectacular recommendation letters from faculty at Towson University, where he was an undergraduate student, and a disconcerting explanation he provided regarding his prior arrest record. Such pre-conditions, according to UMSM, placed him at odds with the admissions policy of the university, and he would have been rejected even if he was a racial minority. In 2001, the court ruled that there was insufficient evidence to suggest that race played a role in the UMSM rejection of Farmer and, accordingly, there were other factors that resulted in the rejection. The case was dismissed by a federal judge (that is, the judge denied Farmer's motion for a partial summary judgment) who agreed with the university that race had played no factor.

Overall, these three cases demonstrate that the fight against affirmative action was and continues to be ever-present, even if national exposure is missing. They set the stage for prominent admissions and affirmative action cases that serve as the focus of this book and subsequent chapters: *Gratz/Grutter v Bollinger* (2003) and *Fisher v University of Texas at Austin* (2013 and 2016). Before we move on to our analysis of these more recent cases, we return to the notion of diversity and its growing impact on the affirmative action landscape in higher education.

## Return to diversity and affirmative action: Where do we go from here?

As stated before, the *Bakke* ruling placed the notion of diversity at the forefront of the fight for and against affirmative action while eliminating the idea that quota-like policies are permissible. The Justices also put to rest the notion that past discrimination can be the reason for using affirmative action policies. In a related case dealing with academic freedom (*Keyishian v Board of Regents*, 385 US 589, 1967), Justice Powell (385 US at 332 [Powell, J.]) wrote in his opinion that, "It is not too much to say that the nation's future depends upon leaders trained through wide exposure to the ideas and mores of students as diverse as this Nation of many people." Thus, the *Bakke* case and others moved the conversation around affirmative action away from mediating present and past discrimination to diversity as an acceptable constitutional rationale for admitting marginalized groups into universities (Alon and Tienda, 2007). While this ruling may seem innocuous and even positive, it set in motion a critical condition that has stunted the growth of affirmative action and possibly set the stage for its ultimate demise.

The fight for and against the constitutional viability of affirmative action continues today. Again, as with the *Bakke* case, the notion of diversity has been at the forefront. In the *Grutter* case against the University of Michigan, Justice Sandra O'Connor penned the majority opinion and stated that "numerous studies show that student body diversity promotes learning outcomes, and better prepares students for an increasingly diverse workforce and society, and better prepares them as professionals" (539 US at 18 [O'Connor, S.]). In this light, it is clear that diversity has become the standard for current cases dealing with affirmative action (Alon and Tienda, 2007), given the stamp of approval by Justice Powell and thus, by the state. Furthermore, it is also clear that an analysis of any debate surrounding affirmative action will have to take seriously the diversity frame in arguing a case for and against the policy.

Despite being part of the dissenting opinion in the *Grutter* case, Justice Kennedy crossed over and supported the notion that diversity is indeed a cultural imperative for students and citizens. He wrote that diversity is essential because it "promotes cross-racial understanding, helps to break down racial stereotypes, and enables students to better understand persons of different races." Administration from both the University of Texas and the University of Michigan committed early to the notion that diversity is essential for young scholars and future employees, as laid out by the *Bakke* case (Green, 2004). For instance, Lee Bollinger, the then President of the University of Michigan, stated,

> We really decided to set out to prove the fundamental premise of *Bakke*, that race is a significant factor in American life, and that significance gives it salience in an educational setting. That is, it is intimately related to our educational goals, and that people really are affected in their education by being in a

diverse environment. So, there are no other ways that we can do this acceptably, then by using race as a factor in admissions. So that has been the thrust and focus of our legal defense.

In line with this rationale, the Supreme Court has agreed with *Bakke* and *Grutter* that diversity is an important characteristic at a university whose goal is to educate and produce graduates who must seek employment in diverse environments. In writing the majority opinion in the *Fisher* case, Justice Kennedy stated that the use of race as fashioned by the University of Texas at Austin was permissible and did not violate the Equal Protection Clause. Along with the "Top 10% Rule" (discussed in more detail in Chapter 5), the University of Texas at Austin's undergraduate system used a more holistic approach in determining admissions when Fisher applied. The holistic approach as applied considered several factors when making decisions about the viability of a student, including their race.

Despite its prominence in the affirmative action debate and seemingly logical underpinning, both opponents and supporters of affirmative action take issue with the diversity rationale. Opponents have condemned it for different reasons. The most prominent argument against the use of diversity is that it reflects actual overt discrimination against whites. This perspective promoted by conservatives poses that such policies are in opposition to the Equal Protection Clause. In this case, it would be the often-used term "reverse discrimination" against whites. This perspective has been referred to as neoliberal in nature because it takes the notion of racial justice as sought out by minorities and promoted by the late great Martin Luther King Jr, and stands it on its head. Now the very idea of using race to ameliorate racial discrimination is in and of itself discrimination that is detrimental to whites. Whites have become the victim, the victim of a policy that discriminates against groups based on race, an inscriptive factor whites do not control.

Most interesting and seemingly counterintuitive, some supporters also struggle with the notion of diversity (Berrey, 2011; Collins, 2011a, b). Ellen Berrey (2011, p 589), for example, noted that "diversity was not a demand of civil rights activists, and it poses some challenges for contemporary activists, who find they must simultaneously use the term and refute it." Diversity to some is seen as a color-blind mechanism that minimizes persistent racism and discrimination; thus, diversity initiatives often miss the boat by de-emphasizing problems minorities continue to live with today. As such, diversity initiatives do very little to eliminate racism and discrimination and are actually seen as doing more harm than good (Bonilla-Silva, 2018). If anything, diversity is viewed as a soft response to the persistent inequality and discrimination felt by minorities in general and African Americans in particular.

Supporters also pose that diversity is problematic because it allows for inaction on the part of universities and university officials. That is, universities often argue that they promote diversity, yet do very little to ensure that campus life is welcoming and supportive for groups who have been marginalized in the past. This lack of attention increases the chances of marginalized students feeling less supported and welcome than is optimal within a diverse campus. As such, the diversity rationale within higher education pulls attention away from racism and discrimination and places students in institutions that do not promote their best interests. The diversity rationale, according to scholars such as Eduardo Bonilla-Silva (2018, p 2), can then be seen as promoting color-blindness by minimizing real techniques that could be used to reduce inequality. Bonilla-Silva (2018, p 2) posed that color-blindness is akin to "racism lite" because no "racist" is needed to maintain racial inequality, and discrimination is built into the structure of society:

> This ideology, which acquired cohesiveness and dominance in the late 1960s, explains contemporary racial inequality as the outcome of nonracial dynamics. Whereas Jim Crow racism explained African Americans' social standing as the result of their biological and moral inferiority, color-racism avoids such facile arguments. Instead, whites rationalize minorities' contemporary status as the product of market dynamics, naturally occurring phenomena, and African Americans' imputed cultural limitations.

In short, people rely on an "anything but racism" argument despite the overwhelming and documented evidence of persistent racial inequalities and examples of discrimination and exclusion (eg, in the workforce and academia).

In a way, such a statement on diversity issued by Justice Powell was an untested fact at the time. Justice Powell argued that diversity related to the racial makeup of a student body would significantly improve race relations on and off campus and prepare students for their post-college careers where diversity is a quintessential part of work and social life. Patricia Gurin (Distinguished Professor and Emeritus Research Director at the University of Michigan) and colleagues stated in 2002 that "until recently, these arguments lacked empirical evidence and a strong theoretical rationale to support the link between diversity and educational outcomes" (2002, p 9). Even in 2009, Nida Denson and Mitchell Chang further stated that understanding the impact of diversity in higher education is still "a relatively new area of educational research" (2009, p 2). Thus, it is clear that very little empirical information existed; therefore, the charge was indirectly made to social scientists that the fight for affirmative action needed to start with the development of empirical evidence to support the argument that diversity is important for the university, students, and citizens alike, and has a real function in our society. Without such evidence, the death of affirmative action would be inevitable.

With that said, whether optimal or not, or whether supporters and opponents agree or not, the diversity rationale will be part of the conversation from now and into the future in the fight for and against affirmative action, particularly in the courts. In most cases, using race as one factor to improve diversity seems almost trivial and the most non-invasive manner to do so. It does not matter—the fight for and against the policy is well under way, and will not be stymied. Interestingly, while proponents see it as too little and very minimal, opponents see it as invasive and a direct assault on their way of life. Throughout the rest of this book, we utilize recent Supreme Court cases to take a systematic and detailed look at these debates within the context of affirmative action and higher education in the contemporary US. We indeed expect to see arguments, pro and con, that draw heavily on the diversity rationale.

## Conclusion

Given the complexity outlined in this chapter, it is clear to see how the landscape of US politics and the Supreme Court has changed. The fight for and against affirmative action in the past provides insights into how we got here and where we are today. While it appears that recent cases could create a positive momentum for future ones dealing with racial preference within higher education, it is clear that the fight is just beginning. Even the smallest attempt, such as a plus factor, to improve the standing of marginalized students and increase diversity on college and university campuses remains under attack. This minimally invasive attempt to improve the chances of minorities is yet seen as unacceptable by many opponents. While the death of affirmative action is not guaranteed, the prognosis is not good, as opponents focus their attention on reverse discrimination and the diversity rationale. Given that the Supreme Court will return to a more conservative bent again under the presidency of Donald Trump, the future is bleak.

The remaining parts of this book focus on the most recent Supreme Court cases: *Gratz/Grutter v Bollinger* (2003) and *Fisher v University of Texas at Austin* (2013 and 2016). In the next chapter, we look particularly at who argues for and against affirmative action in the Supreme Court (via amicus briefs). Are there differences in those who choose to speak out for and against such a polarizing policy, particularly in the courts? We feel the distinction between the entities who label themselves as social authorities on the matter will provide insight into the policy, contemporary politics, and the state of race relations today. We pay particular attention to advocacy groups as their power and reach have magnified over the past half-century. The later chapters of the book then focus on the narratives produced by these entities that support and oppose affirmative action in written documents: amicus briefs. In this vein, we describe the dominant frames and how they are used strategically with other discursive frames in arguments made by both sides of the affirmative action debate.

**Note**

[1]   Certiorari is an order by which a higher court agrees to review a decision of a lower court.

# 4

# Who is Fighting the Fight?

## Introduction

In the 1978 *Bakke* US Supreme Court case, the lead attorney for the university and in support of affirmative action was Archibald Cox, a prominent lawyer with a great deal of experience with the Court (Stefoff, 2006). Cox was a legal scholar and faculty member at Harvard Law School and, for four years, served as Solicitor General under President John F. Kennedy. Kevin McGuire (1993) described Cox as a legal elite who, at the time, had more experience litigating in front of the Court than anyone else in history. The lawyer representing Bakke, Reynold H. Colvin, conversely had much less experience and had never litigated a case at the level of the Supreme Court (McGuire, 1993). Colvin practiced law in a private firm outside the Washington beltway. While credentialed, McGuire (1993) posed that Colvin was not prepared to handle a case of such magnitude because he was focused on results rather than the broader scope of the policy, particularly during oral arguments. Furthermore, Colvin chose not to include more seasoned lawyers to co-litigate the *Bakke* case. While Bakke was not able to afford the long drawn-out affair, Colvin remained his counsel without compensation because of the reach and prestige of the case.

A notable shift in the mode of representation can be seen in the *Hopwood* (1996) and two *University of Michigan* (2003) Supreme Court cases on affirmative action in higher education. For the *Hopwood* case, the University and state were defended by several lawyers, including Betty R. Owens, Beverly Gayle Reeves, and Charles Alan Wright, to name a few. Unsurprisingly, these lead attorneys were either from private firms or employed as faculty at the University of Texas at Austin. Cheryl Hopwood, on the other hand, was represented by several lawyers, including the lead attorney Joseph A. Shea, Jr. Shea Jr was associated with the Center for Individual Rights (CIR), a self-described non-profit public interest group with a conservative agenda that sought to defend "individual liberties against the increasingly aggressive and unchecked authority of federal and state governments" (Green, 2004, p 737). The CIR recognized both the opportunity provided by the case as well as by Hopwood, a student whose academic record and community service was quite notable and exemplary. The founders of the CIR were Michael McDonald and Michael Greve who worked together at the conservative Washington Legal Foundation. As the story goes, the CIR vetted individuals, including Hopwood, who would best represent their claims in the hope of defeating affirmative action. Accordingly, the CIR was instrumental in appealing the *Hopwood* case to the Fifth Circuit Court of Appeals that ultimately ignored *Bakke* and ruled that the use of race even for diversity was not a viable constitutional rationale.

The CIR also provided the lawyers and resources in the anti-affirmative action University of Michigan Supreme Court cases (*Gratz* and *Grutter*). Like Hopwood, Jennifer Gratz and Barbara Grutter, both white students, were contacted by the CIR that filed suit on their behalf against the University and state in 1997 (Green, 2004). Other major players in funding the Michigan cases and the national anti-affirmative action campaign were the Center for Equal Opportunity, Independent Women's Forum, and American Civil Rights Institute, all of which are conservative think tanks. Thus, in the *Gratz/Grutter* and *Hopwood* cases, prominent groups with an interest in the case provided an abundance of resources to end the controversial policy. By contrast, the lead attorneys representing the University in the *Gratz* and *Grutter* cases were John Payton and Maureen E. Mahoney, respectively. Payton was a prominent civil rights litigator who passed away in 2012 while Mahoney was a former deputy solicitor general and a member of a private law firm. These cases are discussed in more detail in Chapter 5.

Generally speaking, lawyers for the *Fisher v University of Texas at Austin* cases (*I* and *II*) seemed to reflect the *Bakke* case. The University of Texas at Austin was represented by a well-credentialed lawyer and former solicitor general under George W. Bush: Gregory G. Garre. Garre had worked for a private law firm and taught constitutional law courses at Georgetown University Law School since 2009. On the other hand, the plaintiff, Abigail Fisher, was represented by Bert Rein, a partner at a private law firm, Wiley Rein (Ho, 2012). Rein had made his name by litigating anti-trust cases where he represented various pharmaceutical companies and airlines. He also served as director of the US Chamber of Commerce. While this background seems a bit strange and unrelated to the topic at hand in this case, the story behind how Rein became lead counsel to Fisher is not. Edward Blum, who helped develop the Project for Fair Representation (POFR), contacted Bert Rein. On the surface, the POFR's mission and its democratic name looks innocent and even quite honorable. However, a closer look reveals this group to be a conservative legal advocacy group challenging the government's use of race and racial preference in several areas including education, voting, contracting, and employment. Blum is also a visiting fellow at another conservative think tank, the American Enterprise Institute, where he assists plaintiffs in hiring lawyers who are affordable and eager to advance their interests. The *Fisher* case is discussed in more detail in Chapter 6 as we move forward.

As suggested in Chapter 3, the Supreme Court has been instrumental in shaping the application of affirmative action in university admissions policies. However, in this chapter, we explore the rise of elite actors and advocacy groups (special interest groups [SIGs] and think tanks) and their role in the trenches fighting for and against affirmative action in Court cases. We highlight the various actors and advocacy groups with an interest in affirmative action cases concerning college admissions and that attempt to lobby the Court via legal documents (discussed further below). We rely on sociological theory to demonstrate the potential impacts of these groups on legal and socio-political decisions concerning racial inequality and related policies, such as affirmative action. We also take it a step further and look closer at the leaders and structure of the organizations as well as their take on affirmative action. We rely on archival data gathered from various sources, including websites, mission statements, and press releases.

## Leading the charge: Groups, advocacy, and affirmative action

For a more thorough understanding of the fight for and against affirmative action in the US today, we argue that it is imperative to describe and examine the primary actors involved in the debate at the highest level: the Supreme Court. We echo the sentiments of Herbert Blumer, who stated in 1958 that special attention needed to be paid to those individuals and organizations that have the ability and resources to reach out and touch the masses. These elite entities with resources play an active role in defining the argument for the masses in years to come. Views on issues, particularly that of race, rarely spontaneously appear; instead, these perspectives are nurtured by messages created by entities that act as social authorities on a particular issue. Indeed, Eduardo Bonilla-Silva (2018) suggested that certain voices are heard simply because they can speak the loudest. Thus, the need to underscore the role of advocacy groups is more significant than ever. Scholars looking at the growth of advocacy groups (SIGs and think tanks in particular) have shown that they have increased drastically since the 1980s. While their impact is often debated in the literature, as political outcomes are complex and hard to gauge, funding for these groups and their work has skyrocketed (McGann, 2007).

So the purpose of this chapter is to assess who and what has led the charge for and against affirmative action in the most recent Supreme Court cases on affirmative action in the 21st century. Stated differently, we are interested in the primary lobbyist of the Supreme Court during cases dealing with higher education and affirmative action – *Gratz/Grutter* and *Fisher I and II*. We focus on those entities that authored amicus briefs in support and opposition to affirmative action. Amicus briefs are seen as "friends of the court" because they provide novel information to the Court as well as elucidate broader social and political implications of the case's potential decision. However, scholars also argue that such briefs act to lobby the Court for a specific resolution (Spriggs and Wahlbeck, 1997; Collins Jr et al, 2015). While the direct impact of these briefs are hard to measure using traditional research methods, Paul Collins Jr, Pamela Corley, and Jesse Hamner (2015) argued that the briefs are important because they become a public record and are used to impact public sentiment and more importantly, legally binding decisions.

This chapter focuses on the totality of groups and individuals who submitted briefs over the University of Michigan (2003) and University of Texas (2013 and 2016) cases.

While we look at all variation in authorship (eg, individuals, civic organizations, universities, etc), we pay particular attention to advocacy groups that have joined the fight for and against affirmative action in the public arena. Concerning opponents of affirmative action, sociology Wendy Moore (2018) stated succinctly that the backlash in the US over policies and initiatives associated with the Civil Rights Movement has been led by elite-backed advocacy organizations, including SIGs and think tanks. According to Moore (2018), these organizations serve as mechanisms for elite whites to negatively frame affirmative action in the public and fight against it in the legal system. While conservative advocacy groups are bemoaned by Moore (2018) and others, we expect supporters to be well represented by such groups as well. Nonetheless, we attempt to answer the following questions and more. Does the type of author vary between supporters and opponents of affirmative action? Is there any qualitative difference between groups fighting for and against the policy at the level of the Supreme Court? What are the organizational characteristics of those who do participate in the debate on both sides, and do they have different goals depending on what position (pro or con) they hold? That is to say, we are interested in whether these advocacy groups are disproportionally associated with briefs in support or opposition to affirmative action.

Scholars in the area of interest groups and think tanks give us reason to believe that these groups will more likely oppose the policy than support it. First, scholars have argued that conservative advocacy groups have been aggressive and successful in gaining support from wealthy constituents and in the production of ideas around social and political issues. In referring to think tanks, the director of the Think Tanks and Civil Societies Program at the University of Pennsylvania, James McGann (2007), argued that in the 1980s and 1990s conservatives and conservative foundations increased long-term funding because they viewed these groups to be instrumental in affecting policy in Washington, DC. Moreover, political scientist Lee Cokorinos (2003, p x) stated that "those who have been leading the assault on affirmative action have been more organized, better funded, and more deliberate than we knew twenty years ago." McGann (2007) pointed out that it took liberal advocacy groups decades to match the strategies and funding initiated by conservatives. Second, advocacy SIGs and think tanks are most commonly associated with the political Right (McGann, 2007). While think tanks exist for both the conservative and liberal political sides, the number of advocacy think tanks pushing a conservative agenda has out-paced that of those pushing a progressive agenda.

In addition to describing the variation in author type (groups versus individuals) and comparing those differences across supporters and opponents, this chapter also focuses on the groups that have the resources to lobby the Supreme Court via amicus briefs. It provides a detailed account of the self-described purpose and structure of these organizations, and highlights the actors involved. This analysis will shed light on the type of organization and the elite actors that run them. Cokorinos (2003) stated that it is a relatively small number of elites who make up the network that so vigorously fights against civil rights initiatives. It is through this analysis that we will provide, at least partially, a view of the state of the debate surrounding affirmative action today by highlighting who supports and opposes such a controversial, yet crucial, social policy.

## Lobbying: The rise of advocacy organizations and the Supreme Court

Given the complexity of the political machine and the proliferation of the media in the US, scholars have argued that organizations have popped up to assist politicians in making decisions and to provide pundits for 24-hour news cycles. Depending on the goal of the organization, and whether they seek to influence policy in a particular direction, this assistance can be viewed (and is often seen) as *policy advocacy*. Advocacy groups have long been part of the political system in the US. Indeed, the 1st Amendment of the US Constitution assured the right of citizens to organize and petition the government. Thus, individuals coming together to promote their best interests through strength in numbers were viewed in quite a positive light, even from the beginning.

Two types of groups have garnered the lion's share of attention in social science research, and we feel they will be highly represented in our analysis: SIGs and think tanks. We will, accordingly, spend most of our time discussing these groups. Generally speaking, the expressed purpose of SIGs is to advocate for a position of interest to their members (if they have a membership). While this type of organization meshes well with a commonsense understanding of advocacy groups (strength in numbers), think tanks maintain a different position in the political system and are viewed in quite a different light. Think tanks are often described, mainly through self-description, however, as policy analysts that provide unbiased information for politicians and even SIGs. This definition implies independence of knowledge creation where think tanks create knowledge for others who fight for and against various initiatives. However, funding needs and the growing polarization in politics has muddied the water and forced many think tanks to take sides and embrace policy advocacy. Sociologist Thomas Medvetz (2012) suggested that the demarcation of think tanks from other advocacy and legal groups is often hard to do, if not impossible. While the purpose of these groups (SIGs and think tanks) seems to be quite different, we will show that many share some of the same characteristics when it comes to structure and advocacy. These similarities and differences become more apparent as we study amicus briefs submitted to the *Gratz/Grutter* and *Fisher I* and *II* Supreme Court cases, and are disconcerting given the distinction as independent and scholarly experts often claimed by think tank leaders.

SIGs (or "interest groups" or "pressure groups") have garnered the most attention in social science research. In the most general sense, Gene Grossman and Elhanan Helpman (2001, p 1) defined SIGs as "organizations that take political actions on behalf of a group of voters." This definition makes it clear that individuals who simply have a similar interest are not considered an interest group. Rather, a SIG exists when individuals come together and attempt to impact political policy; thus, these groups tend to be membership driven. Since the 1970s, the US has witnessed a significant growth in the number of SIGs that represent a wide variety of interests, including business and trade interests (eg, American Iron and Steel Institute), occupational interests (eg, American Federation of Teachers), professional associations (eg, American Sociological Association and National Bar Association), and farm groups (eg, National Farmers Union). SIGs also exist that represent various ideological and social positions, including those focused on religious interests (eg, American Jewish Congress and Christian Coalition of America), gun control (eg, National Rifle Association), the environment (eg, Sierra Club), and gay rights (eg, National LGBTQ Task Force), to name a few. Indeed, Grossman and Helpman (2001) argued that, based on the number and diversity of SIGs that exist today, there are not many governmental policy topics that are not covered by one of these groups.

The activities of SIGs to influence policymakers tend to vary from organization to organization and depend on the resources available to them; however, all activities revolve around providing vital information to policymakers. Indeed, one of the primary measures of success for these groups is how close they get to and connect with influential policymakers.

The most celebrated activity used by SIGs is lobbying, which can take several different forms, ranging from preparing testimony for congressional hearings, writing amicus briefs, meeting with legislators in their offices, or even informally presenting reports to policymakers. Another activity is to educate the public on the impact of policy. This component reflects "lobbying" of citizens, where the group attempts to create the narrative surrounding an issue for the population. SIGs may also directly attempt to fund candidates seeking political office who support their goals. While not as common, SIGs may also demonstrate or protest about various issues. Accordingly, SIGs enlist several activities depending on the goals and resources of the organization to promote their interests.

Another type of organization that has gained prominence in the past 30 to 40 years is that of think tanks. McGann (2007, p 11) described think tanks as public policy research institutions that "generate policy-oriented research, analysis, and advice on domestic and international issues in an effort to enable policymakers and the public to make informed decisions about public policy issues." These groups act as policy experts on various issues and attempt to provide information to politicians to help them make sense of a highly complex social world. This control of information allows them to maintain close relationships with individuals in positions of power, particularly politicians and sometimes even interest groups that need well-researched information. Political scientist Nina Belyaeva (2011, p 125) stated, "The complexity of the decision-making process in modern states created a demand for independent expert support. This demand has been satisfied by new institutes of intellectual, political support- think tanks."

Philosophically speaking, it seems appropriate for think tanks to maintain unbiased positions on policy issues. However, this is not always the case. Medvetz (2012) posed that these groups are under the same pressures as other advocacy groups to stay afloat financially. Thus, think tanks often succumb to the economic pull to become policy advocates. An example of this type of think tank is the Cato Institute. The Cato Institute describes itself as a "public policy research organization—a think tank— dedicated to the principles of individual liberty, limited government, free markets, and peace. Its scholars and analysts conduct independent, nonpartisan research on a wide range of policy issues." So, the Cato Institute's mission is advancing a particular political and ideological perspective while attempting to explain their position as "independent" and "non-partisan." Even though they align themselves with a specific ideology, they still feel the need to promote independence. This is not by accident—appearing neutral gives greater credibility to the message produced by these groups. Medvetz (2012) argued that such a claim of independence is just not feasible given the current funding and political climate. The Cato Institute and other groups like them do more than produce information; they use that information to advocate and impact policy decisions whenever possible.

While these advocacy groups (SIGs and think tanks) vary in type, the demarcation line is not always clear, as a good deal of overlap exists in structure, history, and goals (Creason, 2018). The first commonality is that both SIGs and think tanks have witnessed an explosion in growth since the 1970s in the US. Several social and political factors have been implicated in this (Herrnson et al, 2012; Medvetz, 2012). One, the US political system is open and quite complex, so elite individuals and organizations with resources have the opportunity to interject their ideas into the political process. Two, party polarization and the heightened competition to control the executive and legislative branches at federal and state levels have led to an increased involvement of groups with interests. Finally, the rise of the internet and 24-hour media news outlets has provided greater access to politicians and citizens than ever before. Networks such as CNN, FOX, and MSNBC have particular agendas and need to fill airtime, so, experts with valued information become highly valued. It is not surprising, then, that advocacy groups attempt to use their resources to impact political policy.

A second common characteristic among SIGs and think tanks is that they have some overlap in leadership and organizational characteristics. Both often involve issue-motivated founders and formal staff (including lawyers). The leaders, CEOs or presidents, tend to be the face of the organization, and thus are very connected politically with management and public relations (PR) experience. Many of these organizations tend to have a board of directors who are also well connected politically and are influential in their field. Because funding is so crucial for these groups, the CEOs and board of directors tend to take on dual roles in the organization: both as part of the governing body and as fundraisers.

A third common characteristic is the funding streams for these interest groups. Most receive their operating funds through individual and organizational donations. As noted by Cokorinos (2003), most conservative-leaning interest groups started through wealthy individuals and families dumping millions into a cause to prevent the spread of a liberal agenda. As these interest groups grew, more and more funds flowed in from trusts and foundations set up to channel charitable donations into research and lobbying efforts to support a specific cause. Much of this funding stream is similar for liberal-leaning interest groups as well. Wealthy liberal individuals and families donate to various interest groups directly or through foundations. On a related note, these organizations also have a variety of supporters, including wealthy constituents and established policy analysts and politicians interested in the group's mission.

Finally, the ultimate goal of both SIGs and advocacy think tanks is to lobby policymakers and thus, policymaking. Both SIGs and think tanks do so by controlling information, although to varying degrees. One such place this occurs is in the media. These groups can use both print and electronic media to promote their position on a variety of social and political issues. By being labeled experts in their field, spokespeople use that knowledge to gain quality face time in newspapers and political television programs. Scholars from think tanks often write and submit opinion pieces for newspapers to promote their positions. These groups also use the internet to promote their perspectives, either via personal websites or news websites. Indeed, anytime these groups speak to a social issue, they often provide press releases and organization responses that they promote on their websites.

In terms of organizational structure, there are similarities, but there are also key differences between SIGs and think tanks. For one, funding of SIGs is often dependent on membership (although some are not) while think tanks are not. Second, think tanks attempt to differentiate themselves from common interest groups. Because think tanks want to give the impression of independent scholars, officials tend to have academic backgrounds and hold advanced college degrees (eg, a PhD). Another difference is that interest groups are often created to represent the interests of marginalized groups, including ranchers, farmers, business owners, or just concerned citizens with specific agendas to address what they see are serious affronts to their way of life or business. Think tanks are not created for these purposes. Whatever the makeup of the group, the ultimate mission of SIGs and think tanks is to promote programs and disseminate information.

With that being said, while some organizational structures and tactics may vary, the line separating SIGs and think tanks in terms of purpose is blurry. Operating from a power elite perspective, we argue that the goals, whether manifest or latent, of conservative advocacy groups in particular are to maintain the status quo and promote the interests of the dominant group. However, the role of think tanks in the fight against affirmative action is particularly insidious. These groups produce information meant to advocate, yet, in the same breath, attempt to project a sense of independence and unbiased scholarly quality. This is not the case for SIGs. The efforts of advocacy groups, both SIGs and think tanks, that seek to dismantle prominent racial policies do so without concern for the adverse effects that may impact minorities (Cokorinos, 2003). As we will see in Chapters 5 and 6 where we look at the narratives produced by these groups, rarely do these anti-racial policy groups raise concern for minorities if their efforts lead to the removal of affirmative action in higher education. Notwithstanding, we focus on how these groups attempt to improve the social and economic positions of the dominant group by eliminating affirmative action, a policy most associated with the Civil Rights Movement that strives to improve the life chances of marginalized groups that have historically been discriminated against, socially, politically, and economically, in the US.

## Advocacy groups: The rise of the conservative agenda

The fight against civil rights initiatives by conservative interest groups began as early as the 1960s. Cokorinos (2003, p 16) stated succinctly that "For as long as there has been civil rights law, conservatives have been developing the arguments and instruments to reverse it." This fight was led by conservative politicians who opposed the "liberal agenda" associated with civil rights gains and struggled with the idea that the US National Government would force the desegregation of formerly white spaces against their wishes. However, Cokorinos (2003) posed that efforts to end civil rights initiatives, such as affirmative action, gained traction and became more organized in the 1980s just as major US institutions (higher education, government, and business) were making concerted ameliorative efforts.

Most notably in Cokorinos' (2003) assertions is that the supposed "groundswell" of organized opposition to anti-civil rights initiatives in the 1980s was actually rooted in "strategic political action" of just a few well-connected actors rather than massive grassroots organizing. The impact of these actors should not be understated as they set the agenda and fostered the social and political environment in the US that still reverberates today. Less than two decades after the Civil Rights Movement under the presidency of Ronald Reagan, wealthy white conservatives (with family names such as Coors, DeVos, Scaife, and Hunt) were empowered and mobilizing to fight gains made by the Civil Rights Movement in the 1960s (Moore, 2018).

Cokorinos outlined three factors that led to the ultimate backlash against civil rights initiatives that brings us to the current fight against affirmative action (for a more thorough discussion, see Cokorinos, 2003). One, the Reagan administration ushered in a color-blind orientation toward civil rights policies where commonsense initiatives meant to alleviate racial inequality were vilified. Two, this color-blind agenda was promoted by several veteran opponents of civil rights initiatives embedded in the Reagan administration. Cokorinos viewed these individuals as critical cogs in the anti-civil rights movement in the 1980s and labeled them the "permanent revolution." Finally, political planning by this conservative "permanent revolution" led the charge in loading conservative advocates in the federal judiciary and developing advocacy groups promoting the conservative agenda.

It should be noted that this response among elite conservatives did not occur in a vacuum. These individuals were reacting to the so-called growing liberal and diversity threat posed by moderate Republicans and Democrats who supported change. The funding and development of advocacy organizations that occurred during this era were so definitive that McGann (2007) concluded that the conservative groups had won the war of ideas in politics. Liberals and more progressive advocacy groups found themselves decades behind in planning and resources and forced to match the reaction of this well-organized and funded conservative machine in the 21st century.

Reagan appointees led the charge in the fight against civil rights initiatives such as affirmative action that still reverberates today (Cokorinos, 2003; Collins, 2011b; Moore, 2018). For instance, Reagan appointed Jay Parker, an African American, as transition team head of the Equal Employment Opportunity Commission. Before being appointed, Parker was at the forefront of the South African apartheid propaganda machine, via his company International Public Affairs Consultant, Inc, that sought to continue racial apartheid (Cokorinos, 2003). As transition head, Parker set up a group of young "operatives" in the administration who would eventually play critical roles in the dismantling of civil rights initiatives during the 1980s and 1990s. Reagan's legal strategy to upend civil rights initiatives was led by several key Reagan loyalists, including Ed Meese, William French Smith, and Ted Olson. Meese and Parker brought a cadre of young conservatives into Reagan's Justice Department, including leaders of the conservative Federalist Society (Lee Liberman Otis, Steven Calabresi, and Michael Carnin) as well as leaders from conservative advocacy organizations (eg, Michael Carvin from the CIR). Meese and Parker were also responsible for placing other anti-civil rights people into the Justice Department, including Linda Chavez (staff director at the US Commission on Civil Rights) and Clarence Thomas (chair of the Equal Employment Opportunity Commission). Both Chavez and Thomas espoused color-blind orientations and denounced key civil rights initiatives, including affirmative action. As a Supreme Court Justice, Thomas's clear anti-affirmative-action stance was apparent in his opposition to the policy in the *Gratz/Grutter* and *Fisher* Supreme Court cases. An assistant of Clarence Thomas, Clint Bolick, may have had the most significant impact on the future of this movement. In his book, *Changing Course: Civil Rights at the Crossroads* (1988), Bolick laid the blueprint for how advocacy groups would fight against affirmative action in three areas (politics, media, and in the courts) using a variety of techniques over the next several decades.

The advocacy groups and think tanks that resulted from this conservative movement are still active in the affirmative action fight today. These groups, some of which wrote briefs in the *Gratz/Grutter* and *Fisher I* and *II* cases, included the American Civil Rights Institute, Center for Equal Opportunity, Center for Individual Rights, Institute for Justice, and the Civil Rights Practice Groups of the Federalist Society. This movement has also been instrumental in creating regional litigation organizations that fight against affirmative action today, including the Pacific Legal Foundation, Southeastern Legal Foundation, and Mountain States Legal Foundation. These groups also submitted briefs to the Court in opposition to affirmative action. Indeed, they have focused their efforts on (1) overturning fundamental civil rights decisions; (2) precipitating crisis and division in branches of government and between federal and state; (3) using the rhetoric of individual liberty to turn a wave of public sentiment against these initiatives; and (4) using political contacts to undermine the enforcement of anti-discrimination measures.

While conservatives attempted to hinder efforts to apply affirmative action in employment during the 1970s, Reagan's support of a color-blind US Constitution, as well as conservative-leaning political appointments, created the environment necessary to significantly challenge at least the federal enforcement of civil rights. Moreover, the Reagan era emboldened influential citizens, both wealthy and political, to create advocacy groups to question all applications of civil rights legislation and the application of affirmative action to college admissions policies particularly. In fact, by the end of Reagan's term, the number of advocacy groups out to challenge various government policies focusing on equality grew from around 20 in 1975 to over 200 by 1990 (Cokorinos, 2003).

## Advocacy groups and sociological theory: Blumer's group position theory

The theory of group positioning offered by Blumer (1958) provides a robust theoretical frame to understand the possible influences of advocacy groups. Blumer (1958, p 4) argued that through collective and historical processes majority members develop certain feelings, including those of superiority, a sense that they are "naturally superior or better" than the other groups, perceptions of propriety or entitlement claims over valued resources, and finally, concerns that the minority group seeks to obtain valued resources belonging to the dominant group. That is to say, over time, group members develop a *sense of group position* they should hold relative to out-groups, and it is this sense of group identity that stands at the heart of racial prejudice.

How do members of the dominant group develop this collective sense of group position that is superior to out-group members? Note that this is not an individual-level inter-individual phenomenon, according to Blumer. This sense of positioning transcends the individual and occurs at the macro or group level. Nonetheless, the answer to the question of how this happens is quite complicated as humans are complex and are affected by various external stimuli. While noting the importance of interactions of members of the majority group in producing negative images of the out-group, Blumer (1958) implicated larger macro-level forces in the socialization process. He specifically outlined the significant role of elite actors and groups that have access to the public ear in the process.

From an elite-oriented perspective, elite actors and groups have the necessary resources to access the public and dictate arguments they want the majority to hold on various social issues. Blumer (1958), however, only touched briefly on the role of advocacy groups and the creation of the sense of group position. Nonetheless, he posed that such elite actors and groups have the ability to create and re-create "abstract meanings" that ultimately: (1) allow one group to claim propriety over value public and private resources and (2) dictate the definition of the arguments for the majority on various social issues (Blumer, 1958, p 6). Ken Kollman (1998) noted that the orientation of the mass public is indeed rarely spontaneous, and behind the movement of individuals to protest are elite actors and advocacy groups pushing a standard message.

Most central in Blumer's (1958) argument is the use of "threat." He argued that elite actors and advocacy groups have an impact via the use of threat. That is to say, these entities use threat to valuable resources to stimulate the sense of group position that Blumer identified as the root of the prejudice. Indeed, research we have conducted found that arguments against affirmative action by advocacy groups were saturated with threat frames that raised concern that the resources previously held (eg, elite college seats) by white students were being threatened by groups that had not earned those resources (Carter et al, 2019). The use of threat in arguments is important for several reasons. First, "threat" frames have been shown to stimulate animosity toward a target policy (Kollman, 1998; Bobo and Tuan, 2006). Kollman (1998) argued that conflict expansion through threat is essential for advocacy groups to arouse public anger and get what they want. Second, the use of "threat" is often used to increase interest, which ensures survival of the organization through increased support (Lowery, 2007). Thus, for the reasons just mentioned, it is in the best interests of an advocacy group to stimulate feelings of threat among the majority that they are somehow losing out to groups that are not deserving.

With that being said, the remaining part of this chapter looks at the characteristics of supporters and opponents who submitted an amicus brief to the Supreme Court. Who and what is fighting the fight at the highest level of litigation? We pose that understanding the characteristics of the entities in the debate will shine a light on the discussion itself. However, we go further than just characterizing the groups and comparing supporters and opponents. We pay special attention to advocacy groups, and attempt to provide an insight into these groups (including their leaders) and why they are fighting so fervently for and against affirmative action in higher education.

## Supporters of affirmative action: Advocacy groups, think tanks, and elite actors

Using the organizational framework discussed above to classify advocacy groups (SIGs and think tanks), Table 4.1 reveals that in total there were 44 advocacy groups (of 144 total briefs) that participated in the writing of amicus briefs in *support* of affirmative action in college admissions policies across all cases (including *Grutter*, *Gratz*, and *Fisher I* and *II*).

**Table 4.1:** Amicus briefs of advocacy groups in support of affirmative action submitted to the Supreme Court cases[a]

| Authors of brief amici curiae Supporters* | Grutter 2003 | Gratz 2003 | Fisher 2013 | Fisher 2016 |
|---|---|---|---|---|
| Advocacy groups | | | | |
| 1. Advancement Project | | | ✓ | |
| 2. American Association for Affirmative Action | | | ✓ | |
| 3. American Bar Association | ✓ | | ✓ | ✓ |
| 4. American Civil Liberties Union | | | ✓ | ✓ |
| 5. American Council on Education, et al | | | ✓ | ✓ |
| **6. American Educational Research Association, et al** | ✓ | ✓ | ✓ | ✓ |
| 7. American Federation of Labor and Congress of Industrial Organizations | ✓ | | | |
| **8. American Jewish Committee, et al** | ✓ | ✓ | ✓ | ✓ |
| 9. American Law Deans Association | ✓ | | | |
| 10. American Law Teachers | | | ✓ | ✓ |
| **11. American Psychological Association** | ✓ | ✓ | ✓ | ✓ |
| 12. American Sociological Association, et al | ✓ | | | |
| 13. Anti-Defamation League | | | ✓ | ✓ |
| 14. Asian American Legal Defense and Education Fund, et al | | | ✓ | ✓ |
| **15. Association of American Law Schools** | ✓ | | ✓ | ✓ |
| **16. Association of American Medical Colleges** | ✓ | | ✓ | ✓ |

(continued)

**Table 4.1:** Amicus briefs of advocacy groups in support of affirmative action submitted to the Supreme Court cases[a] (continued)

| Authors of brief amici curiae Supporters* | Grutter 2003 | Gratz 2003 | Fisher 2013 | Fisher 2016 |
|---|---|---|---|---|
| Advocacy groups | | | | |
| **17. Boston Bar Association, et al** | ✓ | | ✓ | ✓ |
| 18. Clinical Legal Education Association | ✓ | | | |
| 19. Coalition to Defend Affirmative Action, et al | | | ✓ | |
| 20. Constitutional Law Scholars and Constitutional Accountability Center | | | ✓ | ✓ |
| 21. Graduate Management Admission Council, et al | ✓ | | | |
| 22. Human Rights Advocates, et al | | | ✓ | ✓ |
| 23. Human Rights Advocates and the University of Minnesota Human Rights Center | ✓ | ✓ | ✓ | |
| 24. Hispanic National Bar Association and the Hispanic Association of Colleges and Universities | ✓ | | | |
| 25. Latino organizations | ✓ | ✓ | | |
| 26. Lawyers Committee for Civil Rights Under Law, et al | ✓ | | | |
| 27. Leadership Conference on Civil & Human Rights and Southern Poverty Law Center | ✓ | | | ✓ |
| **28. National Association for the Advancement of Colored People Legal Defense and Educational Fund, Inc, and American Civil Liberties Union** | ✓ | | ✓ | ✓ |
| 29. National and Texas Latino organizations | | | ✓ | ✓ |
| 30. National Asian Pacific American Legal Consortium, et al | ✓ | ✓ | ✓ | |
| 31. National Center for Fair & Open Testing | ✓ | | | |

(continued)

**Table 4.1:** Amicus briefs of advocacy groups in support of affirmative action submitted to the Supreme Court cases[a] (continued)

| Authors of brief amici curiae Supporters* | Grutter 2003 | Gratz 2003 | Fisher 2013 | Fisher 2016 |
|---|---|---|---|---|
| Advocacy groups | | | | |
| 32. National Coalition of Blacks for Reparations in America, et al | ✓ | | | |
| 33. National Coalition of Educators, et al | | | | ✓ |
| **34. National Education Association, et al** | ✓ | ✓ | ✓ | ✓ |
| 35. National Urban League, et al | ✓ | ✓ | | |
| 36. National Women's Law Center, et al | | ✓ | ✓ | ✓ |
| 37. Nationwide Black Law Students Association | | | ✓ | |
| 38. New America Alliance | ✓ | ✓ | | |
| 39. New Mexico Hispanic Bar Association, et al | ✓ | | | |
| 40. NOW Legal Defense and Education Fund | ✓ | ✓ | | |
| 41. Society of American Law Teachers | ✓ | | | |
| **42. The College Board, et al** | ✓ | ✓ | | ✓ |
| 43. United Negro College Fund | ✓ | ✓ | ✓ | |
| 44. Veterans of the Southern Civil Rights Movement, et al | ✓ | | | |
| Total | 30/46 | 12/46 | 23/46 | 26/46 |

Notes:

* Those entities that submitted briefs to both the *Gratz/Grutter* and *Fisher* Supreme Court cases are in bold.

[a] *Grutter v Bollinger* 2003, *Gratz et al v Bollinger* 2003, *Fisher v University of Texas at Austin* 2013, *Fisher v University of Texas at Austin* 2016.

The remaining 100 support briefs (of 144 total briefs) were authored by individuals and groups not defined as advocacy groups, which we refer to as "various entities." Table 4.2 provides the total number of "various entities" that wrote briefs across each of the four cases. In terms of the total number of authors who submitted briefs from *Gratz/Grutter* to *Fisher*, advocacy groups authored only 31 percent. The clear majority of support briefs (69%) came from quite heterogeneous individuals and groups, including, but not limited to, universities, social science organizations, civil rights organizations, groups of concerned students, social scientists and professors, alumni of various colleges and universities, states, and state and federal legislators from across the US, to name just a few.

Of the 44 groups advocating for affirmative action, we estimate mostly all to be SIGs (most memberships, but some without), non-profit government organizations (NGOs), and some legal advocacy groups. SIGs were represented by various groups including the American Bar Association, American Educational Research Association, American Psychological Association, American Sociological Association, Association of American Law Schools, National Association for the Advancement of Colored People, National Education Association, The College Board, and United Negro College Fund, to name a few. Take the National Education Association (NEA), for example. On its website, it describes itself as the "largest professional employee organization" committed to advancing the cause of public education from pre-school to college. The NEA is led by a president, vice president, and executive director as well as a nine-member executive committee and board of trustees. The NEA also boasts a membership of over 3 million educators.

Examples of legal advocacy groups include the NOW Legal Defense and Education and National Association for the Advancement of Colored People (NAACP) Legal Defense and Education Fund, Inc. Renamed "Legal Momentum," the purpose of the NOW Legal Defense and Education advocacy organization is to "ensure economic and personal security for all women and girls by advancing equity in education, the workplace, and the courts" by providing women with expert legal support (Legal Momentum, 2019). Interestingly, despite the growth in think tanks since the 1990s, only one supporter could be characterized or characterized themselves as a think tank (Constitutional Accountability Center), and it wrote its brief in conjunction with constitutional law scholars. On its website, the Center describes itself as an organization that is educational and quite neutral. It states,

> CAC [Constitutional Accountability Center] produces scholarship showing that the Constitution's text and

history command progressive results. Through our expert commentary, issue briefs, in-depth think tank series, and in testimony to Congress, we inform the public and America's elected leaders with comprehensive accounts of the most contentious and timely topics in modern constitutional and federal law.

As you can see, this organization promotes itself as an education provider without mentioning its clear advocacy actions. Classifying these groups is not always easy as the goals and methods of advocacy often overlap with other advocacy group types. Nonetheless, these advocacy groups more than not met the characteristics of a SIG.

Conversely, Table 4.2 reveals that the other 69 percent of briefs written in support of affirmative action was authored by various entities not classified as advocacy groups (see Table 4.2). We used "various entities" as a label to identify those individuals or groups that represented a one-time consortium to write an amicus brief for a specific case. More specifically, these various individuals or groups tended to be people in the four particular professions (law, politics, higher education, and industry) with a stake in the case. While we do not want to list all examples, here are a few. With respect to law, briefs were submitted by a consortium of law students from accredited law schools, law student associations (eg, Emory Latin American Law Student Association and University of Michigan Law Student Association), by various law schools (eg, Arizona State, NYU, Harvard, Stanford, and Yale), law school deans (eg, Robert Post and Martha Minow), law scholars, and by lawyers themselves. With respect to politics, various politicians (eg, US Senator Harry Reid, Michigan governor Jennifer Granholm, and members of Pennsylvania General Assembly) also filed amicus briefs in support of affirmative action.

Higher education, in general, was well represented in briefs by undergraduate and graduate student consortiums, university professors (eg, Cedric Merlin Powell), and university presidents (eg, chancellor of the University of California). Various universities also submitted briefs, including Harvard, Houston Community College System, Massachusetts Institute of Technology, New York University School of Law, School of Law at the University of North Carolina, and the University of Michigan (during the *Fisher* case). Most, if not all, of these briefs submitted by colleges and universities stated their unconditional support of diversity as an essential goal for shaping the educational outcomes and overall success of students in their respective careers. Such an endorsement would seem to hold much more significance as these entities were clearly social authorities on the matter, and understood the value of education for all citizens.

**Table 4.2:** Amicus briefs of "various entities" in support of affirmative action submitted to the Supreme Court cases[a]

| Various entities* | Grutter 2003 | Gratz 2003 | Fisher 2013 | Fisher 2016 |
|---|---|---|---|---|
| 1. 13,922 current law students at accredited American law schools | ✓ | | | |
| 2. 28 (39) undergraduate and graduate student organizations with the University of California | ✓ | | ✓ | ✓ |
| 3. 65 leading American businesses | ✓ | ✓ | | |
| 4. American social science researchers | | | ✓ | |
| 5. **Amherst College and 27 fellow private colleges and universities** | ✓ | ✓ | ✓ | ✓ |
| 6. Appalachian State University, et al | ✓ | | ✓ | |
| 7. Arizona State University College of Law | ✓ | | | |
| 8. Authors of the Texas Ten Percent Plan | | ✓ | | |
| 9. Bay Mills Indian Community, et al | ✓ | ✓ | | |
| 10. Black Student Alliance at the University of Texas at Austin et al | | | ✓ | ✓ |
| 11. Black Women Lawyers Association of Greater Chicago, Inc | ✓ | ✓ | | |
| 12. Brennan Center for Justice at NYU School of Law, et al | | | ✓ | |
| 13. Brown University, et al | | | ✓ | ✓ |
| 14. California Institute of Technology, et al | | | ✓ | ✓ |
| 15. Carnegie Mellon University and 37 fellow private colleges and universities | ✓ | ✓ | | |
| 16. Cecilia Polanco, et al | | | | ✓ |

(continued)

**Table 4.2:** Amicus briefs of "various entities" in support of affirmative action submitted to the Supreme Court cases[a] (continued)

| Various entities* | Grutter 2003 | Gratz 2003 | Fisher 2013 | Fisher 2016 |
|---|---|---|---|---|
| 17. Cities of Philadelphia and Cleveland, and National Conference of Black Mayors | ✓ | ✓ | | |
| 18. Coalition for Economic Equity, et al | ✓ | | | |
| 19. A coalition of Bar Associations of Color | | | ✓ | ✓ |
| 20. College Board and the National School Boards Association, et al | | | ✓ | ✓ |
| 21. Columbia, Cornell, Georgetown, Rice, and Vanderbilt Universities | ✓ | ✓ | | |
| 22. Committee of concerned black graduates of American Bar Association-accredited law schools | ✓ | | | |
| 23. Council for Minority Affairs at Texas A&M | | | ✓ | |
| 24. David Boyle | | | ✓ | ✓ |
| 25. Dean Robert Post and Dean Martha Minow | | | ✓ | ✓ |
| 26. Distinguished alumni of the University of Texas at Austin | | | ✓ | |
| 27. Dr Robert D. Putnam | | | ✓ | |
| 28. Dupont, IBM, Intel, and National Action Council for Minorities | | | | ✓ |
| 29. Emory Outlaw and Emory Latin American Law Students Association | | | ✓ | |
| 30. Empirical scholars | | | ✓ | |
| 31. Experimental psychologists | | | ✓ | ✓ |
| 32. Family of Heman Sweatt | | | ✓ | ✓ |
| 33. Fordham University, et al | | | ✓ | |

(continued)

**Table 4.2:** Amicus briefs of "various entities" in support of affirmative action submitted to the Supreme Court cases[a] (continued)

| Various entities* | Grutter 2003 | Gratz 2003 | Fisher 2013 | Fisher 2016 |
|---|---|---|---|---|
| 34. Former commissioners and General Counsel of the Federal Communications Commission, et al | | | ✓ | |
| 35. Former student body presidents of the University of Texas | | | ✓ | ✓ |
| 36. Fortune-100 and other leading American businesses | | | ✓ | ✓ |
| 37. General Motors Corporation | ✓ | ✓ | | |
| 38. Harvard Graduate School of Education Students for Diversity | | | ✓ | |
| 39. Harvard University | | | | ✓ |
| 40. Harvard University, Brown University, et al | ✓ | ✓ | | |
| 41. Harvard, Stanford, and Yale Black Law Students Associations | ✓ | | | |
| 42. Hayden family | ✓ | ✓ | | |
| 43. Hillary Browne, students of Howard University School of Law, et al | ✓ | | | |
| 44. Houston Community College system | | | ✓ | |
| 45. Howard University | ✓ | ✓ | | |
| 46. Howard University School of Law Civil Rights Clinic | | | ✓ | ✓ |
| 47. Indiana University | ✓ | | | |
| 48. Intercultural Development Research Association | | | | ✓ |
| 49. Kimberly West-Faulcon | | | ✓ | ✓ |
| 50. King County Bar Association, et al | ✓ | | | |

(continued)

**Table 4.2:** Amicus briefs of "various entities" in support of affirmative action submitted to the Supreme Court cases[a] (continued)

| Various entities* | Grutter 2003 | Gratz 2003 | Fisher 2013 | Fisher 2016 |
|---|---|---|---|---|
| 51. Law School Admission Council | ✓ | | | |
| 52. Law school deans Judith Areen, Katharine Bartlett, et al | ✓ | | | |
| 53. Lawyers' Committee for Civil Rights Under Law, et al | | | ✓ | |
| 54. Leading public research universities | | | ✓ | |
| 55. Legal scholars defending diversity in higher education | | | | ✓ |
| 56. Lt Gen Julius W. Becton Jr, et al | ✓ | ✓ | ✓ | ✓ |
| 57. Massachusetts, Connecticut, Delaware, et al | ✓ | ✓ | | ✓ |
| 58. Massachusetts Institute of Technology, Stanford University, Du Pont, IBM, et al | ✓ | ✓ | | |
| 59. Media companies | ✓ | ✓ | | |
| 60. Members and former members of the Pennsylvania General Assembly, et al | | | ✓ | |
| 61. Members of the Asian American Center for Advancing Justice, et al | ✓ | | | |
| 62. Michigan Black Law Alumni Society | ✓ | ✓ | | |
| 63. Michigan governor Jennifer Granholm | | | ✓ | |
| 64. National Association of Basketball Coaches, et al | | | ✓ | ✓ |
| 65. National League of Cities, et al | | | ✓ | |
| 66. National School Boards Association, et al | ✓ | ✓ | | |
| 67. New York City Council speaker Gifford Miller, et al | ✓ | ✓ | | |

(continued)

**Table 4.2:** Amicus briefs of "various entities" in support of affirmative action submitted to the Supreme Court cases[a] (continued)

| Various entities* | Grutter 2003 | Gratz 2003 | Fisher 2013 | Fisher 2016 |
|---|---|---|---|---|
| 68. New York Law School Racial Justice project | | | | ✓ |
| 69. New York State Bar Association | | | ✓ | ✓ |
| 70. New York State Black & Puerto Rican Legislative Caucus | ✓ | | | |
| 71. New York University School of Law | | | | ✓ |
| 72. New York, et al | | | ✓ | ✓ |
| 73. President and chancellors of the University of California | | | ✓ | ✓ |
| 74. Professor Cedric Merlin Powell | | | | ✓ |
| 75. Professor W. Burlette Carter | | | | ✓ |
| 76. Religious organizations and campus ministries, et al | | | ✓ | ✓ |
| 77. Representative Richard A. Gephardt, et al | ✓ | ✓ | | |
| 78. Representatives John Conyers, Debbie Dingell, Charles Rangel | ✓ | ✓ | | |
| 79. Richard Lempert | | | | ✓ |
| 80. Ruben Hinojosa, member of Congress, et al | | | ✓ | ✓ |
| 81. School of Law of the University of North Carolina | ✓ | | | |
| 82. Senators Tom Daschle, Ted Kennedy, et al | ✓ | ✓ | | |
| 83. Six educational non-profit organizations | | | | ✓ |
| 84. Small business owners and associations | | | ✓ | |

(continued)

**Table 4.2:** Amicus briefs of "various entities" in support of affirmative action submitted to the Supreme Court cases[a] (continued)

| Various entities* | *Grutter* 2003 | *Gratz* 2003 | *Fisher* 2013 | *Fisher* 2016 |
|---|---|---|---|---|
| 85. Social and organizational psychologists | | | ✓ | ✓ |
| 86. Social scientists Glenn C. Loury, Nathan Glazer, et al | ✓ | ✓ | | |
| 87. State of California | | | ✓ | ✓ |
| 88. State of New Jersey | ✓ | ✓ | | |
| 89. States of Maryland, New York, Arizona, California, et al | ✓ | ✓ | | |
| 90. Teach for America, Inc | | | ✓ | ✓ |
| 91. Texas State Senate and House of Representatives | | | ✓ | ✓ |
| 92. The Association of the Bar of the City of New York | | | ✓ | |
| 93. US Senators Harry Reid, et al | ✓ | | ✓ | ✓ |
| 94. UCLA School of Law students of color | ✓ | | | |
| 95. United States | | | ✓ | ✓ |
| 96. United States Student Association | | | | |
| 97. University of Michigan | | | | ✓ |
| 98. University of Michigan Law Student Association | ✓ | | | |
| 99. University of North Carolina at Chapel Hill | ✓ | | ✓ | ✓ |
| 100. University of Pittsburgh, Temple University | ✓ | ✓ | | |

Note:

* Those entities that submitted briefs to both the *Gratz/Grutter* and *Fisher* Supreme Court cases are in bold.

[a] *Grutter v Bollinger* 2003, *Gratz et al v Bollinger* 2003, *Fisher v University of Texas at Austin* 2013, *Fisher v University of Texas at Austin* 2016.

Finally, American industry leaders were well represented in the briefs as well. For example, Fortune 100 and other leading US businesses submitted amicus briefs for the two *Fisher* Supreme Court cases. The companies included in the Fortune 100 brief included Aetna, Inc, General Electric Company, Starbucks, Viacom, Inc. and Walmart Stores, Inc. Also, General Motors Corporation and a consortium of mass media companies (that is, Banks Broadcasting, Inc, Hispanic Broadcasting Corporation, and Yankees Entertainment and Sports Network) submitted briefs for the *Grutter* and *Gratz* cases. All of these briefs highlighted the notion that affirmative action in college admissions led to a more diverse graduate pool from which to draw employees. In turn, these graduates would understand the value of a diverse workplace. Overall, many of the briefs written to support affirmative action college admissions policies came from a groundswell of individuals, civic organizations, universities, businesses, and states from across the spectrum. More importantly, supporters were mostly *not* advocacy groups.

Before we move to opponent briefs, we would like to make a few final comments about the advocacy groups and various entities that did support affirmative action in higher education in these Supreme Court cases. First, concerning who fights the fight in the Supreme Court, the answer is clear, and it is not advocacy groups. Almost 70 percent of briefs come from a heterogeneous group of individuals, politicians, organizations, and groups with an interest in the case. Of advocacy groups that did submit a brief, we classified them mostly as SIGs and legal advocacy groups, a notable distinction that becomes clear as we talk about opponent briefs. This pattern of authorship was apparent for both the *Gratz/Grutter* and *Fisher I* and *II* cases. Second, while these advocacy groups and various entities express an interest in affirmative action across the cases, there was little consistency in terms of submission. That is to say, most of these authors only lobbied for one case or another. Only one various entity and eight advocacy groups submitted briefs for both the *Gratz/Grutter* and *Fisher* cases.

In terms of change in authorship from the 2003 *Gratz/Grutter* cases and the *Fisher* cases, there were some subtle shifts. One, while the number of briefs submitted across the cases increased, the absolute number of briefs and percentage attributed to advocacy groups decreased, from 42 percent (30 out of 71) in *Gratz/Grutter* to 35 percent (26 out of 74) in the *Fisher* cases. Second, no think tanks wrote briefs for the *Grutter/Gratz* cases and only one for the *Fisher* cases. Given the rise of think tanks since the 1990s, this is surprising. We may attribute this "lack of finding" to the growth of the conservative think tank, which we will discuss further below. Finally, while the US President did not support affirmative action in the Michigan cases (George W. Bush), that changed with the *Fisher* cases (Barack Obama). This support from the Executive Branch of federal government may indeed not be there when the next case makes its way to the Supreme Court.

## Case studies

Before we move to an analysis of opponents, we present a brief discussion of the most common advocacy groups that participated in the debate over affirmative action in the cases of *Grutter, Gratz,* and *Fisher I* and *II* (groups that submitted to both are in "bold" type in Table 4.1). In so doing, we unpack the type of organization that fights for affirmative action at the level of the Supreme Court, and highlight the prominent leaders in these organizations. The information provided comes directly from websites provided by the organization as well as archival articles discussing the organization. These organizations often provided detailed "About" statements that outline their overall mission and "Leadership" to describe the current CEOs or presidents and board of directors.

### American Educational Research Association (AERA)

The AERA was founded in 1916 as a professional organization representing education researchers in the US and around the world. Its mission is to strive for advancing knowledge about education, encourage scholarly inquiry, and promote research to improve education and serve the public good (AERA, 2018). It has over 24,000 members, and most are teachers and professors from education and sociological backgrounds. The AERA is a massive organization as it boasts more than 12 divisions and over 155 SIGs attempting to address various issues concerning education. Its advocacy campaigns have focused on encouraging local, state, and federal government to use evidence-based policy, as well as protecting investment in the social and behavioral sciences, and revising rules concerning the protection of human subjects in research. Funding for this organization seems to flow from membership dues, but also from private and public donations.

As of 2018, its leadership has consisted of individuals such as Dr Felice J. Levine, who is highly connected in the academic world. Dr Levine serves as the executive director and had previously served as the executive officer of the American Sociological Association, the national organization of sociologists. Dr Levine also served as the director of the Law and

Social Science Program at the National Science Foundation. Dr Levine is also the associate editor of the *Journal of Empirical Research on Human Research Ethics*. She also serves in other academic capacities, including as a member of the Executive Committee of the Consortium of Social Science Associations, chair of the Board of Directors of the Council of Professional Associations on Federal Statistics, and as secretary general of the World Education Research Association.

The AERA has made affirmative action a central part of its mission. As it stated (AERA, 2018),

> Promoting the use of research to improve education and serve the public good is central to AERA's mission. To this end, AERA's efforts include providing scientific evidence on the benefits of diversity and affirmative action in legal briefs submitted to the Supreme Court; holding Capitol Hill briefings on research issues of importance to the public and policymakers; and issuing research-based positions on educational issues of public concern.

It also has a specific division of membership that has tackled the question of affirmative action internally to address diversity within its membership and service roles. On its website, the AERA has provided links to all of the amicus briefs it has submitted concerning Supreme Court cases and has clearly stated its purpose:

> Since 2003, AERA has filed several amicus briefs that comprehensively lay out the research evidence for the educational benefits of diverse education environments and the positive impact of affirmative action admissions policies on students' educational experiences and their careers. (AERA, 2018)

As suggested above, much of its argument for supporting affirmative action in college admissions policies has focused on research evidence highlighting the benefits that affirmative action can bring in creating a diverse atmosphere for all students. It has also provided a research file focusing on the impact of affirmative action on higher education, and offers several links to over 30 studies supporting its claims. In general, the AERA's message has been consistent: affirmative action has assisted all students concerning their educational experiences, ultimately giving individuals better opportunities in career placement in the US.

## American Jewish Committee (AJC)

The AJC is a SIG that is different from the AERA. Rather than education professionals focusing on advancing educational goals, the AJC consists of various concerned individuals fighting against discrimination in general and discrimination against Jews in particular. As stated in its mission,

> AJC is the leading global Jewish advocacy organization, with unparalleled access to government officials, diplomats, and other world leaders. Through these relationships and our international presence, AJC can impact opinion and policy on the issues that matter most: combating rising anti-Semitism and extremism, defending Israel's place in the world, and safeguarding the rights and freedoms of all people. (AJC, 2018)

Thus, the AJC is focused on advocating for Jewish people, locally and globally, but has also attempted to advocate for legislation it views as at least having an indirect impact on the civil liberties of Jews as a minority group.

The AJC was founded in 1906 by prominent American Jewish legal and academic professionals (AJC, 2018). It is one of the three largest organizations focusing on advocacy for the Jewish community, and has been funded by private donations and various federal and international grants. The other two have included the Anti-Defamation League (that also submitted briefs) and the American Jewish Congress. This particular organization has focused on global diplomacy, legislation, advocacy, coalition-building, and strategic communications to assist the Jewish community in having a collective voice for recognition and civil rights around the world. The AJC was also a partner with the African American civil rights struggles of the 1950s and 1960s and today, focuses on radicalism, extremism, anti-Semitism, and human rights.

The AJC is led by CEO David Harris and President John Shapiro. David Harris is described as a Jewish advocate who regularly meets with world leaders to advance human rights and inter-religious understanding. After growing up in New York City, Harris graduated from the University of Pennsylvania in 1971 and from the London School of Economics with a Master's and PhD degree. John Shapiro was elected President of the AJC in 2016. He was appointed to the AJC's Executive Council in 2005 and served as chair of AJC's Board of Trustees from 2013 to 2016. Shapiro has an extensive background in business leadership. In 1984, he co-founded Chieftain Capital Management, Inc, where he then served as director.

In addition to his work with the AJC, Shapiro served as president of the UJA-Federation of New York and Dalton School. He also served as chair of Lawyers for Children and vice chair of the American Academy in Rome. Shapiro also served on several influential boards, including for Rockefeller University, The Jewish Museum, and The Washington Institute for Near East Policy.

When it comes to affirmative action, the AJC initially submitted an amicus brief objecting to the use of affirmative action in college admissions policies during 1978, *Regents v Bakke* Supreme Court case (Scheer, 2018). Along with other sizeable Jewish interest group organizations, the AJC was against using race as a way to create a quota system for selecting students for college admissions. However, by the 2003 cases of *Gratz* and *Grutter*, it changed its position and agreed with Supreme Court Justice Powell's argument that affirmative action should be used to create a diverse campus that could lead to better education. In its new stance, Jacob Scheer (2018, p 1) stated that the AJC noted that, "…diversity not only provides all students with a richer educational experience but also prepares them for participation in our pluralistic democracy." Scheer (2018, p 1) also noted that, "Jeffrey Sinensky, general counsel for the AJC, further asserted that 'disallowing the consideration of race as one factor among many in university admissions would have the effect of eliminating meaningful diversity on American campuses.'" Thus, the AJC submitted amicus briefs to support the efforts of college campuses that used affirmative action briefs to diversify educational experiences for all Supreme Courts cases starting with *Gratz* in 2003.

## National Association for the Advancement of Colored People (NAACP)

Similar to the AJC, the NAACP was founded in 1909 as a collective response to the anti-black violence and race riots occurring across the US. The NAACP today is home to over 300,000 members. While first called to order by a group of white liberals that included Mary White Ovington and Oswald Garrison Villard, many prominent African American citizens, such as W.E.B. Du Bois and Ida B. Wells-Barnett, assisted in forming this advocacy organization (NAACP, 2018). Today, the NAACP is headed by lawyer and activist Derrick Johnson. Johnson previously served as vice chair of the NAACP National Board of Directors as well as state president for the Mississippi State Conference.

The NAACP's mission has been to "ensure the political, educational, social, and economic equality of rights of all persons and to eliminate race-based discrimination" (NAACP, 2018). Notably, the NAACP was heavily invested in the Civil Rights Movement of the 1950s and 1960s, and continues to support efforts, as it states in its objectives,

> To ensure the political, educational, social, and economic equality of all citizens; to achieve equality of rights and eliminate race prejudice among the citizens of the United States; to remove all barriers of racial discrimination through democratic processes; to seek enactment and enforcement of federal, state, and local laws securing civil rights; to inform the public of the adverse effects of racial discrimination and to seek its elimination; and to educate persons as to their constitutional rights and to take all lawful action to secure the exercise thereof, and to take any other lawful action in furtherance of these objectives, consistent with the NAACP's Articles of Incorporation and this Constitution. (NAACP, 2018)

Like many large civil rights organizations, the NAACP has worked to address issues of inequality and particularly encouraged, through legal actions and lobbying, the use of affirmative action policies in many different institutions. In the Supreme Court cases dealing with affirmative action in college admissions, the NAACP submitted amicus briefs for all the cases examined in this book. It, too, agrees that universities and colleges should recruit the most diverse body of students, to enhance anyone's educational experience and better prepare them for career opportunities. Specifically, when responding to the Supreme Court decision during the *Fisher* cases, it stated:

> This is a major victory for universities, social justice, civil rights, and our nation. It reaffirms the NAACP's longstanding position that schools must remain able to create diverse and inclusive student bodies. The decision confirms that it is in our national interest, as well as the best interest of students, for talented individuals from a variety of backgrounds to receive a close look and a fair chance at overcoming obstacles to higher education. Providing a diverse learning environment benefits everyone. The University of Texas's Admission plan, which was at the heart of the case, is one that was carefully crafted to meet the goal of ensuring the educational benefits of diversity on its campus. The Fisher decision says to America's educational, business, and other institutions that they should be pursing fair and thoughtful ways of fostering diverse participation, and that doing so is not only beneficial, but constitutional as well. (NAACP, 2018)

In short, the NAACP has long believed that affirmative action in college admissions policies is essential, and has supported this wholeheartedly in its briefs and commentary about higher education.

## Opponents of affirmative action: Advocacy groups, think tanks and elite actors

As will be seen below, unlike those in support of affirmative action, advocacy groups play a stronger role, if not the *central role*, in challenging affirmative action at the level of the Supreme Court. This finding is not all that surprising. As described above, scholars have described the role advocacy groups have played and continue to play in dismantling legislature and policies such as affirmative action associated with the Civil Rights Movement (Cokorinos, 2003; Moore, 2018). They have argued that such groups are well funded and highly politicized, and serve at the behest of the elite class. Accordingly, they have also been solely designed to challenge through litigation and other techniques every civil rights and affirmative action policy created since the 1960s and removing the policy entirely from American law and precedent (Cokorinos, 2018).

In contrast to support briefs, advocacy groups (67%) wrote the vast majority of amicus briefs submitted in opposition to the use of affirmative action in higher education.

In further contrast with the support briefs, we estimate that the opponent briefs come mainly from think tank organizations (15 of 38, or 40%) followed by other SIGs and legal advocacy organizations. Indeed, some of the most prominent and well-funded think tanks in the US submitted briefs in this case, including the Center for Equal Opportunity and the Cato Institute. It is not surprising given the controversial nature of affirmative action. These think tanks generally meet the characteristics of a conservative or libertarian advocacy group. Regional legal organizations that fought against affirmative action (eg, the Mountain States Legal Foundation and Southeastern Legal Foundation) in the past were also represented in the briefs submitted to these cases. In many ways, these groups play similar roles as think tanks (eg, they provide information) but with more emphasis on litigation support. For instance, the Mountain States Legal Foundation describes itself on its website as, "Mountain States Legal Foundation is a non-profit, public interest law firm, focused on defending the constitution, protecting property rights, and advancing economic liberty." It is clear that the entities fighting against affirmative action at the level of the Supreme Court through briefs are mainly advocacy think tanks.

**Table 4.3:** Advocacy groups (amicus briefs) in opposition to affirmative action submitted to the Supreme Court cases[a]

| Authors of brief amici curiae Petitioners* | Grutter 2003 | Gratz 2003 | Fisher 2013 | Fisher 2016 |
|---|---|---|---|---|
| **Advocacy groups** | | | | |
| 1. American Center for Law and Justice | | | ✓ | ✓ |
| 2. American Civil Rights Union | | | ✓ (2) | ✓ |
| **3. Asian American Legal Foundation** | ✓ | ✓ | ✓ (3) | ✓ (2) |
| 4. California Association of Scholars, et al | ✓ | | ✓ (3) | ✓ |
| **5. Cato Institute** | ✓ | ✓ | ✓ (2) | ✓ (2) |
| 6. Center for New Black Leadership | ✓ | ✓ | | |
| 7. Center for Constitutional Jurisprudence | | ✓ | | ✓ |
| 8. Center for Equal Opportunity, Independent Women's Forum, American Civil Rights Institute | ✓ | | | |
| 9. Center for Individual Freedom | ✓ | ✓ | | |
| 10. Center for Individual Rights | | | ✓ | ✓ |
| 11. Center for the Advancement of Capitalism | ✓ | | | |
| 12. Claremont Institute Center for Constitutional Jurisprudence | ✓ (2) | ✓ | | |
| 13. Equal Employment Advisory Council | | | ✓ | |
| 14. Judicial Watch, Inc. and Allied Education Foundation | | | ✓ | ✓ |
| 15. Louis D.Brandeis Center for Human Rights Under Law, et al | | | ✓ (2) | |
| 16. Michigan Association of Scholars | ✓ | ✓ | | |

(continued)

**Table 4.3:** Advocacy groups (amicus briefs) in opposition to affirmative action submitted to the Supreme Court cases[a] (continued)

| Authors of brief amici curiae Petitioners* | Grutter 2003 | Gratz 2003 | Fisher 2013 | Fisher 2016 |
|---|---|---|---|---|
| Advocacy groups | | | | |
| 17. Mountain States Legal Foundation | | | ✓ | ✓ |
| 18. National Association of Scholars | ✓ | ✓ | | |
| **19. Pacific Legal Foundation** | ✓ | ✓ | ✓ (2) | ✓ (2) |
| 20. Reason Foundation | ✓ | ✓ | ✓ | |
| 21. Scholars of Economics and Statistics | | | ✓ | |
| 22. Southeastern Legal Foundation, Inc | | | ✓ (2) | ✓ |
| 23. Texas Association of Scholars | | | ✓ | |
| 24. Center for Equal Opportunity, Independent Women's Forum, American Civil Rights Institute | ✓ | ✓ | | |
| 25. Judicial Education Project | | | ✓ | |

Notes:

* Those entities that submitted briefs to both the *Gratz/Grutter* and *Fisher* Supreme Court cases are in bold.

[a] *Grutter v Bollinger 2003*, *Gratz et al v Bollinger 2003*, *Fisher v University of Texas at Austin 2013*, *Fisher v University of Texas at Austin 2016*.

With support briefs, the heterogeneity of actors outside of the advocacy groups ("various entities") was striking (see Table 4.2). However, actors we termed "various entities" who submitted briefs in opposition were much more homogeneous. These individuals were made up mostly of elite actors who take issue with civil rights initiatives such as affirmative action (see Table 4.4). With this in mind, we offer up the following observations. First, at least five of the elite actors who submitted briefs were affiliated with conservative/libertarian advocacy groups. For example, Ward Connerly, who served as an essential leader in the conservative advocacy group the American Civil Rights Institute, wrote his own brief (Cokorinos, 2003). Interestingly, the Institute was extremely active in fighting against affirmative action in state and federal government applications, and Connerly often led the way for these battles. He was also heavily financially supported by the Bradley Foundation, which has significantly funded the Cato Institute.

Another elite actor who has had direct ties with conservative interest groups was Gail Heriot and associates. When she submitted the brief in opposition to affirmative action for the *Fisher I* Supreme Court case, she did so as a member of the US Commission on Civil Rights. Since 1957 this federal government-authorized Commission has sought to examine and change civil rights policy when necessary. Despite the bipartisan efforts of this Commission, Heriot has served on various committees and advocacy groups, such as the Federalist Society, speaking out against affirmative action. Both of these elite actors just sent in personal letters that were indirectly related and supported by the same conservative advocacy groups that also submitted briefs against affirmative action.

These groups were also often led by "token" minorities to demonstrate to the public that the issues of minority discrimination were over, and that policies to encourage more diversity or equality were not needed. This tactic has been prevalent in the literature on conservative advocacy groups (Cokorinos, 2003). For example, the Asian American Legal Foundation, Center for New Black Leadership, Center for Individual Freedom, Center for Individual Rights, Pacific Legal Foundation, and Judicial Watch, Inc were all headed by either females or racial and ethnic minorities. Such leadership is thus surprising given the messages promoted by these groups. Despite the motivation of the policies to improve the educational, social, and economic standing of marginalized groups, they argue on their website that affirmative action policies are irrational and unfair, and the impetus of the new trend of reverse discrimination against whites. These groups also promoted the defunct argument that the policy hurt minorities themselves.

**Table 4.4:** "Various entities" (amicus briefs) in opposition to affirmative action submitted to the Supreme Court cases[a]

| Various entities | Grutter 2003 | Gratz 2003 | Fisher 2013 | Fisher 2016 |
|---|---|---|---|---|
| 1. Allen B. West, Member of Congress and Lt Col, US Army (Retired) | | | ✓ (2) | |
| 2. Current and former federal civil rights officials | | | ✓ | |
| 3. Duane C. Ellison | | ✓ | | |
| 4. Gail Heriot, et al | | | ✓ (2) | ✓ |
| 5. Indiana Institute of Technology Law School | | | | ✓ |
| 6. James F. Blumstein | | | | ✓ |
| 7. Jonathan Zell | | | | ✓ |
| 8. Law professors Larry Alexander, et al | ✓ | | | |
| 9. Richard Sander and Stuart Taylor, Jr | | | ✓ | |
| 10. State of Florida and Governor Bush | ✓ | ✓ | | |
| 11. States of Alabama, Delaware, et al | ✓ | | | |
| 12. United States (Department of Education) | ✓ | ✓ | | |
| 13. Ward Connerly | ✓ | ✓ | | |

Note: [a] *Grutter v Bollinger* 2003, *Gratz et al v Bollinger* 2003, *Fisher v University of Texas at Austin* 2013, *Fisher v University of Texas at Austin* 2016.

Before moving on to the case studies, we would like to make a comment on the differences (or lack thereof) in authorship between the *Gratz/Grutter* and *Fisher* cases. However, we would like to highlight that the absolute number of amicus briefs in opposition submitted for both cases is quite low in comparison with support briefs. First, the number of briefs submitted increased from 18 in the Michigan cases in 2003 to 23 in the University of Texas at Austin cases in 2013 and 2016. This difference can be seen in the advocacy groups as nearly the same amount of various entities submitted briefs across the cases. In total, 12 advocacy groups submitted briefs in 2003 (representing 67% of all opposition briefs filed) while that number increased to 16 in 2013/16 under the *Fisher* cases (representing 70% of all opposition briefs submitted).

Interestingly, only three advocacy groups filed briefs to both the *Gratz/Grutter* and *Fisher* cases, and no various entities submitted to both. With that being said, the real story is not change over time but (1) the absolute number of briefs submitted for and against affirmative action and (2) who was lobbying the Supreme Court and how that contrasted with those supporting affirmative action. Think tanks were the dominant organizations that advocated for the end of the policy while supporters were represented by a heterogeneous groups of students, professors, schools, and politicians, to name a few.

## Case studies

Like the advocacy groups that supported affirmative action, we have provided a short case history for three prominent advocacy groups that submitted briefs during the various Supreme Court cases analyzed in this book. We selected the three interest groups that filed briefs for all four cases from 2003 to 2013. This included the Cato Institute, Asian American Legal Foundation, and Pacific Legal Foundation. We also examined some of the elite actors to provide more contrast between the two camps arguing over affirmative action.

### *Cato Institute*

The Cato Institute is probably the most well-known advocacy group on the list of those writing briefs opposing affirmative action in college admissions policies. It describes itself as a think tank and was founded in 1977 by Charles G. Koch, and was initially funded by the Koch brothers (Cato Institute, 2018). Eighty percent of its funding comes from private donations, not just from influential individuals, but also from large family foundations such as the Bradley Foundation (Source Watch, 2018). The Institute also has several ties to various corporate and political entities around the world, and its board of directors is a virtual "who's who" of the corporate elite in the US (Source Watch, 2018).

Before we discuss its characteristic, we would be remiss not to mention the unique political role the Koch brothers have and continue to play in the US. As described in detail in Jane Mayer's 2016 book, *Dark Money*, the Koch brothers have been instrumental in setting the conservative agenda nationally over the past several decades. Leading a small but largely wealthy group of conservatives, they "poured money, often with little public disclosure, into influencing how Americans thought and voted" (2016, p 4). Their strategy involved the funding of advocacy groups in general and think tanks in particular to promote a free market ideology, lower corporate tax rates, less oversight over industry (particularly related to the environment), and minimal spending on social services for the needy. The financial commitment made by Koch and others, according to Mayer (2016), afforded them a disproportionate amount of power in American politics seldom witnessed.

Unlike the Asian American Legal Foundation, this organization has several missions, and disputing affirmative action is only one of them. As stated on its website, Cato's mission is to "originate, disseminate, and increase understanding of public policies based on the principles of individual liberty, limited government, free markets, and peace. Our vision is to create free, open, and civil societies founded on libertarian principles" (Cato Institute, 2018). Accordingly, it has not veered too far away from the original vision of the Koch brothers, and focused much of its attention on various social issues and social policies including immigration, war, global trade, finance, healthcare, and social welfare. While the Institute has suggested several times that it is not affiliated with any political agenda or policy, it tends to be conservative and libertarian in its approach to any topic it addresses. It has also couched most of its arguments for or against various social issues as a matter of abstract liberalism in which any effort to curtail individual freedoms is discriminatory regardless of existing social and economic inequalities. For example, when it comes to public education and college or university admissions, it tends to view entry and success in these institutions as governed by individual choice, individual effort, and encouraging little to no public interventions in making sure the curriculum or student or faculty body is equally accessible or obtainable (Cato Institute, 2018. It also views the global economy and politics in the same way.

When it comes to affirmative action, the Cato Institute has been on the front line fighting against its use in every institution and in college admissions policies in particular. For the Supreme Court cases under evaluation in this book, the Institute submitted amicus briefs for all four cases opposing affirmative action and in support of the lawsuits. In an article released by the Cato Institute in 2005 after the *Grutter* and *Gratz* case decisions, the Institute's view of affirmative action was as follows:

> Affirmative action defenders frequently and correctly tout the importance of college to the goal of improving life prospects. But preferences at selective schools have not increased college access. They cannot do so because most minority students leave high school without the minimum qualifications to attend any four-year school. Only outreach and better high school preparation can reduce overall racial disparities in American colleges.
>
> Nor do preferences increase the wages of students who attend more selective schools as a result of affirmative action. When equally prepared students are compared, recent research shows that those who attend less selective institutions make just as much money as do their counterparts from more selective schools.
>
> Affirmative action produces no concrete benefits to minority groups, but it does produce several significant harms. First, a phenomenon called the 'ratchet effect' means that preferences at a handful of top schools, including state flagship institutions, can worsen racial disparities in academic preparation at all other American colleges and universities, including those that do not use admissions preferences. This effect results in painfully large gaps in academic preparation between minority students and others on campuses around the country. Recent sociological research demonstrates that preferences hurt campus race relationships. Worse, they harm minority student performance by activating fears of confirming negative group stereotypes, lowering grades, and reducing college completion rates among preferred students. Research shows that skills, not credentials, can narrow socioeconomic gaps between white and minority families. Policymakers should end the harmful practice of racial preferences in college admissions. Instead, they should work to close the critical skills gap by implementing school choice reforms and setting higher academic expectations for students of all backgrounds. (Quoted in Gryphon, 2005, p 1)

Overall, the Cato Institute has viewed affirmative action as not only challenging the civil rights of individuals in accessing college education but as a terrible policy that worsens race relations, as well as disadvantaging minority student performance.

On its website, it has also put out several publications to support new efforts to end affirmative action. For example, it has supported the sale of a recently self-published book by Clint Bolick titled, *The Affirmative Action Fraud: We Can Restore the American Civil Rights Vision?* It released an article supporting US Attorney General Jeff Session's efforts to go after, what it stated as, "affirmative action's institutional racism" (Shapiro, 2017, p 1). Shapiro (2017, p 1) also stated, "There's strong evidence that schools are discriminating based on race in the name of 'affirmative action'." Finally, in a recent article published by *Forbes* magazine on July 5, 2018, written by Neal McCluskey, Cato Institute's Director of Educational Freedom, he argued this about affirmative action in the era of Trump:

> …While most Americans would probably say the ultimately correct position is for government to be color-blind, for centuries most Americans and their governments weren't even close to that and the price paid, especially by African-Americans, has been very steep. But how do we ameliorate the effects of past racially-driven wrongs without policies that take race into account? Finding the answer to that is even tougher knowing that people who did not perpetuate the past wrongs could well end up paying some of the price.
>
> I've argued that the right way to navigate the almost impossible passageway between making up for past sins and repeating them is for private colleges to embrace affirmative action, and publics to essentially admit by lottery. Free people must voluntarily atone for past wrongs, while government must cease any race-conscious decision-making. (McCluskey, 2018)

Interestingly, McCluskey and other arguments made by Cato Institute officials often argue that affirmative action hurts everyone, especially African Americans. More importantly, affirmative action has required "innocent" white Americans and others who did not support slavery or Jim Crow segregation to, as stated, "atone" for "past wrongs." This particular argument about reverse discrimination against whites has become the primary argument for the Cato Institute since 2003.

## Asian American Legal Foundation (AALF)

The AALF was founded in the 1980s to "protect and promote the civil rights of Asian Americans but is dedicated to the principle that Americans of all races and ethnicities have the right to be treated as individuals, free of discrimination" (AALF, 2018). The legal advocacy organization's home office is in San Francisco, California, and much of its first actions were to legally challenge local and state policies that used racial preference as a determining factor of entering public schools or employment. The organization consists primarily of Asian American members and its funding is through private donations by individuals and influential families. It is also one of several Asian American interest group organizations that have tended to fight specifically for Asian American rights and presented a more conservative agenda. For example, it is often in accord with the Asian American Legal Defense and Education Fund and the Asian American Coalition for Education, that has also spoken out against affirmative action and saw it as an affront to Asian Americans' abilities to attend college because they aren't "minority enough" (Guillermo, 2018). In a current lawsuit against Harvard University for using affirmative action admissions policies, the AALF and other Asian American organizations accused the university of "…unfairly rejecting many top-performing Asian American students…" in favor of different racial and ethnic minorities attending school (Fuchs, 2018).

Based on its website information, this organization sees "racial preferences" or affirmative action policies based on race or ethnicity as "unlawfully" subjecting people to racial classifications, which is biased, harmful, and demeaning (AALF, 2018). It also characterized affirmative action as a "dirty little secret":

> The 'dirty little secret' behind every program of preferences is that, in order to provide preferences to individuals of one group, individual of other groups must be 'disfavored.' In College admissions, the burden of affirmative action programs falls heaviest on individual applicants identified as 'Asian American…' At some universities, 4 out of 5 positions awarded to 'minorities' under affirmative action programs would otherwise have gone to Asian American students. This practice is wrong on several levels: it arbitrarily classifies students from a wide range of ethnicities and backgrounds as 'Asian American'; and it discriminates against individuals, who have a constitutional right to be considered as individuals, not as faceless members of a 'race.' (AALF, 2018)

Based on this, the AALF has been against the use of race or ethnicity at any point as an insult to equal opportunity protected by law. It also tends to view Asian Americans as the real victims in the application of affirmative action policies on college campuses, which has pushed it to fight several other battles in school systems to protect solely Asian American civil rights. The view of protecting one specific group's interests and suggesting the utterance of racial categories serious infractions was also echoed by the three largest Jewish interest groups before the *Grutter* and *Gratz* cases in 2003. However, the AALF stayed with this argument, and other interest groups latched on to the discussion of diversity and its benefits. The AALF reaffirmed its commitment to projecting Asian American interests based on the following statement it included from a Princeton University professor, Dr Russell K. Nieli, on its website:

> There is a third factor that may come into play in *Fisher II* [2016 case] that I have written about in an earlier Minding-the-Campus article—the rise of an aggressive Asian legal challenge to racial preferences in college admissions. No longer quiescent or content to play simply the non-complaining 'model minority' role, many Asian-American groups in recent years have come together and taken a page from the history of the NAACP to pursue an aggressive litigation strategy challenging racial preferences on 14th Amendment grounds. This strategy is clearly on display in Fisher II with an outstanding legal brief filed by two Asian-American groups, the Asian American Legal Foundation and the Asian American Coalition for Education, the latter an umbrella group representing 117 separate Asian-American organizations... The AALF/AACE brief urges the Supreme Court not merely to modify *Grutter*'s diversity-enhancement justification for racial preferences, but to overrule *Grutter* entirely and abandon 'diversity' as a legitimate criterion for discriminating based on race. The brief is a model of legal craftsmanship, informed scholarship, and moral punch that announces to the justices—loud and clear—that Asians will no longer take the widespread discrimination against them with indifference or passivity. The Asians are not going to keep quiet anymore when the universities establish the same kind of ceiling quotas against them that they imposed on the Jews in an earlier period of American history (AALF, 2018).

The text from the AALF also added one more dimension to this discussion about opposing affirmative action. In particular, it suggested that the use of racial and ethnic classification has been problematic because government and other social institutions' applications of an affirmative action program has been about quotas, which demonstrates institutional incompetence in understanding constitutional law. It believes that Justices Scalia and Kagan read its briefs and agreed that no public institution or government should determine entry into college based on race or the possibilities of diversity having a benefit on one's education (AALF, 2018). Overall, the AALF has submitted amicus briefs for every Supreme Court case supporting opposition to any institution that uses affirmative action.

## Pacific Legal Foundation (PLF)

The last interest group presented in this chapter is the PLF. Similar to the Cato Institute, the PLF was founded in 1973 on the principles of protecting personal liberties and protecting pro-business causes (Source Watch, 2017; PLF, 2018). This group has been particularly anti-government since it views government as an infringement on personal liberties:

> Governments at all levels undermine liberty by passing laws that interfere with peoples' right to freely associate and express themselves, acquire and use property, or earn an honest living. It is daunting for the average person to defend those rights against the government, with its power and access to substantial resources. That's where we step in. Thanks to our donors' support, we represent all our clients for free. (PLF, 2018)

The PLF has also focused on a variety of issues that it sees as a challenge to property rights, civil rights, or misinterpretations of the US Constitution, which has included addressing the protection of property rights of business and homeowners, free speech, tobacco regulation, environmental regulations, and even the price and trading of gold. Like many other interest groups, it has focused most of its efforts on public media and litigation campaigns to obstruct government policy and interventions. Also, while it does not characterize itself as conservative, it tends to have board members, receive donations, and support political values that are conservative. Finally, like Cato, its funding is from donations from affluent individuals, families, and private foundations (Source Watch, 2017).

Similar to the Cato Institute, the PLF has been very active in critiquing and challenging affirmative action, particularly in college admissions policies. It submitted amicus briefs to all four of the Supreme Court cases discussed in this book. Based on its website information, the PLF has suggested that affirmative action has been an unconstitutional policy and a severe overreach by universities into personal liberties. For instance, in a press release concerning the brief written by the PLF for *Fisher* Supreme Court Case of 2013, the author stated,

> In our brief, we argue that UT [University of Texas at Austin] did not consider several race-neutral alternatives. We demonstrate how leading state universities across the nation have embraced race-neutral admissions policies, and retained the ability to successfully enroll diverse student bodies. Universities have used socioeconomic-preferences, outreach at underrepresented schools, financial aid, educational initiatives, and transfer programs to enroll students from diverse backgrounds. Many schools have used these policies to exceed the level of racial diversity they were able to achieve when they had previously used race-preferences. And these schools' student bodies are more diverse in kind, because they focus on a concept of diversity that is far broader than simple racial diversity. (Boden, 2013, p 1)

Put simply, the PLF viewed the University of Texas' admissions policies that use race as a criterion as invading personal liberties to obtain a college education. More importantly, it has also argued that using race-neutral alternatives (that is, class-based admissions standards) could lead to the same racial diversity that universities want to achieve. Thus, the PLF has often flipped the argument of using affirmative action as solely focusing on race and ethnicity as a marker of preference as a problem of equality for all. It has also argued that the research suggesting race-conscious policies create better racial diversity on college campuses has been "highly dubious and can be achieved through race-neutral policies that do not have the same negative effects as race-conscious policies" (Boden, 2013, p 1).

One final observation of the PLF has been its ability to band together with other organizations to fight against affirmative action. In a press release from 2014 entitled, "Racial preference is set for extinction," the anonymous author pointed out several ways in which affirmative action, or the phrase more commonly used by the PLF, "racial preferences," were set back by state and federal decisions (PLF, 2014, p 1). For example, the author argued that the inability of the California legislature to repeal Proposition 209, which prohibits the government from giving preferential treatment based on race, was a great victory in ending racial preferences. Moreover, the author noted that this effort was successful because of the efforts of a coalition of interest groups that included the PLF, AALF, and Asian American Legal Defense and Education Fund. The author continued with several other state and federal cases in which racial preferences were successfully challenged, but also clearly noted that these successful cases were because of coalition efforts between the PLF and other interest groups against affirmative action. Overall, pointing out these coalitions is vital to show that these interest groups do work together based on common goals and possibly use the same talking points to justify their arguments.

## Conclusion

We offer up several fundamental findings from these observations. One, there are a higher number of individuals, civic groups, and advocacy groups that support affirmative action at the level of the Supreme Court than oppose affirmative action in higher education. This comparison is not even close. The Court is lobbied the hardest by those individuals and organizations that see affirmative action as important in higher education. Relative to supporters in terms of absolute number of briefs submitted, very few groups and individuals took the time and resources to fight against the policy at the level of the Supreme Court. This remains unchanged from the *Gratz/Grutter* cases in 2003 to the *Fisher I* and *II* cases in 2013 and 2016.

Two, since the turn of the century, advocacy groups have played an active role in lobbying the Court through amicus briefs. Given the growth of these organizations in the US and the role they play in the broader political policy process, this is not surprising. Most notably, however, is that advocacy groups seemed to play a stronger role among opponents of affirmative action than they did for supporters. If we were to give voice to entities opposing affirmative action at the level of the Supreme Court, it would be advocacy groups that speak the loudest. Such a finding is indirectly supported by the literature as well. The conservative reaction to the "liberal agenda" post-Civil Rights Movement has been widely discussed above.

As noted, Cokorinos (2003) posed in an almost flippant manner that as long as there has been civil rights legislature, there has been a conservative backlash in different forms all attempting to either stop civil rights legislation or trying to remove them from the law books. Moreover, scholars in the advocacy group literature note the expansion of conservative advocacy in the political world. In referencing think tanks in particular, McGann (2007) argues that this growth out-paced their liberal counterparts to such an extent that be believes conservatives and their organizations have won the war of ideas. McGann (2007) further stated that it took liberal advocacy groups decades to match the funding and organizational resources maintained by conservative groups.

Three, among the conservative advocacy groups, it is advocacy think tanks that made up the majority of authors writing and submitting legal briefs. What does this mean, and how does this reflect on the current state of the affirmative action debate? As noted above, think tanks are viewed by many as independent organizations driven by goals to shine an unbiased scholarly light on policy issues. However, as discussed, funding issues and party polarization have produced dependence of these groups on funding. Medvetz (2012) argued that due to the reliance of these groups, they turn to advocacy, which makes it hard to distinguish them from SIGs. It is evident in this case that certain think tanks are actively pushing a conservative/libertarian agenda. In this light, Cokorinos (2003) described these organizations quite negatively as guns for hire seeking to sell their services to advance the economic goals of the organization and for elite members of society. Attempting to portray oneself in an independent scholarly manner while lobbying the Court with an agenda seems quite insidious considering the possible outcome of these cases: to roll back prominent civil rights initiatives meant to help marginalized groups make education, social, and economic strides. Indeed, as will be seen in the chapters to come, these groups cloak their arguments in neoliberal arguments reminiscent of the Civil Rights Movement of the 1960s (eg, justice, fairness, and no racial discrimination). However, in this world, it is whites who are suffering at the hands of government and undeserving sub-groups.

Four, the comparison of the non-advocacy group (we termed "various entities") for supporters and opponents is quite sobering. As noted above, the amicus briefs were written by a wellspring of heterogeneous groups and individuals ranging from academic organizations, to students, states, politicians, universities, and businesses. It is evident in this analysis that a wide range of individuals and groups, elite and not elite, seemed to believe in affirmative action and its call for diversity in higher education. Conversely, the non-advocacy opponents (various entities) were few, yet quite homogeneous. These individuals tended to be wealthy, well educated, politically active, and conservative. Thus, the various entities that opposed affirmative action were elite conservative policy advocates who were well connected in the conservative world and had an issue with affirmative action in higher education.

Our final point is that it is clear that the fight *against* affirmative action continues to be waged by a select few elites and wealthy white individuals and the organizations they have created. Foundations supported by rich whites are built and maintained to support advocacy groups (eg, think tanks) to promote a particularly ideological perspective. It is readily apparent, then, that one needs only to follow the money to see who opposes affirmative action. In this light, as the death of affirmative action approaches, we need not look far. The voices of elite and wealthy whites are singing loudly.

# 5

# Case Study 1:
# The *Gratz* and *Grutter*
# Supreme Court Cases against
# the University of Michigan

## Introduction

Almost 40 years after the Civil Rights Act was passed and 25 years after
the precedent-setting *Bakke* Supreme Court decision in 1978 concerning
affirmative action in higher education, the Court would once again review
cases that tested the viability of the policy. It is not an understatement
to say that the *Gratz v Bollinger* and *Grutter v Bollinger* Supreme Court
cases came about in a different social context than the *Bakke* case. With
*Bakke*, the Civil Rights Movement had just celebrated a significant victory
in the fight for equality, and politicians and the public were conceding
change, socially and politically. However, in the early 2000s, neoliberal
politics were winning out, and a social and political backlash to civil rights
initiatives, including affirmative action, was well under way and backed
by prominent civic leaders (including the newly elected President George
W. Bush). Moreover, the tragedy of 9/11 fostered an environment that
was not friendly to racial and ethnic differences.

Furthermore, it is also clear that several vital factors worked against
the continuation of affirmative action. First, state judges and Supreme
Court justices who maintained anti-affirmative action views appointed
by Presidents Reagan and H.W. Bush were numerous and spread across
the American judicial system (Cokorinos, 2003). Indeed, the Justices
in the Supreme Court itself held a distinctive conservative majority. It was

H.W. Bush who replaced the civil rights pioneer Thurgood Marshall with Clarence Thomas, who was anti-affirmative action. Second, the president at the time, George W. Bush, supported the removal of the policy in higher education institutions, and often inaccurately characterized the policy implemented by the University of Michigan as a quota system. Finally, just a few years before the *Grutter* and *Gratz* cases, a prominent litigation (*Hopwood v Texas*) in the state courts of Texas ignored the *Bakke* precedent and ruled against the use of affirmative action in admissions policies. The *Hopwood* judges ruled that diversity was not a constitutional rationale, and thus, race could not be considered in higher education admissions decisions. This case, in essence, held that affirmative action violated the Equal Protection Clause of the 14th Amendment. The culminating force of these factors led many political pundits and interested denizens to feel that affirmative action was in its final throws of application, and that the eradication of the policy was imminent.

The purpose of this chapter is to understand arguments put forth by these social authorities (individuals and groups) in support and opposition to affirmative action within a prominent debate on affirmative action in higher education admissions. As described in previous chapters, we are particularly interested in advocacy groups that have the ability and resources not afforded to most individuals to lobby the Supreme Court. We use the *Gratz v Bollinger et al* and *Grutter v Bollinger et al* Supreme Court cases as the site of the first case study. In so doing, we look at how these entities deployed specific arguments and rhetoric within court documents to frame affirmative action to Supreme Court Justices.

While all frames are considered, we focus on two discursive frames that gained prominence in the social sciences literature. First, we assess if and how these entities used color-blind arguments (frames) in the debate for and against the policy. We use Eduardo Bonilla-Silva's (2018) color-blind frames and determine whether they were salient in legal documents—151 amicus briefs for and against affirmative action— submitted for the cases. Second, we assess if and how threat frames were used in these amicus briefs. The color-blind theoretical framework offered by Bonilla-Silva (2018) only hinted at the role of threat within color-blind rhetoric despite its prominence in the social sciences literature. For instance, Bonilla-Silva (2018) did note that whites often framed opposition to affirmative action as a concern for job loss within personal stories. However, social sciences research reveals threat narratives to be prominent in arguments surrounding racial policies in general and affirmative action in particular.

Herbert Blumer (1958) specifically outlined how group threat felt by the dominant group is problematic for society generally speaking and race relations in particular. Indeed, he argued that feelings of threat and concern for loss is a collective response and stands at the heart of racial prejudice held by whites. Pertinent to this research and within his theoretical reasoning, Blumer highlighted that prominent figures and advocacy groups play a key role in the production of these feelings. Bonilla-Silva (2018) also implied that certain social authorities (elite groups and actors) might have a louder voice in producing and reproducing racial ideology. Because affirmative action is a hotly contested racial policy, and because research has demonstrated color-blind and threat frames to be prominent in such debates, we fully expected both frames to be prominent in these legal documents. In so doing, we link the color-blind perspective of Bonilla-Silva with Blumer's group positioning perspective, providing a thorough sociological explanation of how and why prominent individuals and advocacy groups used certain arguments to attack policies that were *racialized* in nature. That is to say, while these entities may have attempted to sway the audience against race-specific policy by minimizing race, racism, and persistent discrimination through color-blind appeals, we pose that they would also try to activate race and racial animosity by invoking tropes of group threat within the same narratives. The audience of these arguments would be made to feel that resources were being threatened by an undeserving group, even while being told that race did not exist. Thus, the emotion of fear would play a vital role in the persuasive arguments.

With that being said, we fully expected the authors of these briefs to use multiple frames of communication to make their arguments and set the line of discussion for the audience. We termed this multi-framing technique *Racialized Framing*. Such a tactic makes sense in a contemporary society that is supposed to be color-blind and post-race. We argue that *Racialized Framing* provided the authors with the cover of color-blindness and neutrality while trying to infuse feelings of threat into the narrative. We feel that these results will provide a more comprehensive understanding of framing techniques used by prominent social authorities (elite individuals and groups). Moreover, we contend that these results will also provide crucial insights into why some arguments gain traction with the public and in the Supreme Court while others do not.

Overall, this chapter will contribute new layers to the discussion of racial attitudes in two fundamental ways. First, by using amicus briefs as our primary data, this research moves the study of racial attitudes away from individual-level social learning to how external factors (institutional and group-based practices) promote a particular racial ideology via rhetorical framing. Sociologist Herbert Blumer (1958) in the past, and other sociologists such as Lawrence Bobo and Mia Tuan (2006) more recently, have argued that to better understand racism, researchers must analyze how broader factors (prominent individuals and advocacy groups) contribute to the problem of racism in the 21st century, especially since the American public believe we live in a post-race society. Sociologist Woody Doane (2017, p 60) succinctly stated: "studying the racial attitudes of individuals can certainly be useful for exploring the prevalence of elements of racial ideologies, but at some point, the analysis needs to return to the macro level or we risk equating ideology with individual beliefs and prejudice." Second, by focusing on how threat interplays with abstract liberal color-blind arguments, this chapter will demonstrate how color-blind rhetoric ties into material and symbolic interests associated with group relations. We take seriously sociologist Meghan Burke's (2016) charge that in order to understand the impact of color-blind rhetoric and to move this research further than simply identifying it, we must understand the material underpinning of color-blind rhetoric—in this case, the threat to valued resources cherished by all racial and ethnic groups.

For this chapter, we present two sections. First, we summarize the two Supreme Court cases under study for this chapter, *Gratz* and *Grutter*. This section will provide specific details about the case, as well as insights into the important actors involved. Second, we present our results, focusing on how groups and various entities framed the question of affirmative action and its continued use within college admissions policies. This section focuses on both supporters and opponents of the policy.

## Summary of the court cases

Two cases involving the use of affirmative action by the University of Michigan were reviewed simultaneously by the Supreme Court, one focusing on undergraduate admissions and the second on graduate admissions. In the mid-1990s, Jennifer Gratz and Patrick Hamacher, white residents from the state of Michigan, each applied to the University of Michigan's undergraduate program. While both students were considered qualified based on their academic credentials, their grades were not sufficient to gain them entrance during the first review. After being denied entry, they sued the university, stating that its admissions policy was discriminatory to whites and unconstitutional because it gave an unfair advantage to individuals of non-white races. The University of Michigan's undergraduate admissions policy in question involved a point system that arguably gave an advantage to racial and ethnic minorities. Potential minority students received 20 points, or one-fifth of the points needed to gain admission to the university, for being a member of an underrepresented minority group. While students could obtain a maximum score of 150 points when applying to the university, a score of 100 generally guaranteed college admission into the undergraduate program.

At about the same time, in 1997, Barbara Grutter, a white resident of Michigan, was rejected after applying to the University of Michigan's Law School. In 1996, Grutter was a non-traditional 43-year-old mother of two young children (aged 7 and 10), and owner of a small business as a healthcare technology consultant. She was a good student who had earned a 3.81 GPA at Michigan State University 18 years before, and a respectable LSAT score of 161 before she applied to the Law School. The mission of the Law School at the time was to maintain a competitive admissions process while being inclusive of individuals from diverse backgrounds. Grutter subsequently claimed that the Law School had rejected her because race was a factor in the decision in the admissions process. By using race in such a fashion, she claimed the University had violated the 14th Amendment of the US Constitution. However, unlike the undergraduate admissions process, points were not automatically assigned to students based on race. Rather, the University used race as one of many factors to consider when admitting students. Thus, race was *a* factor, not *the* factor, in determining admissions.

The University's argument in the *Grutter* case was that diversity was a compelling interest to them and their mission because a "critical mass" of minorities were needed to ensure that underrepresented minorities had a social support network made up of students of similar racial and social backgrounds. They argued that a minority support network would lead to better success and higher rates of completion of the Law School program, a scenario that would benefit the students and society as a whole. The University also argued that affirmative action was needed because diversity enriched the experiences of all students and prepared them to work in a diverse world.

In 2003, because of the overlapping nature of the cases, the Supreme Court heard the arguments of the petitioners for both the *Gratz* and *Grutter* cases together. While the ruling decisions were mixed, their impact on the affirmative action landscape in higher education was undeniable. The rulings created an uneasy feeling among proponents, and reinforced the beliefs of opponents that race should not be a deciding factor in college admissions. In the *Gratz* case, the Court ruled in favor of Gratz and against affirmative action by a margin of 6–3. Chief Justice William Rehnquist, writing the majority opinion, opined that such point systems that allotted a predetermined number of points for being an underrepresented minority were not *narrowly tailored* (words used in the *Bakke* decision) to withstand *strict scrutiny* and was thus unconstitutional. That is to say, the ruling by the Court held that the use of affirmative action as such did not meet the unique needs of the University to encourage diversity, as put forth by Justice Powell in the *Bakke* (1978) case.

Concerning the *Grutter* case, in a 5–4 decision, the Court ruled that affirmative action as implemented in the Law School was constitutional. Justice Sandra Day O'Connor stated in the ruling opinion that the use of race in the case was *narrowly tailored* and was a *compelling interest* of the University and state to ensure diversity. The decision again noted that while quotas were not condoned, the consideration of race in other ways to promote diversity was permissible. The opinion mirrored the concurrent view held by Justice Powell in the *Bakke* case that diversity was still important for universities. While supporters felt the sting of defeat with the *Gratz* case, the *Grutter* ruling provided some sense of relief and ultimately stayed the execution of affirmative action in higher education.

We end this discussion by saying that the lawsuits for *Gratz* and *Grutter* did not occur by chance and were initiated by advocacy groups interested in challenging the continued use of affirmative action. Both cases were vetted and led the Center for Individual Rights (CIR), a non-profit public interest law firm with a stated interest in ending policies such as affirmative action. It viewed affirmative action as providing unfair preference to specific individuals based on gender, race, or other marginalized statuses. While this seems admirable and neutral, this group maintained a staunchly conservative agenda "dedicated to the defense of individual liberties against the increasingly aggressive and unchecked authority of federal and state governments" (CIR Mission Statement). This group was also responsible for several lawsuits against race-based policies, particularly in higher education, including *Hopwood v Texas*. The CIR was also instrumental in removing affirmative action in the state of Michigan via the Michigan Civil Rights Initiative (Michigan 06-2) that was passed in November 2006.

## *Racialized Framing*, revisited: A theoretical approach

Affirmative action policies aimed at addressing historically entrenched racial inequality have been persistently controversial. As noted in Chapter 2, public opinion polling consistently finds a lack of support among whites, and some minorities, for affirmative action as an ameliorative policy in higher education and elsewhere. Social scientists posit that such a lack of support is rooted in the concern that African

Americans are violating traditional values of hard work and trying to get something for nothing (Kinder and Sanders, 1996; Tuch and Hughes, 2011). Various authors have argued that relying on such cultural and non-racial stereotypes have served as "ideological armor" for many whites in their fight against ameliorative policies, allowing them to deny structural determinants of inequality while espousing color-blind views (Neville et al, 2000; Feagin, 2010b; Bonilla-Silva and Dietrich, 2011; Bonilla-Silva, 2018). While research looking at individual-level attitudes toward affirmative action has received most of the attention in the social sciences, we are more interested in the role of external social authorities that have the resources to frame affirmative action for the courts and the public.

As noted previously, sociologist Eduardo Bonilla-Silva outlined several racial frames that amounted to color-blind racism. This phenomenon, as Bonilla-Silva (2018, p 3) suggested, is sometimes described as "racism lite" because racial issues and policies are explained away using non-racial and seemingly benign explanations. Such frames, according to Bonilla-Silva, reflect the dominant ideology of today, and place the blame for inequality at the feet of marginalized groups themselves, ignoring persistent and structural racism and discrimination. More important for this chapter, these frames amounted to a set of rhetorical "tricks" that manifested in the amicus briefs to suggest racism was dead or at least minimalized in the US with the supposed eradication of Jim Crow laws and segregation through federal interventions in the 1960s (for contrary evidence, see Kozol, 2005; Alexander, 2012; Omi and Winant, 2015; Krysan and Crowder, 2017).

Bonilla-Silva (2018) described four frames of thought developed and used by whites, and even some non-whites, to describe racial issues in seemingly non-racial ways:

- *Abstract liberalism:* A frame that uses vague appeals to classic political or economic liberalism, including "individualism" and "equal opportunity," that ignores persistent racism and discrimination. Objections to racial policies based in abstract liberalism can be seen as reasonable or moral.
- *Naturalization:* This suggests that racial stratification is the result of natural social processes where human beings tend to flock towards like others.
- *Cultural racism:* This attempts to attribute social stratification to inherent cultural differences between groups rather than any structural determinants.
- *Minimization of racism:* This suggests that racism and discrimination are marginal social problems today.

While each frame is found in social and political racial discourse, it is the frame of abstract liberalism (eg, justice) that has been most prominent in debates over affirmative action. As described by sociologists Joe Feagin (2006) and Eduardo Bonilla-Silva (2018), these frames are more than just passive aggressive reactions by whites to growing diversity in America. They act as mechanisms that buoy the structure of dominance maintained by the dominant group (whites) in the US.

More critical to this study, both Feagin and Bonilla-Silva (and others) have highlighted the exponential impact of social authorities in producing the dominant racial ideology in the US. Indeed, Bonilla-Silva (2018, p 219) stated succinctly that, "Dominant actors (men, capitalists, whites) by virtue of their centrality in the social system and their superior resources, are able to frame the terrain of debates and influence the views of subordinated groups." Herbert Blumer (1958) also highlighted the role of elite actors (including politicians and interest groups) in producing and reproducing racial prejudice in a society. Blumer noted that such groups are powerful because they have the resources to access the masses. Accordingly, while *frames of thought* are essential because they help individuals make sense of complicated issues, we also have to examine the *frames of communication* produced by social authorities that can set the line of discussion for the masses.

Bonilla-Silva, however, never said that the color-blind frames he observed were the only frames used to argue that race does not matter in America. Past research has also revealed that a critical ingredient in the anti-affirmative action sentiment is fear of loss felt by whites (Renfro et al, 2006; Sweeney and González, 2008; González and Sweeney, 2010). Accordingly, we expect that threat and the accompanying fear may play an active role in the framing of affirmative action by the social authorities. Research does show threat frames to be quite common in frames of communication produced by the media and politicians regarding prominent social issues, including the US–Iraq War (Luther and Miller, 2005; Thrall, 2007), immigration reform (Brader et al, 2008; Fryberg et al, 2012; Carter and Lippard, 2015), and terrorism (Norris et al, 2003). Robert Entman (1997) found that mass media often framed affirmative action as a zero-sum conflict between whites and African Americans. Threat frames and the associated fear of loss are indeed factors that researchers in the area of race and politics should take into account. Social scientists have connected a fear of loss to anti-affirmative action sentiment in interviews (Sweeney and González, 2008; González and Sweeney, 2010) and experimental research (Renfro et al, 2006). Thus, the purpose of using threat to frame affirmative action in such a divisive manner ("us versus them") among social authorities may be to set boundaries among the groups using negative emotions. While negative emotions are indeed part of the racial prejudice puzzle, Blumer (1958) argued that prejudice as a belief is fundamentally about group identification, where groups develop a sense of group positioning that places them at odds with an out-group.

Accordingly, we pose that color-blind and threat frames would be salient in the briefs submitted to the *Gratz/Grutter* Supreme Court cases. We argue that such a multi-framing technique (we termed *Racialized Framing*) is used to both activate race while simultaneously trying to minimize race altogether. While we expect to find this technique among opponents, our analysis will also explore if and how color-blind and threat frames also prop up support briefs. So, in the first part of this chapter, we particularly coded for the four frames outlined by Bonilla-Silva's theory of color-blind racism. In the second part of the analysis we focus our attention on the role of threat in the debate over affirmative action. Findings demonstrate that color-blind and threat frames were indeed found among supporters and opponents alike. However, the difference between the supporters and opponents groups is quite stark. Arguments against affirmative action were infused with both types of frames. Moreover, as will be seen below, the messages produced by opponents were qualitatively different from those produced by supporters, and were meant to produce feelings of group threat.

## Leading the fight for and against affirmative action in the *Gratz/Grutter* cases

Before we move forward with the frame analysis, we would like to state again that the authors of the support briefs as compared to those in opposition were very different. The supporters were very heterogeneous, represented by SIGs (eg, American Bar Association, American Psychological Association, etc), and a consortium of students, universities, politicians, educators, and professors, and businesses. We want to highlight, however, that the majority of supporters were the latter; thus, advocacy groups did not make up the majority of support brief authors. These individuals and groups tended to band together to tackle what they saw as a social justice issue, where racial equality in higher education was under attack. Supporters mainly championed the idea of enrolling more qualified non-white applicants into undergraduate and graduate programs as a way of enriching the lives of minority students, as well as bringing in diverse perspectives that could benefit the university as a whole. And, as stated above, supporters tended to be those with something to lose, such as universities, educators, states, and students.

In contrast to the large number of briefs submitted by supporters, very few briefs were filed for the *Gratz/Grutter* cases opposing affirmative action. Of the few that were submitted in opposition, a clear majority were written by advocacy groups (largely think tanks and some legal defense foundations). As discussed in Chapter 4, many of these are very vocal and well-funded advocacy groups, including the Cato Institute, Pacific Legal Foundation, Center for Equal Opportunity, and the National Foundation of Scholars. These organizations tended to be set up and funded by wealthy family foundations, and often used prominent political and economic figureheads to serve as executive directors. It is also not surprising that these groups are considered hard-hitting conservative and neoconservative or libertarian organizations specifically formed to end affirmative action and roll back civil rights protections developed after the 1960s (Cokorinos, 2003; Omi and Winant, 2015).

Now that we have a general understanding of who is lobbying the Supreme Court via amicus briefs, we turn to what they are saying. We pull from prominent social science theory to explain why certain frames were being used by supporters and opponents. As discussed above, we fully expected the arguments to be very complicated and that authors in support and opposition would pull from dominant multi-framing techniques. However, we are interested in how supporters and opponents differed in their approach. Did opponents rely on color-blind and threat frames more than supporters? Did both pull from these frames? If so, how, and are there any qualitative differences in the content of the frames? Whatever the answers may be will provide an exciting insight into the state of affirmative action as a viable policy in the US today.

## Supporting affirmative action: Color-blind and race-conscious frames[1]

Table 5.1 provides the frequencies for all the themes and sub-themes found in the color-blind arguments made by the supporters.

The support briefs relied almost exclusively on the "diversity is beneficial" frame (Theme 1: 86%), an argument we expected to see based on past court cases. That is to say, these briefs fully embraced the idea of diversity as promoted in *Bakke* by Justice Lewis Powell, and argued diversity to be a compelling state interest because it improves a student's educational experience (Concept 1a: 89%), society (Concept 1b: 68%), the workforce (Concept 1c: 63%), the student's experience (Concept 1d: 42%), and the community (Concept 1e: 14%). For example, a brief from a consortium of 65 leading American businesses stated,

Diversity in higher education is, therefore, a compelling government interest not only because of its positive effects on the educational environment itself, but also because of the crucial role diversity in higher education plays in preparing students to be the leaders this country needs in business, law, and all other pursuits that affect the public interest.

Another example was available in the brief submitted by the American Jewish Committee, that stated, "Diversity is an important component of a well-rounded education, especially in such a pluralistic country as our own… Only if diversity is permitted to continue and flourish in our universities will our children receive the rich and rewarding education that they deserve."

We argue, however, that this "diversity is beneficial" frame really hinges on how the authors dealt with the racism and discrimination felt by marginalized groups. So there seem to be two camps: one that coupled the diversity rationale with the idea that racism and discrimination was a major issue in the past and/or remained a problem today, and one that maintained a color-blind frame orientation the seemed to ignore such issues faced by non–whites. We argue that the distinction between the two camps is important. However, before discussing the findings, we would like to add that the distinction between color-blind and race-conscious was not always clear. Authors may have acknowledged past harms felt by

**Table 5.1:** Color-blind themes and concepts for amicus briefs submitted by supporters for *Grutter v Bollinger et al* (02-241) and *Gratz v Bollinger et al* (02-516)

| Support brief findings 117/151 (78%) | | |
|---|---|---|
| Coded theme or concept | Theme or concept title | Ratio and % of briefs using theme or concept |
| **Theme 1** | **Diversity is beneficial** | **101/117** **(86%)** |
| Concept 1a | Better education | 90/101 (89%) |
| Concept 1b | Better society | 69/101 (68%) |
| Concept 1c | Better workforce | 64/101 (63%) |
| Concept 1d | Better for student | 43/101 (42%) |
| Concept 1e | Better for community | 14/101 (14%) |
| **Sub-theme 1** | **Race-conscious arguments** | **57/101** **(56%)** |
| Concept sub1a | Past racial discrimination | 57/101 (56%) |
| Concept sub1b | Present racial discrimination | 50/101 (50%) |
| **Sub-theme 2** | **Minimizing race arguments** | **48/101** **(48%)** |

minorities yet still minimized the role of racism today, focusing on the "diversity is beneficial" argument. Accordingly, we offer the following observations.

In the first camp, several of the briefs were race-conscious and connected the continued need for such a policy to past and present issues of racism and discrimination while promoting the "diversity is beneficial" frame (Sub-theme 1). Of all the support briefs that mentioned "diversity is beneficial" ($n=101$), 57 percent (Concept sub1a) and 50 percent (Concept sub1b) made detailed references to past or present racial and ethnic discrimination, respectively. For instance, the American Bar Association noted the history of racial discrimination, specifically against African Americans in higher education in the US. The American Sociological Association also noted the long and historical trajectories of racism in the US, and pointed out that school segregation based on race negatively affected the academic achievement of non-whites in comparison to whites. Or, as noted by Amherst College's brief, "It [University of Michigan's admissions policies] should consider the realities of admitting applicants, to serve a highly selective college's mission, in a society in which race still matters in determining a person's available opportunities and life experience, and the effects of discrimination and entrenched segregation still linger."

In referring to the second camp, we argue that almost half of the briefs (Concept 1a: 48%) actually minimized race and issues of racism and discrimination when making the "diversity is beneficial" argument. Along with other scholars (Moore, 2018), we pose that the "diversity is beneficial" frame can be color-blind and have unintended negative consequences when presented in a way that ignores such transgressions. Of the briefs we define as color-blind, they never fully defined diversity as focusing on race and ethnicity in particular, or they never connected diversity to issues of racism and discrimination, past or present. In most respects, the word "diversity" was a proxy for non-white participation in higher education, and a full discussion of why the African American experience was key to keeping this policy was not included.

While these authors were attempting to save affirmative action in higher education and support Justice Powell's diversity rationale, they were also falling into the post-race American trap of using the politically correct color-blind perspective to make their arguments. This further divorced the concept of affirmative action away from past and present discrimination faced by racial minorities. In other words, rather than directly mention why race continues to matter in the US today generally and why it matters in higher education particularly, the authors focused on vague discussions of why diversity is important for students, the university, and society. Thus, using a color-blind argument detracted from the actual problem of racial discrimination many non-whites continue to face in higher education admissions.

We would like to make one more observation about the "diversity is beneficial" frame. In a broader sense, embracing the diversity argument effectively mutes arguments about how affirmative action could concretely and substantially address racial discrimination in higher education. Educators and scholars are thus not able to create thoughtful programs to alleviate inequality that is historically produced. Even when they spoke of past discrimination, the authors of some briefs minimized the role of race by emphasizing the idea that diversity was good for all regardless of race. The Venn diagram below (see Figure 5.1) visually demonstrates that most authors attempted to first support affirmative action within Justice Powell's initial race-neutral argument during the *Bakke* case. Again, Justice Powell's argument suggested that affirmative action could be allowed if the policy was *narrowly tailored* and was not implemented to correct issues of past or present discrimination by favoring non-white applicants. By comporting with Justice Powell's diversity rationale without the context of how racism continues to work today, and by not implicitly referring to the role race continues to play in the US, the bite of affirmative action is negated, and the experience of minority students is silenced. This, combined with arguments that place other types of diversity over arguments of continued racial discrimination, makes affirmative action very vulnerable

**Figure 5.1:** Identified themes in supporter briefs for *Grutter* and *Gratz*

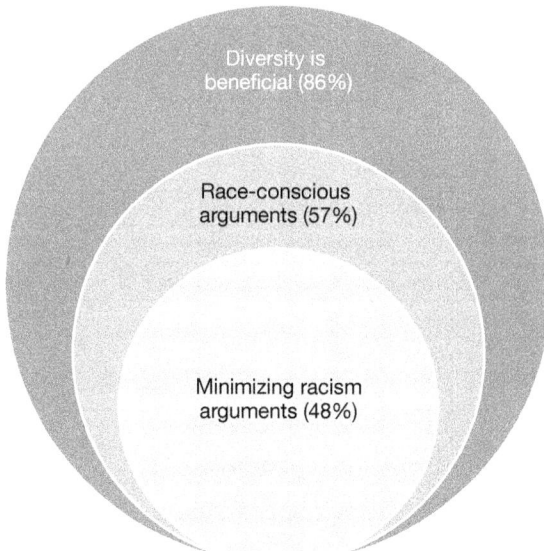

Diversity is beneficial (86%)

Race-conscious arguments (57%)

Minimizing racism arguments (48%)

to conservative courts that seek to kill affirmative action as an ameliorative policy in higher education for good (Herring and Henderson, 2012).

## Opposing affirmative action: Color-blind and race-conscious frames

In stark contrast to supporters, amicus briefs written by authors against affirmative action were infused with color-blind rhetoric (see Table 5.2). These used three of the four color-blind frames identified by Bonilla-Silva (2018) extensively, including abstract liberalism (Theme 1), minimization of racism (Theme 2), and cultural racism (Theme 3).

### Abstract liberalism

Before we move to the findings, we would like to present more detail on Bonilla-Silva's color-blind frames. Bonilla-Silva (2018) states that the dominant ideology in the US today is color-blind. That is, when faced with race and issues surrounding race (eg, inequality, incarceration, etc), most whites and some non-whites attempt to explain away problems using non-racial and even benign explanations. Rather than overt acts of discrimination committed by a few, the real problem in the US today is

**Table 5.2:** Color-blind themes and concepts for amicus briefs submitted by opponents for *Grutter v Bollinger et al* (02-241) and *Gratz v Bollinger et al* (02-516)

| Opponent briefs 34/51 (22%) | | |
|---|---|---|
| **Coded theme or concept** | **Theme or concept title** | **Ratio and % of briefs using theme or concept** |
| Theme 1 | **Abstract liberal arguments** | **27/34** **(79%)** |
| Concept 1a | Racial classifications are dangerous | 27/27 (100%) |
| Concept 1b | Violates equality and meritocracy | 22/27 (81%) |
| Theme 2 | **Minimization of racism** | **25/34** **(74%)** |
| Concept 2a | Diversity has little value | 25/25 (100%) |
| Concept 2b | Diversity achieved/racism in the past | 23/25 (92%) |
| Concept 2c | Race-neutral policies are better | 13/25 (52%) |
| Theme 3 | **Cultural racism — paternalism** | **16/34** **(47%)** |
| Concept 3a | Mismatch to higher education | **14/16** **(87%)** |
| Concept 3b | Mismatch to workforce | **5/16** **(31%)** |

an ideology that minimizes the role of race. Interestingly, Bonilla-Silva (2018) poses that this ideology can be held by racists and non-racists alike, ultimately producing and reproducing the racist system we have today.

One of the most dominant frames implemented in this endeavor is that of *abstract liberalism*, which poses that political and economic liberal ideas are used to explain away racial inequality (eg, lack of a work ethic leads to racial disparities). For opponents, 79 percent (Theme 1: 27 of 34) of the briefs submitted against affirmative action used abstract liberal ideas as the foundation for disputing its use. This happened in two fundamental ways. Among those briefs that used abstract liberal arguments, 100 percent (Concept 1a) suggested that any discussion of race or using racial classifications was dangerous to the core American principle of equality. Thus, opponents were not opposed to affirmative action because they held racist viewpoints; rather, they opposed the policy because it went against cherished principles people held close in the US.

Like many liberal and civil rights organizations attempting to combat continued racial discrimination in the US, several briefs argued that race and ethnicity as a classification system to determine one's academic abilities were erroneous, stereotypical, and discriminatory for *all* people. They also echoed liberal arguments that any classification based on "skin color," as inferred by using affirmative action policies, were clearly "archaic," "damning," "non-scientific," and "inherently suspect." For example, Ward Connerly's amicus brief submitted to the *Grutter* case stated,

> The 'diversity rationale' relies upon and reinforces a rigid and fixed system of racial classification and categorization in a nation of ever-changing and expanding demographics. It is time for America to get beyond 'race' and the 'one drop rule' that underpin 'diversity building.'

Another example was evident in the brief submitted by the Center for the Advancement of Capitalism, which stated "… policies … rely[ing] on using an individual's genetic lineage to assess their character and intellectual capacity. By definition, such a policy is racist … each individual is reduced to a color-coded cipher." The Asian American Legal Foundation's brief for both cases suggested that racial classification led to the exclusion of Asian Americans because they were considered a faceless "yellow horde," as well as the exclusion of Jews for being seen as a "plague."

These arguments echoed the problems of racial classification that have been argued for decades by liberal and civil rights-oriented organizations. However, these briefs flipped this argument on its ear and used it against liberal views of racial justice that sought to improve the life chances of marginalized groups. Michael Omi and Howard Winant (2015) have long argued that such "neoliberal conservative" tactics have been used since the 1980s by politicians and pundits who hold more conservative viewpoints to raise concern for white victimization. Most impressive, these tactics borrow words, phrases, and symbols from the Civil Rights Movement to gain legitimacy, as racial classification has long been held in disrepute based on past transgressions made against minorities in the US. Also, Justice Powell's stance presented in his decision concerning the *Bakke* case on affirmative action stated that the discussion of race and ethnicity should be minimalized, but diversity could be considered. Of course, Justice Powell's argument during this case was also a color-blind approach to addressing racism in the US. In short, it makes sense that both briefs supporting and rejecting affirmative action admissions policies would have to argue that racial classifications were wrong to gain support for their arguments.

The second abstract liberal frame in these briefs suggested that affirmative action challenged American ideals of meritocracy (Concept 1b). Of the briefs that used abstract liberal arguments, 81 percent argued that because racial classifications were deployed through affirmative action, it destroyed merit-based entry into higher education and favored "odious" race-conscious remedies to racial discrimination. More specifically, affirmative action admissions policies directly challenged what the authors of the briefs saw as an infringement on constitutional rights guaranteed to *all* citizens, regardless of skin color. Briefs from the Pacific Law Foundation, law professors, and the US General Counsel emphasized that any affirmative action programs in higher education went against the Equal Protection Clause of the 14th Amendment that "…prohibits states from benefitting or burdening individuals based on race. Equality in the modern day does not suggest or require that 'the less qualified be preferred over, the better qualified simply because of minority origins'" (Pacific Law Foundation for *Grutter*). Thus, racial classification of any sort trampled on individual rights, and more importantly, erased the merits of applicants when universities used "racial favoritism" as a "plus" in admissions to increase diversity on campus (Cato Institute's brief for the *Grutter* case).

Again, while these arguments often matched liberal opinions that racial classification had been structurally discriminatory, the sleight of hand in this rhetoric is important to unpack. For instance, a majority (70%) set up their arguments with a revisionist account of the Civil Rights Movement and its achievements to end racism in education for everyone, regardless of skin color. Fourteen different briefs cited the *Brown v Board of Education* Supreme Court in 1954 as the auspicious beginning to ending racial classifications that created racism in education, and protected both white and non-white students from discrimination. Many of these briefs spent six to ten pages explaining the history of racial discrimination against African Americans in particular, sometimes pointing out racism directed at Hispanics and Asians. Most interesting, the authors never referred to white students specifically, but in subtle ways, it was implied that this same fight for non-white racial justice was, in fact, also a fight for white racial justice. For example, Ward Connerly's brief even went back as far as the American Civil War and slavery, while several others started with the Declaration of Independence as defining moments and documents that ended (or could have ended) racial discrimination for *everyone*.

At least five different briefs suggested that Martin Luther King Jr was for racial equality for African Americans *and* whites, and would have been ashamed of how colleges were using affirmative action to bring about diversity. For example, this was stated in the Claremont Institute's brief for the *Grutter* case:

> These facts reveal that the political opposition to the demands of the Equal Protection Clause is every bit as powerful as the opposition this Court faced in the years following *Brown*. What Martin Luther King said in 1964 is equally true today: 'the announcement of the high court has been met with declarations of defiance. Once recovered from their initial outrage, these defenders of the status quo had seized the offensive to impose their schedule of change'… As Dr King also noted that August day on the steps of the Lincoln Memorial, 'In the process of gaining our rightful place [as beneficiaries of the Declaration's promise of equality,] we must not be guilty of wrongful deeds.'

The Claremont Institute brief also goes on to suggest that Martin Luther King Jr would not have supported any color-conscious policies that could harm any person of color, including white applicants.

What becomes clear is that briefs against affirmative action classified universities as the real perpetrators of racism in the US today. They also clearly argued that racial discrimination was now directed at white applicants because past federal decisions (eg, *Brown v Board*) were only applied to non-whites and, in particular, African Americans. Most interestingly, less than half (47%) mentioned continued issues of discrimination felt by non-whites, a problem consistently found in the social sciences. In short, opponents suggested that affirmative action in higher education should be eliminated because it promoted race-based discrimination and ruined a merit-based higher education entry policy that worked to reward deserving students. We now turn to how these briefs used various discursive frames minimizing racism against non-whites through denouncing diversity and its benefits to student education.

## Minimization of racism

Opponent briefs were also saturated with the "minimization of racism" frame (Theme 2). In *Racism without Racists*, Bonilla-Silva (2018) argued that the minimization of racism is the idea that racial discrimination is no longer considered a central factor or problem affecting non-white minorities' life chances, including educational attainment. He also argued that, rhetorically, this argument could be made in several ways, but the key was to push the conversation away from how race and racism still influenced the lives of non-whites. This color-blind frame only showed up in briefs written against affirmative action.

We found that the most prominent way the briefs reduced the significance of racism was to denounce the notion that diversity mattered at all in higher education. This argument is important in one particular context related to the Court, which has stated that there should be a deadline for diversity to be achieved and, once this has occurred, affirmative action should be removed from admissions decisions. Thus, the use of affirmative action in higher education should have a timetable that is determined by the need for the policy. While this means that supporters were likely to argue for the continued need for diversity, opponents had to denounce diversity as entirely invaluable for anyone in higher education. This also means that opponents had to ignore that non-white applicants continue to face issues of racist exclusion and discrimination in higher education, thus skirting the real problems faced by minorities and the privilege afforded to white students in the admissions process.

Based on our analysis, 74 percent (Theme 2) of all briefs submitted against affirmative action denounced the universities' efforts to use race as an admissions criteria to increase racial and ethnic diversity. Some argued against it because diversity would not have the benefits suggested by the University of Michigan (Concept 2a: 100%). They also argued that diversity had already been achieved with the current student body makeup (Concept 2b: 92%), and race-neutral policies were the best way of creating a diverse student body (Concept 2c: 52%).

The first dismissive frame these briefs used suggested that the University of Michigan's notions of diversity were too vague and thus, intentionally stereotypical and exclusionary in attracting a diverse student body based solely on racial classifications. Thus, the policy is not beneficial. The authors took to heart Justice Powell's statement in his decision about the *Bakke* case that using affirmative action policies must be *narrowly tailored* to argue its usage in college admissions. For example, former Governor of Florida, Jeb Bush suggested that since the University of Michigan did not narrowly define their definition of diversity, the university's "… admissions policies gave preferences on race and ethnicity, and appear to have simply assumed that those [racial] categories necessarily corresponded to particular viewpoints." In other words, and as Ward Connerly wrote in his brief, "'Diversity' is essentially a code word…" for racist admissions policies assuming that non-whites offered diverse viewpoints and, in particular, whether they needed an unfair advantage getting into school. What these comments suggested was that because diversity was vaguely defined, it was about race, and that is racist, just like racial classifications. This made sense in these authors' minds if we tie this argument back to what we previously noted, in which their abstract liberal arguments categorized all racial classification as discriminatory. Besides, diversity does not work if the goal is to bring in "diverse" opinions and backgrounds with the assumption that race or skin color is the only proxy for said diversification.

A second frame that consistently came up, applied to minimize Michigan's desire for a diverse-student body, was that diversity had already been achieved in recent years. This argument reached back to the discussion on how past federal interventions through Supreme Court rulings on equal access to education had sufficiently dealt with structural racism. As noted in the brief submitted by the Center for New Black Leadership, decisions from *Brown* and *Bakke* provided plenty of ways to support non-white and expressly, African American, student access to opportunities to enter higher education. At least three briefs provided statistics that showed that the University of Michigan had admitted several African Americans and Hispanics into their undergraduate and Law School programs in recent years, and as one stated, "…this was sufficient progress in creating a diverse student population."

Many of these briefs argued that race-neutral admissions policies were better at recruiting a diverse population. This was couched in the notion that, as stated by the Center for Equal Opportunity and Ward Connerly, universities did not necessarily want or need racial diversity but instead they needed "perspective" diversity. In this sense, perspective diversity was considered the best way to increase diversity awareness and critical thinking skills for all college students. For example, in former Governor Jeb Bush's brief, the authors argued that Florida had enacted several race-neutral admissions policies focusing on income, first-generation, and non-traditional categories to recruit a diverse student population for the University of Florida system. They also nefariously echoed liberal arguments regarding inequality that more must be done to assist with academic achievement *before* students applied for college. However, they argued that using income and other factors would produce the same racial diversity that the University of Michigan wanted without using race as the proxy.

Overall, the point is clear that diversity is not a public interest because it has been vaguely defined, too focused on racial diversity, or there has been little to no direct support of diversity equaling a better education for *all* students. Although there could be some argument that the universities do need to be specific in what they mean by diversity, opponent briefs consistently minimized the importance of racial diversity as a way to get more non-whites into college and negate continued racism and discrimination in the admissions process. However, again, in the minds of these authors, the college admissions process had become fairer in higher education since *Brown* for most non-white minorities, and was thus not needed. It is at this point that the authors suggested that the higher education process had become unfair, particularly for whites. As the Claremont Institute brief suggested, liberal politicians, organizations, and universities had become "defenders of racial discrimination" by using affirmative action admissions policies based on race, and were now the real enemies because they "…refuse to implement the demands of the Equal Protection Clause."

## Cultural racism and paternalism

Another robust color-blind frame found in opponent briefs was that of cultural racism (Theme 3: 47%). This poses that non-whites, to a great extent, continue to experience inequality because of their flaws as a culture (that is, single parent families, lack of ambition, laziness, etc). As pointed out by Bonilla-Silva (2018), neoliberal arguments against current issues of structural racism often rely on "blame the victim" narratives. These decry a lack of commitment, personal drive, or even, ironically, being a victim of past racism that they cannot recover from generationally due to these same reasons (eg, lack of drive). For example, the Claremont Institute suggested that affirmative action was racist and a paternalistic practice by universities because they assumed non-whites "are incapable of competing without a big brother—a white big brother—to guide them."

Another example was found in former Governor Jeb Bush's brief where his team argued that higher education was not the place to battle structural racism in education; this fight was more appropriate in primary and secondary education realms. Although civil rights and anti-racist organizations would agree with this sentiment, this brief and others took it a step further. Bush's brief and others, for example, suggested that it was the priority of the residents of Florida to address the "achievement gaps" between non-whites and whites before university admissions so that non-whites would not face great disappointment in higher education when they dropped out of college. Here, a theme of paternalism comes through loud and clear. Again, this color-blind theme only presented itself among the briefs against affirmative action.

As discussed in Mary Jackman's (1994) research monograph, *The Velvet Glove*, there has been a long history of paternalistic endeavors by white American society to assist African Americans and other minority groups in being successful economically and educationally. Rather than using power and brutality to control minority groups, Jackman (1994) argued that paternalism has been a constant mechanism to control and maintain power in politics. Social control over racial and ethnic minorities is thus cloaked in a legitimate concern or love for the wellbeing of minorities. However, what paternalistic actions by well-intentioned whites have done to non-whites is, first, to consider them incapable of achievements and success *without* assistance. More importantly, the paternalistic approach suggests that they could not achieve success without the help of white America in particular.

The most common paternalistic argument used in the briefs was that African American and other non-white college applicants were not prepared for the rigor of higher education and would thus fail (Concept 3a: 87%). For instance, the brief submitted by the Claremont Institute stated that,

> For a state-run institution of higher learning to do this is unconstitutional as well as unjust, not just for the Barbara Grutters of the world but for the preferred minority students who are plucked—Michigan paternalistically uses the word 'chosen,'—by the University of Michigan from academic institutions where they would be competitive and thrust into an environment where they are forced to compete with students of significantly stronger academic credentials. When one considers how pervasive is the use of race in college and law school admissions nationwide, the problem becomes intolerable.

This brief suggested that affirmative action for non-whites would put them in educational environments unprepared, placing them in direct competition with "white" students who had better academic credentials. It should be clear here that the Claremont Institute not only viewed non-whites as unprepared academically, but also unable to compete because non-whites were individually just "way less-qualified," as they noted later in their brief. In fact, they argued that if it were not for affirmative action policies, there would likely be no non-white applicants because they just could not compete against white applicants. Thus, "they need help" but not through "race-biased policies."

Ironically, opponent arguments maintain some basis in reality but miss out on a basic understanding of inequality, and how it is produced and reproduced particularly along racial lines. Academic achievement gaps have continued to widen between whites and non-whites (except for Asians) (see Kozol, 2012; Downey and Condron, 2016). For virtually every academic achievement measure obtained, white students outscore African American and Latino students. While this trend is due to a multitude of causes (eg, biased standardized tests, racism and discrimination in schools), most social scientists and public educators argue that white and non-white students have very different experiences within the education system in the US. Even with the supposed end of racial segregation in schools, African American and Latino students faced and continue to face unequal experience in education, including inadequate funding, teaching staffing, and curriculum. It is not surprising, then, that social sciences research has found integration to be mostly a myth. Jonathan Kozol (2012) argues that racial integration has never really happened, and poor or low-income schools, that are often majority-non-white, have continued to suffer in the US. Of course, while poor, white schools have faced some of the same disparities, it has not been at comparable rates to non-whites (see Owens, 2018). Ann Owens (2018) recently found that only affluent white families with children in private schools have the best educational outcomes. Their achievement scores are higher than any non-white scores in private or even high-income public school districts.

All of this irony gets lost in the briefs because while opponents recognized the achievement gaps, they failed to discuss the systemic factors that produced these results. The briefs then proceeded to use the partial evidence against non-whites to suggest that these facts should *exclude* them from higher education opportunities. Again, as former Governor Jeb Bush suggested, along with the Reason Foundation, higher education was not the place for non-whites until they had addressed their achievement gaps in lower grades. As the Pacific Legal Foundation stated in their brief, "… minority groups cannot be expected to meet the same standards as other students." Thus, as they also state, "…we must make a better education system for all…" but it should not be done in higher education.

This dismissive and paternalistic frame did not stop there. These briefs also hammered the point home of a "mismatch" by pointing out that affirmative action would place under-prepared non-white students in schools where they would struggle to succeed. This "mismatch" would not only hurt them in the classroom, but also as they moved into the job market (Concept 3b: 31%). Here the argument was simple. As noted by the Center for Equal Opportunity brief, if non-whites were to graduate from college, their "academic inadequacies" would reveal themselves at work. Thus, as argued by a brief submitted by the Department of Education, "top jobs, graduate schools, and the professions…" that take in these underprepared graduates could lead to being let go due to "inadequacies in skills." Or, as the Center for Equal Opportunity argued, non-whites who graduate will be "professionally uncompetitive" and thus, will not even be selected in a highly competitive job market. Interestingly, not one brief mentioned that there are thousands of white American students who suffer from underachievement, which makes their "everyone suffers" argument convincingly color-blind. What became clear in these statements was that *only* non-whites were underprepared and needed help before entering higher education in comparison to white applicants.

Like the support briefs, those arguing against affirmative action in these Court cases had themes that overlapped to build their discursive persuasions. As noted in Figure 5.2, abstract liberal arguments of dismissing both racial classification and the goal of diversifying a university's student body served as the anchor in the arguments. Then, the authors of opposing briefs relied greatly on the notion that racism was a thing of the past, and minimally directed their talking points at issues facing white students (which becomes a threat narrative, as we discuss below). Finally, and quite different from supporters using a color-blind rhetoric, these briefs turned

**Figure 5.2:** Venn diagram of color-blind themes among briefs opposing affirmative action

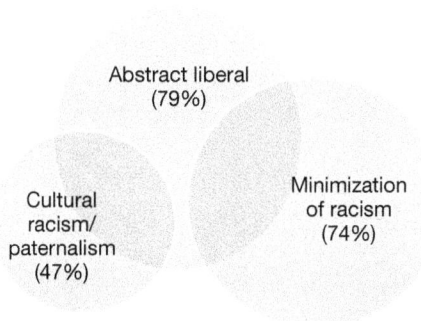

to paternalistic arguments, where they expressed concerns for minorities, particularly African Americans, and their abilities to successfully navigate higher education, given their background. This paternalistic argument drew on seemingly genuine concerns regarding the growing educational achievement gaps expressed by progressives seeking social justice (see Kozol, 2005), without mentioning the systemic issues faced by non-whites of racism and discrimination. Nonetheless, the paternalism narrative became a way to avoid directly explaining the continued issues of structural racism and focus more on discussions of how merit should be the top or only criterion necessary to determine college admissions.

Overall, what we found was that briefs for and against the use of affirmative action in college admissions policies used color-blind rhetoric to make their arguments. On the one hand, supporter briefs used color-blind rhetoric to avoid discussing race and racism to stay in line with the Supreme Court precedent regarding the import of diversity set by Justice Powell during the *Bakke* case. On the other hand, briefs against affirmative action deployed color-blind rhetoric more often to avoid any direct conversations about race, racism, and continued racial discrimination. It would not be an overstatement to say that the briefs in opposition to affirmative action were saturated with color-blind arguments, and seemed to rely on them exclusively. Ultimately, however, by both sides deploying color-blind perspectives, the result was that these briefs continued to downplay past and present issues of racism and discrimination for non-whites in higher education for the Court Justices and for the public.

## Veiled threat frames in the affirmative action debate: The *Gratz/Grutter* cases

As noted above, we proposed that color-blind rhetoric would be accompanied by threat rhetoric. We argue here that the concomitant use of color-blind and group threat frames is intentional. The purpose of using such a multi-framing technique is to activate racialized peril (and ultimately animosity) while trying to suggest that race does not matter in shaping higher education admissions. We termed this tactic *Racialized Framing*. Below, our results support this argument.

### Supporting affirmative action: Veiled threat frames

We first present our results on how notions and discussions of group threat showed up in supporters' briefs during the *Gratz* and *Grutter* cases (Table 5.3). While coding for the various frames of group threat as suggested by Blumer (1958), we assumed such language would be found in opponent briefs. However, we were surprised that supporters of affirmative action used threatening arguments (frames) to make their points as well. It should be noted that their use of threat was quite different from how opponents used threat. Support briefs did not use threat to create a sense of group position or to suggest any prejudice towards a singular racial or ethnic group. In fact, much of their arguments rested on the notion that ending affirmative action in college admissions processes would threaten or ruin a century of work attempting to correct social inequality created, in part, by structural racism. This was clear in the brief submitted by the School of Law of the University of North Carolina, which stated, "…the good faith efforts of a full generation of public university admissions officers—who have acted year in and year out in every state, with the full sanction of governors, legislatures, and university chancellors to broaden access to public higher education—would be irreparably injured by an adverse ruling from this Court." Thus, while we find threat in support briefs (see Table 5.3), we are not suggesting that these threats follow Blumer's theoretical arguments as they did with opponents' briefs. Rather, supporters were more about protecting a marginalized group and universities' right to serve those students instead of, as noted in Blumer's theory, creating clear divisions of "us versus them" to incite prejudicial thoughts and actions.

**Table 5.3:** Group threat themes and concepts for amicus briefs among supporters for *Grutter v Bollinger, et al* (02-241) and *Gratz v Bollinger, et al* (02-516)

| Support brief findings 117/151 (78%) | | |
|---|---|---|
| Coded theme or concept | Theme or concept title | Ratio and % of briefs using theme or concept |
| **Theme 1** | **Threat to US Constitution** | 48/101 (48%) |
| Concept 1a | Free speech/academic freedom | 44/48 (92%) |
| Concept 1b | Equal Protection Clause/14th Amendment | 16/48 (33%) |
| **Theme 2** | **Threat to university goals** | **42/101 (42%)** |
| Concept 2a | Diverse education | 28/42 (67%) |
| **Theme 3** | **Threat to society** | **32/101 (32%)** |
| **Theme 4** | **Threat to minorities** | **20/101 (20%)** |
| Concept 2a | Stereotype threat | 2/20 (10%) |
| Concept 2c | Professional lag | 2/20 (10%) |
| **Theme 5** | **Threat to profession** | **15/101 (15%)** |

One of the most prominent themes in the support briefs was the "threat to the US Constitution." Almost half (Theme 1: 48%) of all supporters' briefs argued that ending affirmative action in college admissions policies would seriously disrupt the civil rights protections afforded by the US Constitution. Within the briefs that focused on a threat to the Constitution, almost all (Concept 1a: 92%) suggested that affirmative action created a diverse student body that allowed them to use their rights to free speech and academic freedom. Several briefs (Concept 1b; 33%), including ones submitted by the National Association for the Advancement of Colored People (NAACP) and American Civil Liberties Union (ACLU), also pointed out that the use of affirmative action helped to support constitutional rights guaranteed by the 14th Amendment in which every person is allowed equal access to higher education, regardless of their race or ethnicity. Some even argued that if the Supreme Court struck down the use of affirmative action in public universities, this would be an infringement on state sovereignty; however, this argument was in less than 20 percent of the briefs.

Another threat frame that stood out in the support briefs was that if the Court was to disallow the use of affirmative action in admissions policies, universities would struggle to meet their goals (Theme 2: 42%). In particular, these briefs focused on the threat to a diverse education (Concept 2a: 67%). For instance, the brief submitted by 65 leading American businesses noted that the end of affirmative action in college admissions policies would narrow the search for students with the most promise. The Association of American Law Schools briefs stated that law schools' and universities' use of affirmative action was "critical to achieving their missions of carrying out research as well as serving avenues of upward mobility for talented students. That support depends on public confidence that the schools are open to talented individuals of all races." Indiana University's brief also agreed by stating, "Any blanket prohibition on race-sensitive admissions would frustrate a time-tested process built in reliance upon the flexibility permitted by *Bakke*, and replace it with a blind judicial ideal detached from the realities of the law school environment. Such inflexibility would ultimately defeat the school's compelling interest in diversity."

While relevant, the following threat frames were less frequently included in the briefs. First, some briefs (Theme 3: 32%) suggested that ending affirmative action was a threat to the society we were seeking to become that promotes equality regardless of race. As the NAACP and ACLU stated in their briefs, "If there is any hope for this country to continue to make racial progress, it lies, at least in part, in the unique ability of colleges and universities to bring together persons of all racial backgrounds to achieve the educational benefits of diversity and, ultimately, to create a more just, racially integrated society." Second, support briefs also posed that removing the policy would lead to backsliding into a more racist and stereotypical higher education experience for non-whites. For example, the brief submitted by the UCLA School of Law Students of Color stated,

> Discrimination is prevalent in our society, otherwise diversity would have occurred naturally. Most of the country's elite educational institutions have already recognized this problem and addressed it. They should be allowed to continue to do so because the present lack of diversity is a direct result of America's history of racial and gender discrimination. Diversity cannot be completely separated from integration. The fact that Black and Latino students are marginalized and presumed to be inadequate is a function of the intrinsic racism prevalent in our society. Affirmative action is simply a mechanism to mitigate the psychological injuries caused to students by these racial stereotypes. Integration is designed as a partial remedy for the stifling effects of this racism. As students of color in the UC system can attest, the assumption of inferiority exists regardless of the existence or nonexistence of an affirmative action program. By matriculating a critical mass of minority students, schools can create an educational environment in which students can achieve their full potential because they no longer suffer under assumed inferiority.

As noted above, without affirmative action, non-white students could be excluded from higher education once again. Moreover, non-whites could continue to face severe psychological injuries because of stereotypical assumptions from the American public, contributing to a long cycle of assumed inferiority (that is, stereotype threat theory). Finally, several briefs from various attorney and bar associations suggested that the removal of affirmative action from higher education would cause a "precipitous decline in the number of lawyers from under-represented racial and ethnic groups" who could actually help to rectify severe racial and ethnic injustices in the American criminal justice system (Theme 4: 15%).

Again, the notions of group threat suggested by Blumer were absent among the supporters' briefs in the *Gratz* and *Grutter* cases. Figure 5.3 provides a Venn diagram demonstrating the connections between threat themes. These focused heavily on the constitutional rights afforded to citizens with expansions into how these rights were important for universities, minorities, and society as a whole. While rare, they also suggested a holistic threat to professions not being able to recruit skilled and diverse candidates to work in a diverse world. In short, the erasure

**Figure 5.3:** Venn diagram of threat frames identified in supporter briefs

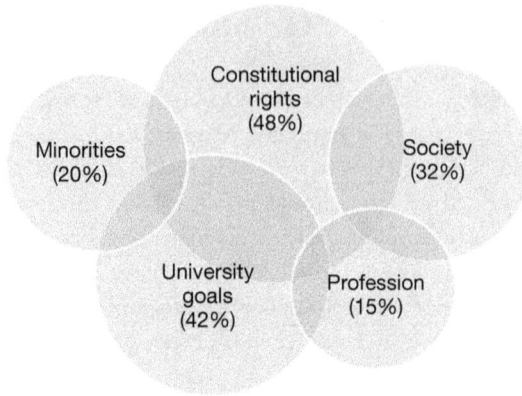

of affirmative action in college admissions policies was seen as going against and an insult to American democratic and egalitarian ideologies, something that supporters believed that the American public and Court justices should believe in and support.

*Opposing affirmative action: Veiled threat frames*

Although threat was part of the briefs in support of affirmative action, much of it was about a threat to the university mission of diversity and the abilities of non-white students to better themselves and achieve racial and ethnic equality not allotted to them otherwise. However, the briefs submitted to the *Gratz* and *Grutter* cases speaking out against affirmative action in the University's admissions policy took threat in a completely different direction (see Table 5.4).

As suggested by Blumer (1958), social authorities that have access to resources, like those writing these briefs, could use rhetoric to recommend to a group that their way of life, values, and access to resources were at risk. More important, this rhetoric could indicate that one or several "inferior" groups that were not deserving were responsible for changing or taking away any said ways of life, values, or resources. In some respects, influential actors can suggest a zero-sum game of two groups fighting over long-held privileges and resources. Within the briefs against affirmative action, the authors provided words and passages that suggested a threat to the group yet appeared to cover up these arguments with color-blind rhetoric. Unlike support briefs, opponent briefs set up a dichotomy of "us" (white America) versus "them" (non-white America). This happened in every brief submitted in three different ways.

**Table 5.4:** Group threat themes and concepts for amicus briefs among opponents for *Grutter v Bollinger, et al* (02-241) and *Gratz v Bollinger, et al* (02-516)

| Opponent briefs 34/153 (22%) | | |
|---|---|---|
| Coded theme or concept | Theme or concept title | Ratio and % of briefs using theme or concept |
| **Theme 1** | **Threat to White American values/life** | **32/34   (94%)** |
| Concept 1a | Unconstitutional | 32/32   (100%) |
| Concept 2b | Harm to society (in general) | 16/32   (50%) |
| Concept 2c | End of meritocracy | 12/32   (37%) |
| Concept 2d | National solidarity | 8/32   (25%) |
| Concept 2e | Encourages national eugenics | 2/32   (6%) |
| **Theme 2** | **Threat to white resources** | **22/34   (65%)** |
| Concept 2a | Reverse discrimination in education | 22/22   (100%) |
| Concept 2b | Reverse discrimination in jobs | 12/22   (54%) |
| **Theme 3** | **Victimized minorities** | **16/34   (47%)** |
| Concept 3a | Harm to minorities/paternalism | 16/16   (100%) |
| Concept 3b | Stereotypes/stigma | 14/16   (87%) |

The first and most prominent frame of group threat mentioned in the briefs against affirmative action was the notion that these policies endangered American ideals (Theme 1: 94%). Note here the word choice and how it moved the arguments from abstract liberal notions of principles and values to those notions being threatened by an undeserving group. Every brief that took on this notion of a threat to American values agreed that affirmative action was an assault on the US Constitution (Concept 1a: 100%) and, as stated directly by several briefs, "a major national problem." As noted earlier, many briefs pointed out that affirmative action went against the 14th Amendment and its Equal Protection Clause that protected citizens from unjust treatment based on protected classes of citizens, such as the consideration of race or ethnicity in decisions about academic admissions. For example, former Governor Jeb Bush's brief stated, "Our Constitution demands that the government treat each with equal dignity and respect, regardless of his or her race or ethnicity … anything else would be unconstitutional … and un-American." They also pointed out that any Court ruling that continued to support affirmative action based on race or ethnicity would violate or take away Americans' constitutional rights. To the contrary, briefs in support of affirmative action argued the opposite, that affirmative action was a tool to ensure federal government would apply these protections to every citizen.

Another example showed in the National Association of Scholars' brief: "Academic freedom and 'educational judgment' cannot be turned into a license to subvert an *individual's* right to protection under the Fourteenth Amendment because some educators believe that doing so advances the interests of some or all racial groups." Further on, this brief pointed out that to challenge the US Constitution was an assault on American rights. Fourteen different briefs used the actual words "assault" or "threat" when discussing the impact of affirmative action on the US Constitution. These words were never used by the briefs in support of affirmative action, even when talking about actual threats to college goals or non-white educational outcomes. The Pacific Legal Foundation used these words interchangeably, and pointed out that any affirmative action program was "fundamentally inconsistent with this Court's [Supreme Court] Equal Protection rulings" because if they allowed affirmative action to continue, it would "threaten American doctrine set by its forefathers."

Ten other briefs suggested that affirmative action in college admissions policies endangered the very principles set forth by "America's forefathers," and thus, as stated by the Equal Opportunity Center's brief and website explanation of the *Grutter* and *Gratz* cases, "...continuing affirmative action would be the end of America as a protector of individual rights and freedoms..." The Claremont Institute brief also suggested that affirmative action even went against the Declaration of Independence, which established the "principle of inherent equality that underlies and infuses our Constitution ... the most important American ideal." It also suggested that Thomas Jefferson, who wrote the Declaration of Independence and owned slaves, would not stand for affirmative action since it took away rights from American citizens to be judged on their merits. These arguments suggested that the US Constitution and its tenets of equal rights and protection were under siege and could be lost if the Court agreed with the University of Michigan's "unconstitutional" and "undemocratic" admissions policies.

It should be pointed out that social science scholars have found that when neoconservative groups want to protect their "white" rights, they often pull the "neoliberal card" of preserving the original tenets of the Constitution and suggest that any question of its validity and reliability becomes an assault on America itself (see Omi and Winant, 2015). Scholars have also argued that whites have often argued for sticking to the purity of the Constitution because before the 13th and 14th Amendments, the Declaration of Independence, the US Constitution, and the supposed forefathers referenced mainly established laws to protect white men and, in particular, only affluent white men (see Berry, 1995; Sanders and Adams, 2003; Feagin, 2010b; Omi and Winant, 2015). As stated by Omi and Winant (2015, p 76), "White rule in North America, before and after 1776, has always been riven by racial conflict." They also suggested that in order to keep whites in dominant positions, white elites have had to find ways to increase fears of the "other" to recruit subordinate whites to their cause to stop the "injustices" against whites that came with giving non-whites freedoms, civil rights, or any opportunities to access higher education and the workplace. Thus, any call to save the Constitution and its rights often refers back to a time of white supremacy. As suggested by Charles W. Mills' (2017) book, *Black Rights/White Wrongs*, American forefathers never had in their minds when penning the Constitution that black slaves or any other non-white race would be equal to whites; nor did they view poor whites as equals.

Coupled with this rhetoric about challenging the sanctity of constitutional protections, a second way the briefs suggested group threat was inciting the notion that affirmative action harmed society. That is to say, as indicated by the Cato Institute, affirmative action "erodes the national fabric and commitment to equality of opportunity." Again, word choice (along with the ideas) suggested loss of resources, and advanced the argument past abstract liberal notions. In this case, however, it is a loss of societal principles and standards rather than any tangible resource. Around 50 percent of the briefs (Concept 2b) that suggested this argued that affirmative action destroyed higher education's prestige, and ended efficiency and collaboration across businesses and within the labor force. Two briefs even suggested it would lead to civil unrest and mistrust for decades to come. However, many postulated that affirmative action's application to higher education rattled and ruined the foundations of American meritocracy and individual freedoms (Concept 2c: 37%). The Center for Equal Opportunity stated succinctly,

> The value of anything must consider its liabilities. And the liabilities attendant to the use of racial and ethnic preferences are substantial: They are personally unfair and set a disturbing legal, political, and moral precedent to allow State racial discrimination; they create resentment; they stigmatize the so-called beneficiaries in the eyes of their classmates, teachers, and themselves; they foster a victim mindset, remove the incentive for academic excellence, and encourage separatism; they compromise the academic mission of the university and lower the academic quality of the student body; they create pressure to discriminate in grading and graduation; they breed hypocrisy within the school; they encourage a scofflaw attitude among college officials; they mismatch students and

institutions, guaranteeing failure for many of the former; they obscure the real social problem of why so many African Americans and Hispanics are academically uncompetitive; and they get state actors involved in unsavory activities like deciding which racial and ethnic minorities will be favored and which ones not, and how much blood is needed to establish authentic group membership.

Although there is much to unpack from this quote, it should be noted that affirmative action or racial preferences of any sort for these authors were generally harmful to American society and its institutions because they, as stated by the Center, gave "an appreciably greater chance" of college admission of African American applicants over white applicants. Moreover, affirmative action goes against "American values of fairness and logical decision-making," as stated by Ward Connerly. Of course, this position raises a few eyebrows given the long history of academic advantage experienced by white applicants when applying to college.

These authors also saw affirmative action as being immoral, hypocritical, and hurting non-whites more than other groups. As suggested by the Cato Institute, affirmative action actually "cheapen[ed]" the experience of higher education and ended the prestige of higher education in the US. Even more important, this brief, like many others (94%), suggested that affirmative action destroyed (white) American society's access to education and the privilege of being selected based on merit versus, as stated by the Center for Equal Opportunity brief, "how much blood." Interestingly, this brief brings in a mention of race as a genetic trait, which subtly suggested a link between genetics and academic achievement and thus, a possible issue of genetic or cultural heritage among African Americans.

Another example of this worry about the end of meritocracy was clear in Ward Connerly's brief. He argued that affirmative action attacked America's "culture of equality" that had attempted to make merit the common measurement of an individual's worth and determine the acceptance of someone into higher education. However, as he wrote, any use of affirmative action had erased America's efforts to address racial inequality through meritocratic applications for the last 60 years. Twelve other briefs also used this argument, suggesting that, as noted by the brief submitted by the Center for the Advancement of Capitalism, "the solution to the problem of racism is individualism...;" they also suggested that the Declaration of Independence was right to suggest that "all men are created equal," but this had been washed away by affirmative action, which did not judge applicants on merit but rather on "biological parentage."

A few briefs also hinted at the notion that affirmative action challenged national solidarity in the US (Concept 2d: 25%). The Claremont Institute's brief threatened that affirmative action had allowed the "government [to] legally discriminate against some citizens for the benefit of others" and would lead to a severe mistrust in the government and shake the foundations of American unity under one government. The briefs by the Pacific Legal Foundation, Jeb Bush, and New Black Leadership argued that college applicants might have to apply internationally because of the unfair practices of affirmative action, which would lead to a loss of talented Americans in the workforce or a transnational movement where the US "will be lost in a transnational and global economy." Even two briefs threatened that affirmative action was an exclusionary practice supported by "bogus blood measurements," and that some populations (that is, whites) would face exclusion resembling the Jim Crow era (Cato Institute and the Center for Equal Opportunity). Note again here the word choice and how it implied a loss for the dominant group and their culture.

Overall, these briefs continually provide threat narratives that American society would be at least challenged if not substantially harmed by the continuing use of affirmative action in college admissions policies. Often dramatic in their tone and insidious in their word choices, they suggested that affirmative action had and would continue to destroy the "culture of equality" presented within the US Constitution and its various institutions. What becomes more and more evident is that, while they want everyone to be judged based on merit, they only saw white applicants as having any merit. Ironically, as they were making strong arguments for a true color-blind orientation, they made color-coded racial appeals. They also clearly attempted to activate race using racial threat frames to infuse emotion into the debate. So the question remains, which group would be most threatened by universities continuing to use affirmative action? We believe the next section provides more of the answer.

## *Reverse discrimination: Threatening white access to higher education*

Most briefs (Theme 2: 76%) submitted against the use of affirmative action by the University of Michigan suggested that reverse discrimination against white applicants was a severe problem. According to the Cato Institute, affirmative action policies allocated "valuable economic and personal benefits" to non-whites over whites. Any attempts universities made to categorize applicants by racial classifications was a direct attack on the equal protection of white applicants, and allowed a new regime of racial discrimination against whites (Concept 2a). As stated by the Center for Equal Opportunity, any affirmative action program, "… threatens a permanent institutionalization of racial and ethnic discrimination … favoring minorities over applicants who are deserving of entrance." The Cato Institute also argued the same, by stating,

> In fact, the Law School and its parent institution [University of Michigan] act to ensure that 'race matters'—and that it will continue to 'matter' in Michigan's publicly funded colleges and universities—by allocating valuable, state-subsidized opportunities on the basis of one's race, and by promising those awards on the proposition that individuals with a particular skin color or ethnic background are likely to articulate particular views in the classroom. Respondents' [University of Michigan] preferential admissions policies, if upheld, can only serve further to delay the realization of the sacred constitutional promise of equal opportunity: the 'dream…'

As noted previously, this brief used several color-blind rhetorical phrases, including a debunking of the argument for diversity, as well as arguing against racial classification. Moreover, the briefs clearly signaled that affirmative action was mainly hurting white applicants by using catchphrases such as "racial balancing," "racial favoritism," and "race-conscious remedies," that excluded, as one brief stated, "the new minority group," subtly referring to whites in their various arguments. All of this shifts the potential damages or threat of affirmative action away from non-whites to white applicants. These briefs even go so far as to suggest that Dr Martin Luther King Jr's "I have a dream" speech could be applied here, in which white applicants now faced the crushing problems of racism in an American institution.

The brief submitted by the Department of Education agreed that affirmative action hurt white applicant chances. They stated, "The Law School's [of the University of Michigan] admissions policy would permit race-based discrimination in perpetuity." They suggested that the future of higher education was a "race-based policy that … favored unprepared minority groups [African Americans and Hispanics) enormously …" over "high-achieving and desiring" white and Asian applicants. They ended their brief by suggesting that any policy using affirmative action would "unfairly burden innocent third parties," who, by their estimation, were white and Asian applicants. Several top lawyers in the US agreed with this statement in their brief when they stated, "… 'diversity' is a race-balancing interest that would, by its terms, require race discrimination for eternity …

race would be the deciding factor between the admission of one applicant and the rejection of another with equal or better qualifications." And, while they never stated it directly, white applicants were assumed to be the equally or more qualified applicant, since they spent the rest of their brief providing statistics suggesting non-whites were not academically prepared for higher education, or that diversity was not beneficial for students in higher education. As noted in Ward Connerly's brief, whites were now the "un-preferred students" in a university "obsessed with diversity."

Overall, what was evident in these briefs was that affirmative action threatened white access to higher education (a highly valued resource in the US). Stated succinctly by the Pacific Legal Foundation for the *Grutter* case, affirmative action policies used by the University of Michigan "perpetuate[d] unequal treatment on the basis of race for the purposes of racial balancing" for white applicants, not non-white applicants. In fact, they clearly argued that minorities received a "plus factor" (that is, special consideration) because the University assumed that they had diverse perspectives and life experiences that would enrich student learning. However, they later argued that whites had the same diverse backgrounds equal to the racism many non-whites had faced, mainly because of the rise of affirmative action that allowed public institutions to "outright reject an applicant based on skin color."

The most critical finding in discussions about reverse discrimination was that the briefs were intended to make sure that the Supreme Court Justices understood that the real problem facing the US was, as one brief stated, "rampant racism" against "un-preferred students" (that is, white applicants). Moreover, they emphasized, as indicated by the Center for Individual Freedom, that the "inalienable rights" of whites to access higher education were being threatened by affirmative action admissions policies. Ironically, however, while many of the briefs suggested that the Court should strike down these policies because they were not "color-blind," their arguments highlighting supposed racist discrimination against whites encouraged the Justices to actually be race-conscious of whites losing what these authors characterized as an "inalienable right" reserved for more-than-qualified white applicants.

### *"The soft bigotry of lower expectations": Paternalistic threats*

The final threat narrative deployed by the authors writing against affirmative action policies used by the University of Michigan was to emphasize a paternalistic threat towards non-whites (Theme 3). As noted earlier, around 47 percent of the briefs argued that admitting non-whites into public colleges and universities was foolhardy because non-white applicants were academically underprepared for higher education. In other words, there was a mismatch between non-white academic skills and the rigor of college. Thus, affirmative action set non-whites up for inevitable failure. However, we also found that these briefs took it a step further in their arguments and word choices by emphasizing how dangerous affirmative action was to not only non-whites flunking out of school, but could also lead to more long-term negative effects (Concept 3a). As noted by Ward Connerly's brief, using affirmative action to get underprepared non-whites into universities as a paternalistic effort to atone for past racial discrimination was "soft bigotry of lower expectations." As former Governor Jeb Bush argued in his brief, accepting and then allowing non-whites to drop out of college did nothing but perpetuate the economic and social inequalities that persist between whites and minorities in America.

Of the briefs that used paternalistic arguments, most argued that affirmative action led to possibilities of non-white underemployment and continued discrimination because of stereotype threat (Concept 3b: 87%). For example, the Center for Equal Opportunity's brief mentioned earlier for its color-blind paternalism suggested that non-whites would not fare well in higher education (citing drop-out statistics from various universities) and would thus fail in the workplace. It also argued that if non-white students did graduate, they might still be "uncompetitive" in professions (eg, doctor, attorney, or engineer) that viewed non-whites as stereotypically incapable of doing the work.

Other examples of paternalistic threat were found in the brief submitted by the Claremont Institute. Several times it pointed out that non-white applicants were not well-prepared for higher education, and universities were devious in using these students to increase diversity on their campuses as they would ultimately fail to meet their needs. It also argued that universities would probably not give them "a proper education" leading to gainful employment. It furthermore contended that stereotypes were reinforced for students on campus by admitting students based on race, and that white students would avoid interacting with their "less-qualified" counterparts. The Center for Equal Opportunity agreed with this sentiment, and stated in its brief, "Greater diversity might lead to exposure to people with different ideas or experiences, but ... the tradeoff actually is more division and racial discrimination ..." based on stereotypes perpetuated by affirmative action policies. The brief submitted by several lawyers suggested the same, that universities using affirmative action admissions policies "would also generate educationally detrimental stigma and hostility ..." among students. Later on they sufficiently threatened that these policies would lead to racialized hostility, stigmatization, and violence that would carry on throughout the non-white student's life.

Several other briefs pointed out the negative impacts on a student admitted under affirmative action programs. For instance, the briefs submitted by the African American Leadership Forum and the Center for New Black Leadership suggested that any non-white student admitted under an affirmative action policy would internalize that they were less qualified and would thus take fewer chances to apply for competitive jobs or occupations. They also argued that society and employers would shame them because of the general prejudice towards non-whites; thus, universities should admit non-white students on merit alone so that they could be confident and fight back against these false assumptions.

Overall, these threat frames created by opponents fit Blumer's discussion of group threat. As noted in Figure 5.4, white American values and white resources were the most prominent themes to emerge from the document, and showcased how the authors wanted to make a strong case that whites were now the victims of racism caused by institutional discrimination vis-à-vis college admissions policies in higher education. However, they attempted to downplay this argument by deploying what seem to be sympathetic pleas (that is, paternalism) to the Supreme Court concerning how affirmative action hurt non-whites. They even suggested that it was racist to expect that undereducated and underprepared minorities could serve the rigor of college education.

Another important conclusion based on the opponents' briefs was the infusion of group threat for white Americans within broader color-blind narratives that attempted to minimize the role of race or racism. Figure 5.5 visually demonstrates the relationships between the color-blind and threat frames. Opponent briefs in particular camouflaged any threat narratives

**Figure 5.4:** Venn diagram of threat frames in opponent briefs

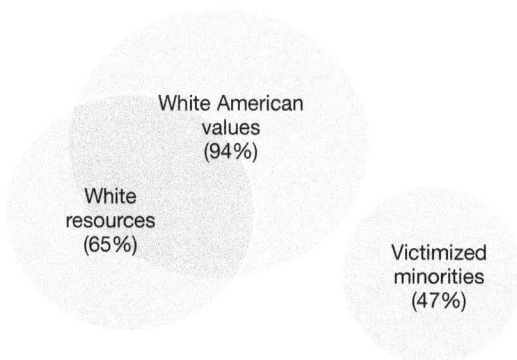

151

**Figure 5.5:** Thematic connections between color-blind rhetoric and group threats among opponent briefs for *Grutter* and *Gratz*

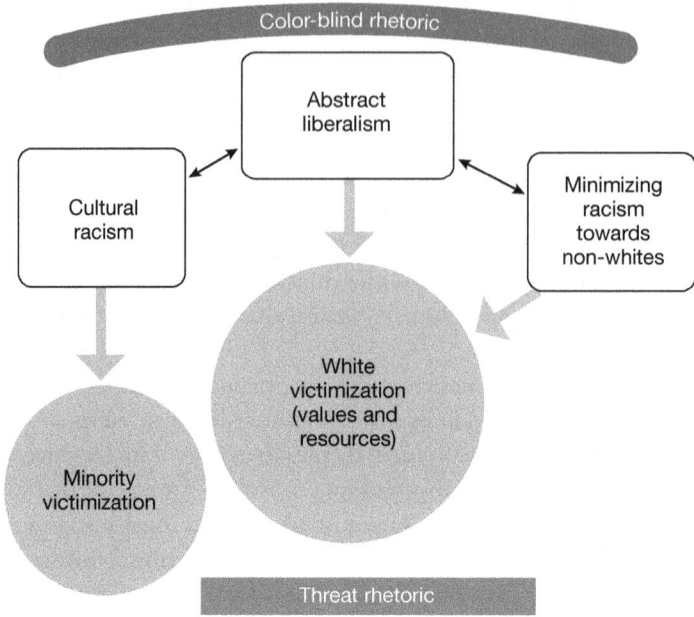

with color-blind rhetoric first, but making sure readers could understand that racism was not a problem for non-whites but a new problem for whites, particularly in applying for college admission. They often suggested that African Americans and Latinos were "healing" from a racist past, and now liberal agendas within universities were taking this correction of racial justice too far. In a paternalistic fashion, they suggested it would continue to hurt underprepared minorities and further exclude whites from opportunities. They were hinting in particular that non-whites were undeserving of entry into higher education because their lack of skills and resources would lead to a waste of a precious resource such as higher education. This also became another way for opponent briefs to skirt the continuing issues of racism and increase concerns about how reverse discrimination was the real issue in this debate over affirmative action in college admissions policies.

## Conclusion

Sociologists Eduardo Bonilla-Silva (2018) and Charles Gallagher (2013) argued that individuals, and white America in particular, have attempted for decades to level the playing field on the discussion of racial discrimination. They want you to believe that it is not only minorities who struggle with racial discrimination; they, too, have suffered. Indeed, whites and some non-whites have suggested that whites and non-whites all suffer the same amounts of discrimination in the US today. Racism is racism and discrimination is discrimination regardless of race. Gallup (2018) polls indicate that both whites and non-whites view racism as less significant in shaping life chances, and somewhat agree that whites can face racism too. As noted by Omi and Winant (2015), if influential whites can explain away the problems of racism for non-whites and whites, they have been able to reinforce the notions that racism is dead or at least diluted, and meritocracy should reign supreme. Omi and Winant also suggest that for whites to continue to be dominant and privileged in this post-race society, they have to accept that racism is real, but also make the US think that it is entirely possible that racism can be used against other groups, namely, whites.

Therefore, if the authors of these briefs had been able to convince the Supreme Court that affirmative action harms everyone (that is, leveling the playing field), then the policy should be unconstitutional, and there would be no use for it in higher education. More importantly, the policy should be removed if they convinced the Justices that affirmative action could and would ruin the lives of non-whites and increasingly ruin opportunities for well-deserving whites who worked hard and did things the correct way. However, as Omi and Winant (2015) have argued, when Americans get rid of race-based policies to correct racial inequality, there is usually a boom of white privilege shortly after. From our observations, it is clear that the debate on both sides has become fully color-blind based on the overwhelming uses of these tropes. It has also allowed a select few highly influential opposing advocacy groups to gain traction in the debate. These groups have pushed the narrative that affirmative action hurts white chances of retaining their well-earned and historically established privilege of entry into higher education.

Sociologist Wendy Moore (2018) agrees, and argues that this rhetoric has been successful in whittling away the effectiveness of affirmative action as a tool for racial equity in higher education. The abstract liberal arguments promoting diversity have been mainstays in the most prominent Supreme Court cases dealing with affirmative action. Moore's (2018) examination of the arguments made during the *Gratz* and *Grutter* cases found that while the Court ruled in favor of using affirmative action,

> … the Court held that diversity in education is a compelling enough interest that some consideration of race might be used for affirmative action admissions policies, but that policies employing mechanical formulations like those in the undergraduate admissions at the University of Michigan were

not permitted by the Constitution because they infringed upon the rights of 'innocent whites' (eg, Gratz); however, considerations of race as a non-uniformly, whole-person review wherein race is considered as a 'plus' factor were permissible (eg, Grutter). Thus the Court affirmed the abstract liberalist framing of 'diversity' as a basis for a very limited, amorphous affirmative action admissions policy.

In short, even though affirmative action was not ruled to be unconstitutional, those against affirmative action policies were at least emboldened to suggest that affirmative action was a problem. Affirmative action was also a growing problem because it challenged white privilege, which was directly argued several times in these briefs as an "inalienable right" for whites to access higher education. In this light, by using *Racialized Framing* techniques, opponents were able to both minimize race through color-blind rhetoric and also activate race through threat while attempting to end the policy in higher education in general, and at the University of Michigan in particular.

## Note

[1]   This chapter and the following on the *Fisher* cases relies on critical discourse analysis (CDA) to assess the ways supporters and opponents frame arguments for and against affirmative action within amicus briefs. This technique attempts "to unpack the ideological underpinnings of discourse that have become so naturalized over time that we begin to treat them as communicative, acceptable and natural features of discourse" (Fairclough, 1989, p 20). Each individual brief was treated as an individual unit of analysis. A count was made that established how many briefs utilized specific frames and how many of the frames were utilized in any given brief. A total count was made of the number of times a given frame was used throughout the briefs. For each frame, the proportion of the briefs in which they appeared was also noted. In essence, this quantitative data provide context, describing the most and least common arguments made by the various entities.

We used both open and focused coding (Charmaz, 2006). Open coding allowed us to outline the dominant frame(s) for this case. It also produced a number of concepts that were then grouped under specific categories or themes that could later assist in directing an in-depth analysis of thematic relationships or patterns across categories. This helped us to note the similarities and differences in arguments about immigration across respondents. After concepts were established via open coding, specific examples were noted and counted using focused coding to create themes. Focused coding allowed us to search in particular for "color-blind" and "group threat" frames deployed in arguments for and against affirmative action in this court case. To ensure greater reliability, all briefs were coded by both authors individually. We then compared our coding to identify any inconsistencies in indicators we see in the data. On review, we noted less than 5 percent of our individual coding had inconsistencies, and these were resolved after some discussion.

# 6

# Case Study 2:
# The *Fisher* Supreme Court
# Cases against the University
# of Texas at Austin

## Introduction

The next and most recent case to challenge affirmative action in college admissions policies in the Supreme Court was the *Fisher v University of Texas at Austin* (2013 and 2016). Similar to Chapter 5, the purpose of this chapter is to understand precisely what supporters and opponents argued about this controversial policy. That is, how did they frame the debate surrounding affirmative action? We focus again on the amicus briefs submitted by social authorities to the Supreme Court that had an interest in the outcome of the cases. While we were interested in variation in the types of frames used in these two cases (*Fisher I* and *II*) relative to the *Gratz* and *Grutter* cases, we mainly focused on the authors' continued use of both color-blind and group threat frames to state their positions.

While some nuanced changes were observed from *Gratz/Grutter* to *Fisher*, our findings revealed a great deal of consistency from case to case, and that the briefs continued to rely on these pernicious frames to characterize the policy. Both supporters and opponents of affirmative action deployed color-blind arguments. However, opponents relied more heavily on them while also suggesting that the policy was a threat to the dominant group. Among the opponents' briefs in particular, threat frames suggested that whites in general and white college applicants and students in particular were losing in a country consumed by liberal agendas of diversification and entitlements only afforded to unqualified and ill-prepared non-whites. This finding is consistent with those found in Chapter 5. Nonetheless, in this chapter, we outline the similarities and differences as we describe the key frames used in the debate.

Although 25 years separated the *Gratz* and *Grutter* cases (2003) from the *Bakke* (1978) Supreme Court case, only 10 years elapsed between *Gratz/Grutter* and *Fisher*. While this relatively short time period between cases raised concern among supporters, the societal context was even more disconcerting as it seemed ripe for the final removal of the policy in the US. The President at the time, Barack Obama, who at one time had been a strong advocate of affirmative action, expressed lukewarm support for the continuation of the policy, implying that class-based preferential treatment may be more appropriate (Kahlenberg, 2008). Furthermore, the Supreme Court itself leaned Right of center and seemed poised to remove the policy from higher education altogether; Justice Antonin Scalia even came out publicly against it.

Similar to past cases, the *Fisher I* and *II* cases dealt primarily with how a college admissions policy used race as a factor to increase diversity at the University of Texas at Austin. As can be derived from previous chapters, the type of arguments viewed as acceptable in the quest to label affirmative action as helpful or harmful has evolved, at least in litigation at the level of the Supreme Court. This evolution has led to an era where affirmative action policies in colleges must be *narrowly tailored* to the institute's strategic goals and pass the *strict scrutiny* of the courts. If implemented, affirmative action must be shown to be a compelling interest to the state, and use the least restrictive means to achieve its goals. As such, one interpretation was that to implement this policy, an organization must make all accommodations to not harm the white majority population who would otherwise be admitted based on merit. Any policy had to carefully weigh out merit and the need for diversity without impacting white majority communities. Accordingly, college admissions policies looking to increase diversity and opportunity for underrepresented populations could not rely on quotas or "extra" point assignments based on race or ethnicity, as these are seen to adversely affect the white majority.

Before we provide a discussion of how color-blind and group threat frames played out in the recent amicus briefs, we first outline the *Fisher* case, and attempt to provide the context and rationale behind it, reiterating who was at the helm in fighting for and against the policy. We then turn to the dominant arguments (frames) made for and against affirmative action in the amicus briefs, and describe how they were similar or different from arguments made in the *Gratz* and *Grutter* cases. We hope to tell the story of the case (the actors involved and the arguments in the debate) in such a fashion that it will provide an insight into the state of race relations and affirmative action in higher education in the US today. While we would like to be able tell an uplifting story of change and hope, this doesn't seem to be the case for affirmative action. Narratives surrounding the policy continue to be quite insidious, particularly among opponents, and this negativity seems to be only growing more agitated and heated over time.

## *Fisher v University of Texas at Austin*: **A summary**

Admissions practices in the state of Texas in general and at the University of Texas at Austin (UT Austin) in particular related to diversity have undergone several changes over the past few decades. Before 1996, the university relied mainly on an "Academic Index" to select students. This was based primarily on a student's academic qualifications, including their SAT score and high school grades. In the process of choosing students for enrollment, preference was given based on the candidate's race. However, this all changed in 1996. A ruling by the Fifth Circuit of Appeals Court (*Hopwood v Texas*) held that such a policy violated the Constitution's Equal Protection Clause, making it unconstitutional. Since the Supreme Court declined to hear the case, the decision covered the use of race in admissions in only three states (Louisiana, Mississippi, and Texas) under the jurisdiction of the Fifth Circuit. Nonetheless, this case and its ruling cast a long shadow over affirmative action in higher education and its future, and dictated how UT Austin had to recruit students and promote diversity.

The *Hopwood* ruling, in essence, ignored *Bakke* and held that race could no longer be used as a factor in higher education admissions, even to ensure greater student diversity. In its place, the university developed a new admissions policy that ignored race and based admissions on a "Personal Achievement Index." This was a holistic review of an applicant and looked at several characteristics, including the quality of their essays, leadership abilities, work experience, as well as other extracurricular activities. The admissions process also considered other "special characteristics" that looked at an applicant's background, with their race omitted from consideration.

In response to the 1996 *Hopwood* case, Texas state legislators (Texas House Bill 588) passed the "Top 10% Rule" in 1997 that guaranteed graduating seniors who ranked in the top 10 percent of their high school automatic admission to any state-funded university of their choice. The legislators posed that such a color-blind solution was fair and could maintain diversity without making decisions based on race. The *Hopwood* decision was rather short-lived and was effectively overruled by the 2003 *Grutter v Bollinger* Court decision. *Grutter* ruled that the use of race, and thus affirmative action, was permissible by the University of Michigan Law School. Thus, the *Grutter* ruling reinforced the *Bakke* standing and upheld the notion that universities have a *compelling interest* in creating a diverse environment as long as a point or quota system was not used in the process.

After the *Grutter* ruling, UT Austin sought approval of the board of regents to again consider race in the admissions process. The new admissions process was accepted by the board, with race used as one factor to fill the seats not filled by students granted admission by the "Top 10% Rule." UT Austin placed a cap on students to enter based on the "Top 10% Rule" at 75 percent—that is to say, only 75 percent of incoming students in any given class could be admitted. The new admissions policy that considered race would only impact the remaining 25 percent of incoming students. Practically speaking, this equated to very few seats left available. While UT Austin maintains an "Academic Index" that looks at academic qualifiers (eg, SAT score), it also considers a "Personal Achievement Score" that considers race under "special circumstances" among other factors (for a thorough discussion of the *Fisher* case, see Jayakumar et al, 2015).

The decision to reinstate affirmative action by UT Austin was not made lightly and without reason (Jayakumar et al, 2015). First, minority representation in admissions never recovered to the pre-affirmative action ban level. Second, two studies conducted by the school highlighted issues it had with diversity, with one finding a lack of diversity in small and medium-size classes across the university. Another study found that minorities were more likely than their white counterparts to feel isolated and report that the University lacked beneficial diversity. Accordingly, UT Austin decided to modify and add to their race-neutral admissions policy by including race as *one* factor, but not the *only* factor, in admissions decisions. They argued that "central mass" was necessary, and that race should be a primary measure of diversity.

Fast forward to 2008—two white students, Abigail Noel Fisher and Rachel Multer Michalewicz, applied but were not accepted to UT Austin. While 81 percent of the incoming freshman class seats in that year were accounted for by the "Top 10% Rule," students could gain admission by scoring high on standardized tests and demonstrating other valued characteristics, such as leadership skills. Along with family characteristics, race *was* also considered when accepting students. Given that their high school grades were not sufficient to get into the top 10 percent of their school, Fisher and Michalewicz were forced to compete unsuccessfully with other students for the final 19 percent of available seats (Jayakumar et al, 2015).

Both Fisher and Michalewicz filed a suit against UT Austin that same year (although Michalewicz withdrew from the lawsuit in 2011). Both students claimed that the use of race under affirmative action was inconsistent with the *Gratz* ruling and violated the Equal Protection Clause of the 14th Amendment, which protected citizens from unnecessary discrimination based on race (Jayakumar et al, 2015). The University countered Fisher's claim by arguing that using race and affirmative action in such a fashion was *narrowly tailored* to meet the needs of the University as outlined in the *Grutter* case, and was necessary to produce a more diverse campus environment.

Like *Gratz* and *Grutter*, the *Fisher* Supreme Court case did not just organically develop from years of student frustration. Instead, the case became a reality primarily out of efforts put forth by an advocacy group, the Project on Fair Representation (POFR). The POFR is a conservative legal defense foundation created by Edward Blum, a well-known conservative strategist discussed in previous chapters. This was not Blum's first foray into the affirmative action lawsuits; Blum maintained a clear anti-affirmative action agenda and has initiated many lawsuits challenging affirmative action and other race-based cases in recent years. For example, Blum was instrumental in the 2013 Supreme Court case (*Shelby County v Holder*, 570 US 2, 2013) that successfully contested provisions of the Voting Rights Act of 1965. Blum also founded an offshoot of POFR, Students for Fair Admissions (SFFA), that has been instrumental in a current lawsuit against the use of affirmative action by Harvard University, a case some experts predict will eventually make its way to the Supreme Court.

In 2009, a Fifth Circuit Court of Appeals upheld the admissions policy proposed by the University and stated that it was *narrowly tailored* and met the strict standards promoted by the *Grutter* case. However, in 2012, the Supreme Court decided to review the lower court decision on *Fisher v University of Texas at Austin* and placed it on the Court's docket for that year. The decision to hear the case by the Court was troublesome to supporters for several reasons. First, the Court has only heard four cases dealing with affirmative action since the 1970s. Given that this Court is highly polarized with a conservative majority, and that they have recently overturned prominent civil rights legislature (eg, the Voting Rights Act), supporters were rightly concerned. Second, the Court typically takes on cases that are well developed in the lower courts, leading to confusion and disagreement about the proper interpretation of the Constitution. Cases heard in the Supreme Court also usually have a large following, deal with the rights of a large segment of the population, and are often class action in nature. The *Fisher* case did not meet any of these conditions. Third, Fisher, as a plaintiff, no longer had an interest in attending UT Austin, and only requested that her application fee be reimbursed. Thus, the choice to hear this case in particular concerned supporters because it seemed to be a break from the norm, implying that the Court wanted to make a statement and severely restrict or even end the use of affirmative action in admissions policies. Finally, the case was of concern because Justice Elena Kagan recused herself due to her role as Solicitor General in the Obama administration, where she had penned an amicus brief in support of the policy (Jayakumar and Garces, 2005). This recusal was offset to a certain extent by the untimely passing of Justice Scalia in early February 2016, before the final ruling in the summer of 2016.

Oral arguments were heard in October 2012, and the Court's opinion was rendered in June 2013. In a 7–1 decision, the Court vacated and remanded the original Fifth Circuit Court of Appeals ruling. Writing the majority opinion, Justice Kennedy stated that such a verdict was handed down because they felt the original Court of Appeals did not do *due diligence* and apply *strict scrutiny* when analyzing the University's admissions policy. Justice Ruth Ginsburg provided the only dissenting opinion, in which she argued that the admissions policy held by the University was quite flexible (using both a neutral policy, the "Top 10% Rule," and one that would consider race). Furthermore, she argued that even though race was used in the admissions process, it was only used as one factor in a sea of many others (Jayakumar et al, 2015).

In November 2013, the Fifth Circuit Court once again heard oral arguments, and, in 2014, ruled in favor of the University and the use of race once again. It noted that the holistic approach that only considered race as one factor in admissions was consistent with the University of Michigan *Grutter* case and thus, constitutional. This ruling set the stage for the Supreme Court to take up the issue again in 2015 (docket number 14-981). In June 2016, in a somewhat surprising fashion, the Court supported the lower courts' decision by a 4–3 margin, ruling that the University's use of race was constitutional and did not violate the Equal Protection Clause of the US Constitution. While proponents of affirmative action see this as a victory, the fight against its use in higher education appears to be far from over.

The ruling by the Supreme Court was a mixed bag of sorts. On the one hand, affirmative action in higher education lived to see another day. The decision was held in high regard by many students, faculty, and universities that have strong social justice orientations and believe race continues to play a substantial role in producing unequal social and economic outcomes. Universities could continue to seek out diversity by using race as a factor among others when making admissions decisions. On the other hand, diversity is still an abstract and divisive idea, even among progressive camps. Many elite, private, and public universities continue to struggle recruiting minority students, are now focused on promoting diversity for diversity's sake and ignore issues of past and current racial discrimination. We feel that this is a systemic failure that places affirmative action in a precarious state and minimalizes the lived experiences of minorities and marginalized groups that continue to fight against discrimination. Nonetheless, it is now clear that universities are in the diversity business, whether that has a solid foundation or not.

## Leading the fight for and against affirmative action in the *Gratz/Grutter* cases

Before we move on, we would like to reiterate how different the authors were who penned amicus briefs for and against affirmative action in the *Fisher I* and *II* cases (see Chapter 4 for more discussion). Similar to the *Gratz* and *Grutter* cases, supporters tended to be heterogeneous and represented by SIGs (eg, the American Psychological Association) and other individuals and groups scattered across the public and private sectors with an interest in affirmative action. The entities included state and federal government representatives, student organizations, judges, lawyer bar associations, Fortune 100 businesses, professors, law schools, and colleges, and universities. As in the *Gratz/Grutter* cases, the majority of the briefs were written by the various groups and not by formal advocacy groups.

Again, like the *Gratz/Grutter* cases, the diversity and number of affirmative action supporters stand in stark contrast to the limited number of homogeneous opponents (with opponents submitting fewer briefs than supporters). The clear majority of opponents were advocacy groups (mainly think tanks and legal foundations), including some of the most prolific groups in the US today. For instance, the Cato Institute, Center for Individual Rights, and Pacific Legal Foundation, among others, all advocated against the use of affirmative action through amicus briefs. Social sciences research has suggested that think tanks in particular have gained status as experts on specific political issues, and have close relationships with those in positions of power (Medvetz, 2012). The remaining brief authors were not just average citizens with an interest, but were elite individuals (often associated with advocacy groups) with financial resources, including university professors and a US Representative.

Thus, as with the authors who wrote briefs 10 years prior for the *Gratz* and *Grutter* cases, those in support tended to be an array of groups and individuals who believed in social justice whereas opponents tended to be limited to a few elite actors (prominent actors, think tanks, and legal foundations) with an agenda to eliminate affirmative action in higher education. We now turn to arguments or frames from the opposing sides.

## Supporting affirmative action: Color-blind and race-conscious frames

Table 6.1 provides the frequencies of all themes and sub-themes (frames) dealing mainly with color-blind arguments made by supporters. As we found in Chapter 5 that focused on the *Gratz* and *Grutter* cases, briefs submitted in support of affirmative action generally concentrated on the "diversity is beneficial" for higher education frame. The overwhelming majority (Theme 1: 96%) of the 133 support briefs highlighted three significant benefits of general diversity: (1) a higher-quality educational experience (Concept 1a: 97%); (2) better preparation for the workforce and professional life (Concept 1b: 80%); and (3) better preparation for leadership in civic society (Concept 1c: 77%). Interwoven within these themes is the notion that diversity exposes all students to a variety of perspectives that will enhance their critical thinking and problem-solving skills as well as their adaptability in diverse social, professional, and

**Table 6.1:** Color-blind themes and concepts for amicus briefs submitted by supporters for *Fisher v University of Texas at Austin*

| Support brief findings 133/184 (72%) | | |
|---|---|---|
| **Coded theme or concept** | **Theme or concept title** | **Ratio and % of briefs using theme or concept** |
| **Theme 1** | **Diversity is beneficial** | **128/133** **(96%)** |
| Concept 1a | Better education | 125/128 (97%) |
| Concept 1b | Better workforce | 102/128 (80%) |
| Concept 1c | Better society | 98/128 (77%) |
| **Sub-theme 1** | **Abstract liberal arguments** | **78/128** **(61%)** |
| Concept sub1a | General diversity is key | 78/78 (100%) |
| Concept sub1b | Dismissive or racial diversity | 21/78 (27%) |
| **Sub-theme 2** | **Race-conscious arguments** | **54/128** **(41%)** |
| Concept sub2a | Past racial discrimination | 49/54 (91%) |
| Concept sub2b | Present racial discrimination | 29/54 (88%) |

community settings. The American Jewish Committee summed up the general perspective promoted in the support briefs: "Diversity in higher education is of vital importance not only to schools themselves but also to our society, given the critical impact education has on shaping students to become citizens and leaders in our country."

The overwhelming focus on diversity among support briefs is not coincidental. As noted in Chapter 5, Supreme Court Justice Lewis Powell proclaimed that affirmative action could not be used as a mechanism to make up for social discrimination, but rather, its only appropriate use was to promote diversity. Thus, consistency in the use of the diversity rationale across *Gratz/Grutter* and *Fisher I* and *II* suggests that supporters felt relegated to this argument due to the *Bakke* case and other past rulings. As noted previously and will be described more below, this seemingly benign focus on diversity by universities can have detrimental effects for non-white students. Regardless, we now focus on how supporters used the diversity argument specifically to save affirmative action.

## Abstract liberalism arguments

We pose that while the diversity arguments are expected (due to the *Bakke* ruling), they become an abstract liberal argument as described by Eduardo Bonilla-Silva when they ignore present and past issues of racism and discrimination (Sub-theme 1: 78 of 128). Wendy Moore and Joyce Bell (2011) specifically argued that the diversity rationale amounts to color-blindness when it divorces the problem (lack of minority participation) from historical and contemporary forms of racism and discrimination. By doing this, we can never get at the real problem but simply continue to throw Band-Aids on a gaping wound. This problematic framing was also found in the *Gratz/Grutter* briefs. For instance, we find that most support briefs submitted to the *Fisher* case (Concept sub1a) posed general diversity to be key without any discussion of the broader issues of racism or discrimination, past or present. For example, the American Association for Affirmative Action writes:

> Even a small number of diverse candidates can have an outsized impact on the overall diversity of an admissions class by furthering UT Austin's important goals of promoting cross-racial understanding, helping to break down racial stereotypes, promoting learning outcomes, better preparing students for an increasingly diverse workforce and society, and enabling students to better understand persons of different races.

Similarly, a brief submitted by the Amicus Curiae Society of American Law Teachers states, "A diverse student body also creates a learning environment that better prepares students—both minorities and non-minorities—for the workforce." These emphasize the benefits of diversity in education for preparing (presumably all) students for the diversity they are likely to encounter in their future employment and social lives. Within this frame, affirmative action is beneficial because diversity in the college classroom will help universities produce graduates who are better prepared to meet the demands of their future jobs. Affirmative action is therefore framed as a policy that is not necessarily designed to benefit minorities, but rather, as a mechanism to help universities fulfill their function in society. In doing so, it benefits businesses and corporations that need culturally competent employees, thereby contributing to the economic structure and society as a whole.

While promoting the diversity frame of argumentation, 21 of the 78 briefs (Concept sub1b) even seemed to dismiss race altogether. This frame was unique to the *Fisher* cases. For example, the College Board brief stated, "Success is dependent upon an individual's ability to engage with the diversity of all kinds, be it diversity of ideas or cultures or diversity in race and ethnicity." This excerpt dismisses race as an important rationale for supporting affirmative action, emphasizing instead "all kinds" of diversity as enhancing higher education. In this argument, diversity is important because it brings with it differences in ideas that students can be exposed to in the classroom. It suggests that it is not the race of the students per se that is important, but rather, a diversity of ideas. Briefs in this sub-theme use color-blind framing to minimize the unique significance of race historically and in the US today.

## Race-conscious frames

Less than half of all the support briefs (Sub-theme 2: 54 of 128) promoted diversity while using race-conscious frames. These briefs bring race to the forefront in their arguments to support affirmative action rather than cloaking race under a rhetoric that focuses on diversity or denying race altogether. The majority of support briefs in this sub-theme (Concept sub2a: 49 of 54) used race-conscious frames to argue that affirmative action is needed to remedy past discrimination in the US. Of the 49 briefs that discussed past racial discrimination, 18 mentioned the *Brown v Board of Education* decision as a significant racial event in shaping the present issues of affirmative action in higher education. For example, the United Negro College Fund wrote:

> In 1954, this Court declared in *Brown v Board of Education*,
> 347 US 483 (1954), that segregated schools were inherently
> unequal, and thus racial segregation and discrimination in
> education could no longer be defended against a constitutional
> challenge as 'separate but equal.' Unfortunately, transforming
> that decree into reality has proved difficult at all levels. *See*
> *United States v Fordice* ... (holding that a State must take
> affirmative steps to eradicate prior de jure segregation, and 'that
> the adoption and implementation of race-neutral policies alone
> [do not] suffice to demonstrate that the State has completely
> abandoned its prior dual system').

This excerpt draws on the *Brown* case to emphasize Supreme Court
decisions to eradicate racial segregation in education, bringing historical
race policies to the fore. It also makes explicit that race-neutral policies
are insufficient for establishing racial equality in education. In this way,
race-conscious frames are utilized to support affirmative action.

Another 10 of the 49 briefs that used race-conscious frames pointed out
the legacy of slavery in negatively impacting African Americans, arguing
that affirmative action could "right this wrong." A brief submitted by
two organizations working together, Constitutional Law Scholars and
Constitutional Accountability Center, states:

> At the same time, in writing the text, the Framers recognized
> that, after a century of racial slavery, the Constitution could
> not be simplistically color-blind. Faced with the task of
> fulfilling President Abraham Lincoln's promise of a 'new birth
> of freedom,' and integrating African Americans into the civic
> life of the nation, the Framers of the Fourteenth Amendment
> concluded that race-conscious efforts were appropriate to
> further 'the legitimate interest the government has in ensuring
> all people have equal opportunity regardless of their race'...
> The Fourteenth Amendment's Framers time and again rejected
> proposed constitutional language that would have precluded
> race-conscious measures designed to assist African Americans
> in the transition to their new status as equal citizens.

This brief draws on the history of slavery and efforts to integrate African
Americans into US society post-emancipation to justify support for
affirmative action. It uses a race-conscious frame by highlighting the
historical significance of race, and expresses explicit opposition to color-
blind policies.

While less common, 29 of the 54 support briefs that used race-conscious frames (Concept sub2b) presented affirmative action as a way of mitigating current racial discrimination, particularly in the realms of higher education, in the state of Texas, and in the US more generally. For example, the brief submitted by the Council for Minority Affairs at Texas A&M et al states, "Race still matters in American society today. Individuals continue to be treated differently based on their race in many contexts, and the reality shapes the experiences of many young people applying to and attending UT and other colleges and universities." Similarly, the brief submitted by the Lawyers Committee for Civil Rights states: "Race continues to play a significant role in individuals' experiences in many realms of society. Because of both the reality and perception that race matters throughout society—in education, employment, criminal justice, healthcare, and many other sectors—race continues to inform and shape the individual identities of people of color." Thus, support briefs that drew on race-conscious frames to support affirmative action highlighted the potential benefits of such policies to minorities, and presented them as a mechanism for reducing the effects of past and persistent racism and discrimination.

In summary, nearly all support briefs emphasized the value of diversity for improving the quality of education, the workforce, and society in general. A majority used the color-blind frame of abstract liberalism to focus on the general value of diversity while either minimizing race or erasing its significance altogether. Abstract liberalism was the only one of Bonilla-Silva's color-blind frames identified in the support briefs. None of the other three frames (naturalization, minimization of racism, and cultural racism) were identified in the data. This is also true of support briefs submitted to the *Gratz* and *Grutter* cases.

While the use of the diversity rationale without regards to the structural determinants of inequality is considered a color-blind argument, it is clear that affirmative action supporters use the diversity argument to follow the standard set by past rulings and ultimately improve the chances of minorities who have less access to elite universities. Also less common but still prevalent among the support briefs is the use of race-conscious framing, where racial inequality and discrimination are highlighted as a rationale for supporting affirmative action. The use of color-blind frames in the manner identified in the support briefs and the use of race-conscious frames stand in stark contrast to those used by opponents of affirmative action, as will be seen in the following section.

While similar arguments were made from *Gratz* and *Grutter* (Chapter 5) to *Fisher*, there were some notable differences in degree. Looking at the "diversity is beneficial" concept, a more significant proportion of briefs in *Fisher* stated that diversity was needed for education, the workforce, and society. It seems that the support briefs for the *Fisher* case made a concerted effort to demonstrate the import of diversity and how it helped. Moreover, a greater number of abstract liberal (color-blind) arguments were made among *Fisher* supporters (61% of briefs) than were observed for *Gratz and Grutter* supporters (48%). Remember that for a diversity argument to be considered abstract liberal, it needed to minimize the role of race or discrimination in its arguments. We see this again in the ways in which all arguments in these briefs build on abstract liberal support of diversity as beneficial (see Figure 6.1). Interestingly, a greater percentage of support briefs in *Gratz* and *Grutter* made race-conscious arguments compared to the support briefs in the *Fisher* cases. This trend implies that more contemporary arguments have gravitated toward the minimization of race and racism through more abstract liberal arguments of diversity.

**Figure 6.1:** Venn diagram of color-blind themes in support briefs for the *Fisher* cases

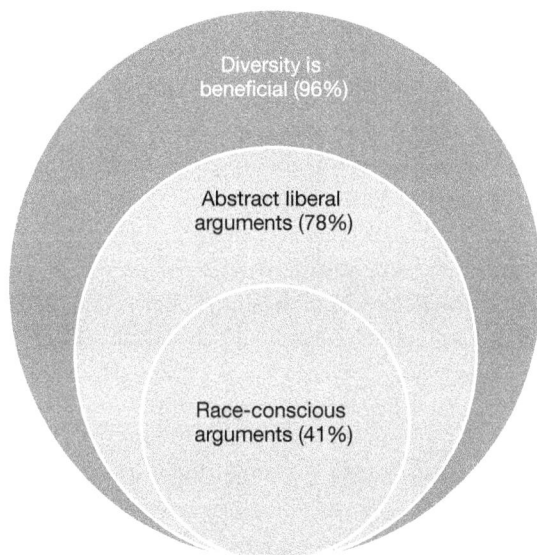

## Opposing affirmative action: Color-blind frames

Similar to arguments made by opponents in the *Gratz* and *Grutter* cases, opponent briefs submitted in support of Fisher's lawsuit against UT Austin were saturated with color-blind frames (see Table 6.2). Of the 51 opponent briefs, 100 percent utilized at least two of the four

**Table 6.2:** Color-blind themes and concepts for amicus briefs submitted by opponents for *Fisher v University of Texas at Austin*

| Opponent briefs 51/184 (28%) | | |
|---|---|---|
| **Coded theme or concept** | **Theme or concept title** | **Ratio and % of briefs using theme or concept** |
| **Theme 1** | **Abstract liberal arguments** | **42/51** **(83%)** |
| Concept 1a | Racial classifications are dangerous | 35/42 (84%) |
| Concept 1b | Violates equality and meritocracy | 19/42 (45%) |
| **Theme 2** | **Minimization of racism** | **42/51** **(83%)** |
| Concept 2a | Diversity already achieved | 21/42 (50%) |
| Concept 2b | Diversity has little value | 18/42 (44%) |
| **Theme 3** | **Cultural racism/paternalism** | **33/51** **(65%)** |
| Concept 3a | Mismatch to higher education | 30/33 (91%) |
| Concept 3b | Mismatch to workforce | 21/33 (63%) |
| **Theme 4** | **Naturalization** | **14/51** **(28%)** |
| Concept 4a | Self-segregation | 8/14 (57%) |
| Concept 4b | White responses | 7/14 (50%) |

color-blind frames identified by Bonilla-Silva (2018). The abstract liberal frame was the most common, appearing in 42 of the 51 briefs (Theme 1). This poses that opposition is based only in principle and has nothing to do with race. For instance, those who wrote in opposition to affirmative action argued against consideration of race, suggesting that this was both a violation of the Constitution and a risk to society by reinstating institutionalized racial discrimination. Of the 42 briefs that included abstract liberalism arguments, 84 percent posed that racial classifications of any kind were dangerous (Concept 1a). For example, the brief submitted by the Mountain States Legal Foundation states:

> This case involves the level of judicial scrutiny a court should apply when reviewing the university's racially discriminatory admissions policy, an issue of extraordinary and fundamental importance to the nation: 'racial classifications of any sort pose the risk of lasting harm to our society,' which 'may balkanize us into competing racial factions [and] carry us further from the goal of a political system in which race no longer matters.'

The argument here is that racial classification is dangerous for society, posing a risk of long-term harm. As noted in Chapter 5, with respect to the opponents' arguments, many of these briefs used sleight-of-hand rhetoric that placed whites as those in need of racial justice. These briefs also raised the concern that racial classification would lead to stereotyping of groups that would benefit from the policy.

Similar to the *Gratz* and *Grutter* arguments, opponents posed that racial classification also violates the spirit of equality and meritocracy (Concept 1b). This frame was identified in 19 of the 42 briefs that centered on the notion that affirmative action programs undercut the central promise of equal opportunity in the US. The arguments that comprised this theme were in many ways the most salient of anti-affirmative action rhetoric borrowing from the social liberalism of the civil rights era, and specifically from the ideology of Dr Martin Luther King Jr, as evident in the brief submitted by the think tank the American Civil Rights Union:

> The greatest warrior in the 20th century for equality under the law, the very principle embodied in the Constitution's Equal Protection Clause, was the Reverend Martin Luther King, who called for a day when every American would be judged by the content of their character rather than the color of their skins. But Petitioner Fisher was judged for admissions to UT by the color of her skin, in violation of the Equal Protection Clause.

This excerpt draws on abstract liberalism to argue that the principles of equality were violated by considering race in college admissions. It combines color-blind framing with civil rights rhetoric to portray affirmative action as not only unconstitutional, but also counter to the wishes of prominent civil rights activists.

Briefs in the abstract liberalism theme stated that affirmative action policies institutionalized "racial discrimination," "unequal treatment," and "unfair advantage." For example, a brief submitted by the Cato Institute stated:

> … the Court's precedents require that the necessity of racial classifications be supported by a 'strong basis in evidence,' not just generalized assertions of interest. The concerns that motivate this requirement—racial neutrality, individual dignity, and accountability—apply with special force to public universities' use of racial classifications to achieve 'diversity,' a vague and potentially limitless goal that may provide cover for politically-motivated or invidious discrimination.

As this excerpt demonstrates, opposition briefs never mentioned directly which group(s) might receive "special treatment" or experience discrimination by affirmative action policies. However, groups were often implied, as can be seen in the Center for Constitutional Jurisprudence brief: "America will lose out in its fight for equal treatment if unfair advantages are dolled to groups that have been crippled by the welfare state... We must make sure we stick to our principles of equal treatment for all, or we will all lose..."

## Minimization of racism

Also consistent with the *Gratz* and *Grutter* arguments, the second most common theme among opposition briefs is the "minimization of racism" frame, which was implemented by disputing the efficacy of affirmative action in higher education (Theme 2: 83%). The most common way in which this was done was first, to claim that racial diversity had already been achieved (Concept 2a: 50%) or second, that it added little value (Concept 2b: 44%) in American universities and colleges. Many of the briefs that make the "equality has been achieved" argument attributed UT Austin's relatively diverse student body not to its affirmative action policy, but to Texas' "Top 10% Rule" program, which guarantees admission to a state-funded institution, including UT Austin, to any student who is ranked in the top 10 percent of their high school graduating class. Citing a previous case, the briefs from the representatives of the petitioner herself, Fisher, suggest:

> The necessity of using racial classifications is doubtful when racial classifications have a minimal impact on school enrollment... Small gains suggest the UT 'could have achieved its stated ends through nonracial means.' That is not speculation in this instance. As explained above, UT's prior race–neutral plan, including the reliably high level of minority enrollment produced by the Top 10% Law, already has, in fact, resulted in an 'ever-increasing number of minorities gaining admission' to UT.

As this excerpt demonstrates, briefs that used the minimization of racism frame argue that race is no longer relevant in society. Therefore, racial equality has already been achieved, and policies that emphasize race only provide opportunities for institutionalized discrimination.

## Cultural racism

The third color-blind theme is cultural racism (Theme 3). This was also prevalent in arguments made in the *Gratz and Grutter* cases. In both cases, opponents posed that their anti-affirmative action view was partly borne out of concern for African Americans. Among opponent briefs, 65 percent argued that affirmative action created a culture of entitlement and underachievement among minority students. This argument fits under a cultural racism theme because they are not suggesting that minorities are biologically or intellectually incapable of succeeding in college, but that admission by affirmative action would produce cultural differences leading to failure. As in the *Gratz* and *Grutter* cases, these briefs utilized *paternalism* in their color-blind frame, suggesting that racial and ethnic minorities should be spared the consequences of affirmative action because of the potential for underachievement. We described in detail the role of paternalism in social control in Chapter 5.

The claim that minorities suffer academically under policies of affirmative action also comes in the form of the suggestion that they are "academically mismatched" with institutions that are beyond their skill level (Concept 3a). As a result, minority students become demoralized and fall behind in what they see as a futile effort to keep up with their more academically prepared white peers. For example, a brief submitted by UCLA law professor Richard Sander and lawyer and journalist Stuart Taylor Jr states:

> For decades, it was unclear whether very large preferences generally benefited the preferred students (through the positive peer effects of very able classmates) or, on balance, harmed them by subjecting them to academic 'mismatch' (because teachers would aim instruction at the median student, and those with weaker preparation would fall behind and learn less). A growing array of evidence suggests that mismatch effects predominate.

Claims that affirmative action harmed minorities by setting them up for failure in higher education were prevalent in 30 of the 33 briefs that discussed this mismatch.

Perhaps the most patronizing of the claims made within the briefs was that students admitted to colleges and universities under affirmative action were not just underprepared, but that they would also be disincentivized from working hard. For example, the brief from Abigail Thernstrom et al states,

> ... the evidence indicates that race-based admissions negatively impacts black and Latino students by increasing students' self-doubts about their abilities to succeed academically, by creating disincentives for minority students to work hard due to students' expectations that they will receive favorable treatment on the basis of race in the future.

This suggests that affirmative action breeds a culture of laziness among minority students, who will have no incentive to work hard based on their expectation that affirmative action policies will guarantee them a job when they graduate. As evident in this quote, 21 of 33 briefs (Concept 3b) in the cultural racism theme stated that affirmative action would diminish minorities' ability to succeed in the workforce after college. These claims are paternalistic in that they suggest that the US government is responsible for protecting minority students from such an insidious disincentive to work by prohibiting race-conscious policies such as affirmative action.

## Naturalization

The least common color-blind frame identified in the opposition briefs is naturalization (Theme 4). This was not found in the *Gratz/Grutter* opponent briefs. Briefs in this theme (28%) argued that race-conscious policies had unintended consequences that would result in the inevitable natural tendency of human racial groups to factionalize or self-segregate. Two distinct concepts were utilized in this frame. The first (Concept 4a: 57%) was that diversity in higher education would lead to self-segregation among minority students, resulting in these students "foregoing benefits that would result from studying with better-prepared peers" (Scholars of Economics and Statistics). This theme draws on the assumptions that group segregation is natural, that all minority students are less prepared than all white students, and that consequently, minority students will perform poorly because they will gravitate toward their same-race underprepared peers.

Additionally, diversity was argued to harbor the racial discord (Concept 4b: 7 of 14) that ascribed to innate human tendencies toward distrust and tribalism. The most salient example of this was found in the Thernstrom et al brief, which stated:

> Contact between people of different racial and ethnic groups is more likely than not to lead to tension, ethnic conflict, and a tendency to self-segregate and harbor deep suspicions of

outsider groups than it is to further intergroup cooperation and trust. Human beings are tribal, as observers often say, and simply bringing people who identify with different groups together in the same location can lead to tension and conflict at least as often as to harmony and mutual respect…

While less common than other concepts, this suggested that diversity in higher education would create real problems of internal conflict and violence within the classroom and university setting. Thus, affirmative action is framed as having detrimental consequences for all students.

While these color-blind frames (minus the naturalization that was not found in the *Gratz/Grutter* cases), as outlined by Eduardo Bonilla-Silva (2018), were highly prevalent in all Supreme Court cases included in this analysis, we pose that there was a difference in proportion across them. Each of the three frames—abstract liberalism, minimization of racism, and cultural racism—were more prevalent in *Fisher* than they were in *Gratz* and *Grutter* (see Figure 6.2). Given that opponents suffered a tremendous loss in the *Grutter* case, it could very well be that they focused more intensely on denouncing racial classification, minimizing the impact of race and diversity, and raising concern over harms to minorities. It could also be that arguments have simply become more developed and established in American lexicon over time. As such, the rhetoric was amped up on each of these fronts, and opponents of the policy added the fourth color-blind theme of suggesting any "anti-white" policies would lead to a natural backlash against non-white students. This theme assisted in increasing what we noticed in *Gratz* and *Grutter*, an intensification of

**Figure 6.2:** Venn diagram of color-blind themes in opponent briefs for the *Fisher* cases

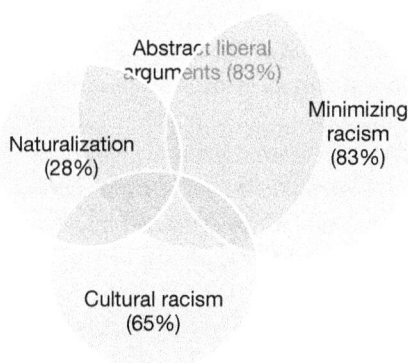

Abstract liberal arguments (83%)

Minimizing racism (83%)

Naturalization (28%)

Cultural racism (65%)

threatening rhetoric in the more recent *Fisher* case. Accordingly, we now turn to the nuanced ways opponents used threat to frame their arguments.

## Veiled threat frames in the affirmative action debate: The *Fisher* cases

While it is clear from these findings that opponents wanted to minimize the discussion of race and racism, past or present, within the debate over affirmative action, it is also clear that these social authorities purposefully used group threat frames within the color-blind rhetoric to activate racialized group positioning and thus, racial animus. We labeled this multi-framing technique *Racialized Framing*.

Noteworthy in our analysis of opponent briefs is that *Racialized Framing* as described is even more insidious because it does not focus on persistent racial inequality and discrimination faced by non-whites; instead, opponent arguments push a narrative to the public and the Supreme Court that race no longer matters and, rather than be helpful to minorities, is actually a threat to more "deserving" students. Thus, the real problem is systematic discrimination against white Americans. This style of argumentation is not that surprising. Herbert Blumer (1958) argued that racial prejudice and ultimately, discrimination is rooted in group identification and feelings of group competition. That is to say, those who identify as white develop a sense that they are superior to out-groups and then develop concerns that out-group members are threatening valued resources. In this case, admissions to higher education and corresponding status are the valued resources, and opponents seem to understand that a fear of loss is essential to get people to react and move on their feelings. This finding is consistent with the work of Robert Entman (1997), who also argued that threatening rhetoric (frames) is key to producing emotions for and against an issue and thus, winning social and political debates.

With this revelation in mind, this chapter, along with Chapter 5, has urged for a re-conceptualization or at least additions to how race and racism scholars should explain white reactions to individual and structural racism. Looking solely at the arguments from a color-blind perspective, it is clear that opponents attempted to minimize the role of race using various rhetorical frames (see Bonilla-Silva's color-blind types) to eliminate the policy. However, a closer look reveals nuanced and threatening language within those color-blind frames that, we argue, is an attempt to activate racial animosity and push Supreme Court Justices (and the public, for that matter) to turn on the policy and strike down affirmative action in higher education. Notably, the call for ending any race-conscious policies that equalize access is really about white Americans' perceptions that valued resources are at risk, and that their privileged access to them may be at an end if affirmative action continues.

Accordingly, the rest of this chapter further demonstrates how threat frames played a prominent role in color-blind rhetoric, particularly in the arguments made by those opposing affirmative action in college admissions policies. Interestingly, both supporters and opponents alike used color-blind language and discussed issues of threat. However, we will show that opponent briefs' veil of color-blindness was an attempt to hide their racist concerns from the watchdogs of political correctness, and to avoid outright rejection from Supreme Court Justices since it needed to follow Justice Powell's 1978 color-blind arguments. In short, word choices and phraseology empirically noted by other researchers examining racial animosity (Bobo, 2000) sent signals to white America and the Supreme Court that affirmative action in higher education threatened "their" (white Americans') resources.

## Supporting affirmative action: Threat to American principles of equality and justice

Briefs submitted in support of affirmative action used threat frames. However, these arguments, like those in the support briefs filed for the *Gratz* and *Grutter* cases, focused more on describing the potential pitfalls of eradicating affirmative action by further marginalizing non-white students, and more generally, going against American principles of equality. They continued to highlight the positive outcomes generated by affirmative action, and frame its elimination as the potential risk—or threat—of losing out on these benefits for those who could benefit from the programs. These threats were stated overtly, but not in the subtle ways we later see among opponents' briefs against affirmative action. Furthermore, threat, as used by supporters, were not meant to create group position and thus group conflict via "us" versus "them" arguments.

The most prominent threat frame used in the support briefs (Theme 1: 93%) was that eliminating affirmative action posed a significant threat to the core missions of higher education (see Table 6.3). Briefs that used this frame emphasized the importance of diversity for adequately educating students. For example, a brief submitted by the League of Cities et al states, "Higher education institutions have a historically rooted public mandate to prepare the nation's leadership to address society's most important concerns ... racial and ethnic diversity is necessary to meet this

**Table 6.3:** Threat themes and concepts for support briefs

| Support brief findings 133/184 (72%) | | |
|---|---|---|
| Coded theme or concept | Theme or concept title | Ratio and % of briefs using theme or concept |
| Theme 1 | Threat to university goals | 128/133 (93%) |
| Concept 1a | Diverse education | 111/124 (90%) |
| Theme 2 | Threat to minorities | 100/133 (75%) |
| Concept 2a | Stereotype threat | 85/100 (85%) |
| Concept 2b | Professional lag | 46/100 (46%) |
| Concept 2c | No leadership in minority communities | 39/100 (39%) |
| Theme 3 | Threat to society | 81/133 (61%) |
| Concept 3a | Professional homogeneity | 49/81 (60%) |
| Concept 3b | Civic conflict and disengagement | 49/81 (60%) |

Note: $N$ = 133.

mandate." In this brief, as in others, diversity is framed as a requirement for universities to fulfill their function in society. Lack of diversity in higher education is framed as a veiled threat to universities (Concept 1a). The argument that diversity is necessary for quality education was often justified by the Court's previous rulings in the *Bakke* and *Grutter* cases, which ruled that diversity was a compelling state interest for public university programs. In this way, the veiled threat frameworks go hand in hand with the color-blind abstract liberalism frame of the importance of diversity for promoting the goals of American universities.

The second most common threat frame used in support briefs was that ending affirmative action posed a threat to racial and ethnic minorities, which was identified in 75 percent of the briefs (Theme 2: 75%). The veiled threat to minorities frame suggests that minorities would face increased discrimination in a racist American society without affirmative action. These briefs argued that losing affirmative action would be a threat to minorities through continued stereotyping (Concept 2a: 85%), problems of professional lag (Concept 2b: 46%), and a lack of leadership in minority communities (Concept 2c: 39%). A brief submitted by Teach for America stated, "A pipeline of diverse leaders [created by affirmative action] is needed to break the cycle of racial disadvantage." This veiled threat frame suggests that ending affirmative action would assure the continuation of deprivation in minority communities.

The final threat frame used in support briefs was that eradicating affirmative action would be detrimental to society (Theme 3: 61%). This veiled threat took two primary forms. The first, identified in 49 of the 81 support briefs (Concept 3a), focused on threats to a society based on lack of minority representation in the workforce, resulting in professional homogeneity. For example, the American Bar Association brief stated, "Because the public's perception of the legal profession often informs impressions of the legal system, a diverse bar and bench create great trust in the law." This excerpt highlights the importance of diverse representation in the legal profession for generating public trust in the legal system, suggesting that reducing diversity in this realm would threaten public trust and thus, endanger society as a whole. The second form, also identified in 49 of the 81 support briefs (Concept 3b), argued that ending affirmative action would incite either racial conflict or civic disengagement at a university in question and elsewhere.

Overall, the threat frames identified in the support briefs for the *Fisher* cases suggested that eliminating affirmative action would cause a potential threat to higher education, minorities, and society in general. Identifying the risks of potential harm to higher education and general society was often utilized in conjunction with the color-blind abstract liberalism frame that emphasized diversity as beneficial and correspondingly, the absence of diversity was a threat to American principles of at least allowing equal access to higher education (see Figure 6.3). It was also apparent that there was a noticeable shift from *Gratz* and *Grutter*. The level of threat to these components seemed to be heightened in the *Fisher* cases, which may be the result of the split decisions with the *Gratz* and *Grutter* cases. This level of threat may also reflect the growing concern that affirmative action, a policy often linked to civil rights, is on the verge of being swept away by a conservative backlash.

**Figure 6.3:** Venn diagram of threat frames in support briefs for the *Fisher* cases

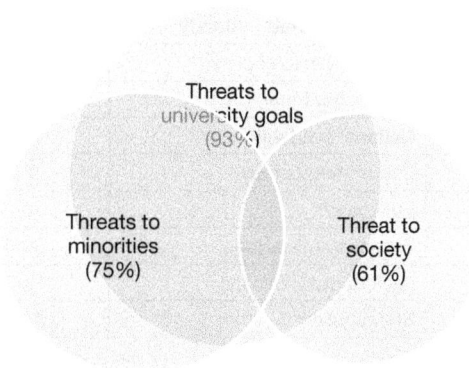

## Opposing affirmative action: Veiled threat frames

Briefs submitted in opposition to affirmative action also used veiled threat frames; however, the utilization of these frames was quite distinctive in skirting the issues of race and racism in higher education as it impacted non-whites (see Table 6.4). The briefs utilized these frames to emphasize the potential harms associated with the continuation of affirmative action policies (see Figure 6.4). They also highlighted the negative outcomes created by affirmative action, and framed its continuation in terms of risk of threat. In the opposition briefs, threats were sometimes stated overtly, but most of the time, the notion of threat towards white privilege in higher education was veiled within a color-blind rhetoric.

### The threat to white resources

The most common veiled threat identified in the opposition briefs was the notion that affirmative action policies threatened the valued resources of white Americans (Theme 1: 78%). The most common veiled threat in this theme was the notion that "reverse discrimination" or preferential treatment based on race was a real threat to the dominant group (Concept 1a: 83%). These briefs posed that the use of affirmative action

**Table 6.4:** Veiled threat themes and concepts for opponent briefs

| Petition briefs 51/184 (28%) | | |
|---|---|---|
| Coded theme or concept | Theme or concept title | Ratio and % of briefs using theme or concept |
| Theme 1 | Threat to white resources | 40/51 (78%) |
| Concept 1a | Reverse discrimination | 33/40 (83%) |
| Theme 2 | Threat to (white) society | 38/51 (75%) |
| Concept 2a | Vague harm to society | 20/38 (53%) |
| Concept 2b | Unconstitutional | 20/38 (53%) |
| Concept 2c | National solidarity | 18/38 (47%) |
| Concept 2d | End of meritocracy | 16/38 (42%) |
| Concept 2e | Eugenics | 10/38 (26%) |
| Theme 3 | Threat to minorities | 30/51 (59%) |
| Concept 3a | Lack of qualifications | 26/30 (88%) |
| Concept 3b | Stereotypes | 14/30 (47%) |

Note: $N = 51$.

**Figure 6.4:** Venn diagram of threat frames in opponent briefs in the *Fisher* cases

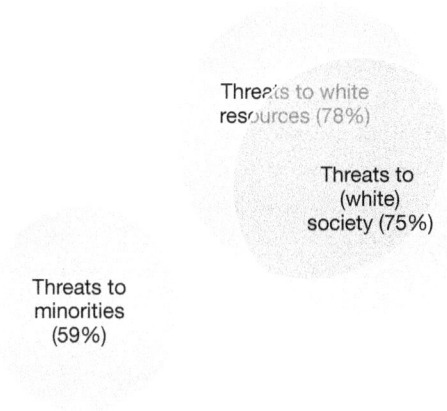

Threats to white resources (78%)

Threats to (white) society (75%)

Threats to minorities (59%)

in higher education admissions was a form of race-based discrimination rather than a remedy to it. However, it was whites, rather than minorities, who were being discriminated against. They posited that affirmative action policies resulted in highly qualified (white) applicants being denied admissions based on their race. These arguments highlight the veiled threat frame that cast affirmative action as threatening the status of the dominant group by taking away admissions to college that whites had rightfully earned through their qualifications. While on the surface the notion that universities should not "discriminate based on race" may not necessarily reflect "reverse discrimination," we argue that such language is merely slippery abstract liberal rhetoric, as described by Bonilla-Silva (2018), and clearly reflected the concerns of white Americans feeling that their "race" was now being used to discriminate against them in the admissions process. In this way, affirmative action was framed as a threat to white prosperity and valued resources.

### *The threat to (white) society*

Opposition briefs also used veiled threat frames to argue that affirmative action policies posed a harm to society (Theme 2). Over half of the opposition briefs (Concept 2a: 53%) evoked some form of threat that continuing affirmative action would cause a significant, yet vague and unspecified, harm to society. They tended not to provide much specific information on the injuries that may come, but noted the problem regardless. For instance, a brief submitted by the Pacific Legal Foundation et al poignantly stated, "Discrimination based on race is 'illegal, immoral, unconstitutional, inherently wrong, and destructive of a democratic society.'" A brief by the Mountain States Legal Foundation similarly added that "racial classifications of any sort pose the risk of lasting harm to our society."

The second most common threat to society that was used in the opposition briefs was the notion that affirmative action threatened the US Constitution or body politic (Concept 2b: 53%). Opposition briefs in this category posed that the use of affirmative action in higher education had broader implications for endangering the Constitution and US people as a whole. For instance, a brief submitted by the Mountain States Legal Foundation posed that allowing the use of affirmative action in college admissions would effectively "destroy confidence in the Constitution and idea of equality." A brief by the Scholars of Economics and Statistics added that "because classifications based on race are potentially so harmful to the entire body politic, it is especially important that the reasons for any such classification be clearly identified and unquestionably legitimate." Similarly, a brief by the Cato Institute posed that "classifications based on race are potentially so harmful to the entire body politic." While aiming their concerns at broader society as a whole, these briefs specified that affirmative action threatened the Constitution, which would lead to the destruction of public confidence in the government.

Another veiled threat identified in the opposition briefs was that affirmative action threatened national solidarity (Concept 2c: 47%). Opposition briefs in this category noted the odious nature of racial division by claiming that affirmative action caused racial hostility and conflict, thereby creating divisions within society. For example, a brief submitted by the Mountain States Legal Foundation posed that affirmative action policies "endorse race-based reasoning and the conception of a nation divided into racial blocs, thus contributing to an escalation of racial hostility and conflict." Similarly, the Pacific Legal Foundation noted, "Poisonous intergroup relations and real dangers to the fabric of society have also been produced by affirmative action." The Cato Institute further argued that "unless they are strictly reserved for remedial settings, they may, in fact, promote notions of racial inferiority and lead to a politics of racial hostility." Opposing briefs used this veiled threat frame to suggest that continued use of affirmative action would result in increased racial conflict, thereby threatening national solidarity and posing harm to the fabric of US society.

Opposition briefs also used veiled threat frames by arguing that affirmative action challenged core American values and ideals of meritocracy (Concept 2d: 42%). These briefs argued that by using race as a factor in college admissions, affirmative action interfered with the ability of individuals to advance solely on their merit, creating an uneven academic field. For example, a brief prepared by the Louis D. Brandeis Center for Human Rights Under Law stated:

> In devaluing the hard work of deserving students on account of race, these policies foment racial strife, undermine our society's basic meritocratic values, and deprive all Americans of the benefits that might be expected from channeling educational resources at those students exhibiting the greatest merit.

Similarly, a brief submitted by the Texas Association of Scholars added that the diversity argument in support of affirmative action was based on a culture of "merit and assimilation." The briefs in this category draw on the dominant stereotype that white people were harder working, and would therefore naturally have more "merit" than racial and ethnic minorities. Continuing affirmative action policies would thereby disrupt the meritocratic ideals that are at the foundation of US society. Finally, opposition briefs that used a veiled threat frame to position affirmative action as a threat to society argued that such policies encouraged a eugenics paradigm (Concept 2d: 42%), where racial preference ultimately led to extreme devaluation of a group. This frame harkened back to Nazi Germany.

Like the briefs submitted for the *Gratz* and *Grutter* cases, these opponents against affirmative action wanted to emphasize the infringement these programs had, not just on American values, but on white American values too. Again, the authors implied that the ideologies and national solidarity were a result of white American "forefather" efforts, particularly using the "creators of the US Constitution" as the measurement of the pure principles of democracy, freedom, and equality. Through color-blind rhetoric, they also used tropes of American exceptionalism to point out that it was the "greatest country on earth" as long as it did not bow to diversity and affirmative action. Thus, the argument here became one of sticking to the American principles of yesteryear, referring back to cherished times of the 1700s or 1950s, when African Americans were enslaved or facing Jim Crow. The idea is simple—white American values were the "gold standard," and any challenge was an affront to white values. More importantly, since this language was as prominent concerning the *Fisher* cases as with the *Gratz* and *Grutter* cases, these authors wanted white America to remain in control of the narrative of what was equal and right, or who would receive the privilege of higher education.

## Threat to minorities

Again, like the *Gratz* and *Grutter* cases, a prominent third veiled threat frame identified among opposition briefs was that affirmative action posed a threat to minorities (Theme 3: 59%). This theme was a completely separate argument from how affirmative action would impact white applicants or white America. Briefs that used this theme contended that affirmative action must be eliminated because it harmed minorities, and the role of the US government was to protect them. Briefs in this theme again drew on a paternalistic sentiment, which Mary Jackman (1994) has argued is often used as a mechanism to maintain political control over minority groups. Jackman posed that paternalism allows groups to cloak domination in terms of genuine concern or love rather than violence. Jackman indeed argued that once violence is needed to control minorities, then all control is lost. As we saw in the *Gratz* and *Gutter* arguments, paternalism or suggesting that minorities were further victimized by affirmative action, was a ruse to avoid sounding racist and a way to steer conversations to how all applicants were harmed by college admissions policies when race was used as a criterion for admissions.

In briefs submitted to the *Fisher* cases, the most common way in which veiled threat frames suggested that affirmative action posed a threat to minorities was by arguing that colleges and universities would produce underqualified minority graduates who were inadequately prepared for the workforce (Concept 3a: 88%). Many drew on the mismatch hypothesis, which argued that affirmative action would lead to the admission of underqualified students into higher education institutions, setting these students up for failure. This position is perfectly outlined in a brief submitted by Gail Heriot et al:

> When the highest schools on the academic ladder relax their admissions policies in order to admit more underrepresented minority students, schools one rung down must do likewise if they are to have the desired number of minority students, too. The problem is thus passed on to the schools another rung down, which respond similarly. As a result, underrepresented minority students are overwhelmingly at the bottom of the distribution of entering academic credentials at most selective schools.

While this position seemed to be concerned with the outcomes for minorities, it assumed that minority applicants were less prepared while negating the benefits accrued by minorities through affirmative action. Instead, it petitioned the Supreme Court to protect minorities from failure by eliminating affirmative action.

The second way in which veiled threat frames suggested that affirmative action posed a threat to minorities was by expressing concern that these policies would lead to greater stereotyping of minorities (Concept 3b: 47%). For instance, a brief submitted by the Louis D. Brandeis Center for Human Rights Under Law stated,

> The University's policy does not promote diversity. It promotes racial and ethnic stereotyping by making generalizations that equate an applicant's race or 'Hispanic or Latino ethnicity' with his or her viewpoints, backgrounds, and experiences.

The Pacific Legal Foundation similarly noted that "racial classifications destroy our very form of Constitutional government by requiring governments to stereotype individuals, assuming they act in accordance with their race." With a more specific argument about the future experience of minorities, a brief by the Current and Former Federal Civil Rights Officials insisted that the use of racial preference required minorities to be a "specimen of a particular race or ethnicity." This veiled threat frame warned that affirmative action increased racial and ethnic stereotyping by presuming a connection between one's race or ethnicity and their behaviors and experiences. Such connections, they warned, were detrimental to minorities in the US.

Accordingly, as with the support briefs, the level of threat expressed by *Fisher* opponents was significantly greater than the level of threat expressed by opponents in *Gratz* and *Grutter*.

This shift toward greater fear-mongering (that comes from threatening rhetoric) seems to parallel contemporary identity politics, which appear to be becoming more extreme over time, particularly on racial issues such as terrorism, immigration, wealth inequality, and police brutality. It was clear that opponents infused threat more fluidly in *Fisher* than they did in *Gratz and Grutter* just a short decade before. Even when couched in color-blind rhetoric, threat frames were also easier to see and pull out of the opposing narratives in the *Fisher* cases than in the *Gratz* and *Grutter* cases. In short, along with the *Gratz* and *Grutter* results, we contend that veiled threats are and will continue to be prominent racialized frames in the debate to end affirmative action in college admissions policies.

## Conclusion

The purpose of this chapter was to assess if and how color-blind frames were used in debates surrounding affirmative action in higher education by supporters and opponents. This project also sought to evaluate other framing strategies, including how threat frames were used by these entities. We focused specifically on 184 amicus briefs submitted to the Supreme Court case *Fisher v University of Texas at Austin* written by supporters and opponents to affirmative action. Furthermore, this chapter also wanted to begin a comparison of rhetoric used during the *Gratz and Grutter* (2003) cases with the more recent *Fisher* cases (2013 and 2016).

Generally speaking, our findings clearly demonstrate a multi-framing technique used by supporters and opponents. That is to say, the discourse in both support and opponent briefs used multiple frames including "color-blind" and "threat" frames. However, the support briefs mainly relied on color-blind arguments promoting diversity, of which many downplayed or ignored discussions of racial discrimination and racism in higher education. As explained by Moore and Bell (2011, p 602) in their study of Supreme Court cases on affirmative action admissions policies in higher education, "Nearly the instant that 'diversity' in education became a rationale by the [Supreme] Court as an interest so compelling as to justify the use of race-conscious policies like affirmative action, the concept gets de-racialized; securely fitted into the color-blind sub-frame." They also pointed out that because Justice Powell's arguments for these cases suggested that the concept of diversity was grounded in a frame of diversity in which any type mattered, it then significantly reduced the prominence of race, eroding the necessity to address historic and continued racial discrimination.

In contrast, the opponent briefs were saturated with color-blind rhetoric, and in so doing all four color-blind frames described by Bonilla-Silva (2018) were noted in the text. The most prominent frame was the abstract liberalism that was concerned with justice (no preferential treatment or reverse discrimination). Authors of these briefs were clear that the continued use of affirmative action would be detrimental to society as a whole and unfair to hard-working individuals who did things the right way (eg, reverse discrimination). This general notion of concern for reverse discrimination and injustice is consistent with the work on media framing of affirmative action (Gamson and Modigliani, 1987; Richardson and Lancendorfer, 2004), and a staple in research assessing individual-level racial prejudice and beliefs about inequality (Kinder and Sanders, 1996; Bobo and Tuan, 2006). While abstract liberalism was the most prominent, the other frames were also used in conjunction with the opponent frames to minimize the structural causes of inequality.

Embedded in the abstract liberal argument were threat frames, particularly among opponents (see Figure 6.5). Given that a majority of petition briefs posed that affirmative action in higher education admissions threatened the very foundation of US society and the position of the majority in the academy (through reverse discrimination), we can argue that this implied, at least implicitly, that there was a strong proprietary claim to this resource. Threat would not go far if the proprietary claim on behalf of the dominant group was not established (Blumer, 1958). The tapping into feelings of the proprietary claim through threat is quite similar to debates over immigration reform, where opponents attempt to draw support by describing the resulting threat to various resources posed by undocumented immigrants, including education, healthcare, and other governmental benefits claimed by the dominant group (Carter and Lippard, 2015; Chavez, 2008).

The use of threat in the briefs submitted to the Supreme Court by opponents was quite complicated and nuanced. As noted above, the briefs spoke vaguely of a "lasting harm" that would befall US society as a whole unless affirmative action was banned in higher education. One brief posed that affirmative action would be "unhealthy for society at large" if

**Figure 6.5:** Thematic connections between color-blind rhetoric and group threats among opponent briefs for the *Fisher* cases

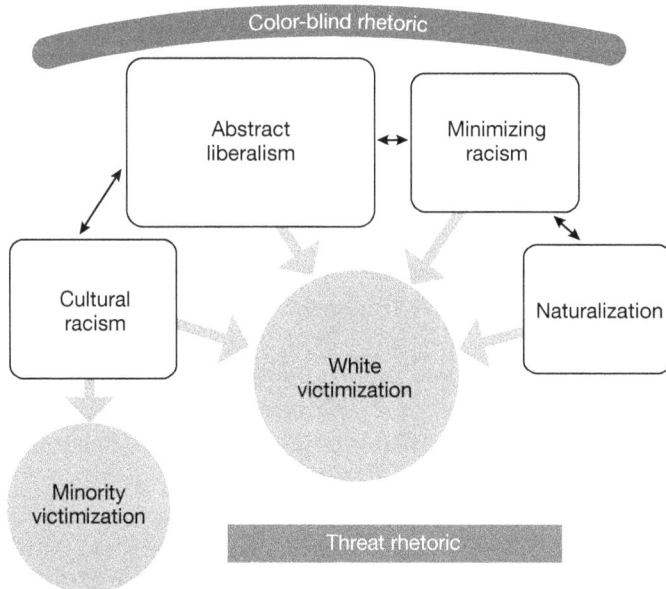

allowed to continue. Others spoke of affirmative action as "destructive of a democratic society" and a danger to "the fabric of society." The combination of this frame (threat to society) with reverse discrimination (threat to the majority) implies that not only would affirmative action threaten the culture in our society but it would also threaten resources the majority deserve due to merit. We argue that the use of threat in this manner has one major purpose: using the rhetoric of classical liberalism (injustice and unfairness), to create the notion that affirmative action threatens the dominant culture and resources of the dominant group. This finding is consistent with Entman (1997) who found affirmative action to be consistently framed as competition for valued resources. This finding also supports the notion that these briefs wanted to activate animosity by emphasizing the positional and competitive nature, whether it be material or symbolic, to group relations.

The opponent briefs did not stop with these fundamental arguments (threat to society and to the majority). They also included a discourse that described affirmative action as a threat to minorities themselves. These seemingly anti-minority briefs created arguments that, on the surface, seemed to want to protect and even promote the best interest of minorities. The use of this frame has also been found in the media when framing the policy (Gamson and Modigliani, 1987). In the most general sense, the briefs created very paternalistic arguments against affirmative action. Jackman (1994, pp 382–3) most poignantly stated "in the cause of preserving the modus vivendi, dominants have little wish to enter into battle with subordinates over the distribution of resources. They prefer to hold them in a coercive embrace, and to fail that; they endeavor to contain subordinates' incipient challenge with principles and reason."

Interestingly, while opponent arguments did not directly attack the culture of minorities, other discursive techniques were used to argue against the use of affirmative action. First, the petition briefs reminded readers about the harmful nature of eugenics. That is to say, certain briefs highlighted that, unlike today's hospitable racial climate, we did not want to return to a culture where racial antagonism was high and racial preference palpable (eg, in Nazi Germany). Second, the briefs omitted any positive outcomes that have occurred due to affirmative action policy for minorities. Given the warnings regarding the negative effects of racial preference and the omission of positive outcomes, it is clear that the authors made an argument that they wanted to protect minorities from themselves paternally.

With this said, we make a few final observations. One, it is clear that supporters and opponents ramped up their color-blind and threatening rhetoric in *Fisher* relative to *Gratz and Grutter*. This shift seems to have paralleled broader changes in US politics, where identity politics and fear are ever-present. Second, these findings provide support for our theoretical framework: authors, particularly opponents, clearly attempted to use *Racialized Framing* to minimize race as it stands today while also attempting to activate race or racism through the use of threat.

# 7

# Conclusions

While the *Grutter* and *Fisher* decisions appear to signify victories for supporters of affirmative action, the future looks grim, with some scholars arguing that affirmative action as an ameliorative policy is already dead (Moore, 2018). Wendy Moore (2018) argues that years of political and legal attacks, particularly by elite conservative whites and related advocacy groups, have relegated affirmative action to a call to arms among conservatives rather than it being a significant ameliorative policy that could improve the lived experiences of disadvantaged groups and reduce inequality. In other words, affirmative action no longer serves as an effective tool to increase racial equality. This conclusion is not surprising given that even the most minimal use of race as *one* factor (not *the* factor) in the higher education admissions process is demonized by conservatives who will not stop until any "preferential treatment" associated with race is ended. This raises eyebrows considering the historical benefits afforded to whites by excluding non-whites for hundreds of years from higher education, and because there are still ways in which white applicants receive preferential treatment outside of their racial classification (eg, via legacy admissions). Furthermore, this move is also disconcerting, given the persistent state of racial inequality in the US today that continues to hold back millions of non-white Americans. While in past cases the Supreme Court has upheld the use of race as *one* factor but not *the* factor in higher education admissions, this will probably not happen in future cases.

As described in detail in this book, the fight for and against affirmative action in higher education revolves around the notion of diversity and what it means to both white and non-white students. Does diversity in general and racial diversity in particular serve a compelling interest to colleges and universities as well as the state? The answer to this question in the Supreme Court has been "yes" up to this point, but this is not a resounding "yes" due to several split decisions. How an affirmative action policy must be implemented today requires it being narrowly tailored to address a clear need or goal of the institution. However, despite having to pass strict scrutiny and despite its minimal impact, conservative politicians along with many citizens continue to push forward with an anti-affirmative action agenda. The conservative elite have not only fought against the implementation of diversity initiatives, but also against the very idea of diversity, which we found consistently throughout our analysis. We also found that diversity has been discursively identified as a proxy for racial classification in the eyes of its opponents.

Our findings have also presented further shifts toward ramping up color-blind and threat-based frames for supporters and opponents to use in their rhetorical and ideological toolbox. We found in particular that supporters from *Grutter/Gratz* to *Fisher* had to rely more heavily on an abstract liberal approach in an attempt to convince the Supreme Court (and arguably, the American public) that affirmative action would negate all the benefits of higher education, regardless of race of student. Many of these briefs shied away from arguments that pointed out past and present issues of structural racism in higher education, and shifted towards an argument (largely encouraged by the 1978 *Bakke* case) of diversity as an educational benefit for all students, regardless of race. Thus, race, and structural racism, was no longer the problem, as suggested in earlier cases reaching back to the 1954 landmark decision of *Brown v Board of Education*. Rather, the issue was about supposedly protecting all students' rights to access higher education, thus encouraging a blind acceptance of equality among all students, regardless of past, present, and future racial discrimination. More importantly, anti-affirmative action groups and individuals argued that no university or state should create policies that use race as a factor (even a minimal factor) in college admissions' decisions because this went against US constitutional protections and American ideals of meritocracy. Overall, this twist in the argument often suggested that all college applicants, and especially white applicants, deserve equal protection under the law and would suffer from state-sanctioned discrimination that occurs when affirmative action policies are in place.

This twist in the equal protections argument ran counterfactual to the narratives proposed by supporters of affirmative action that do see persistent issues of past and present discrimination facing non-whites. These supporters suggested that non-white applicants faced serious issues of discrimination, structurally and individually, in access to higher education. More importantly, they, too, wanted college applicants to receive equal access to protections, but only focused on the groups that faced rampant past and present discrimination. However, because of the 1978 *Bakke* decision that suggested race could not be the sole factor of college admissions decisions *and* that state arguments to increase diversity on college campuses had to be narrowly tailored, the Supreme Court considered arguments expressed by supporters about past and present racial discrimination moot. Any argument that focused too much on race could not fully compete against the seemingly color-blind notions of equality for all, since the federal government had effectively dismissed racism in the past and present as a dead issue. This shift meant that those in favor of affirmative action had to water down arguments and promote the "diversity is beneficial" perspective while ignoring specific issues of racism and discrimination faced by minorities in higher education today. As such, little discussion of system racism (and ways to combat it) played out in the legal documents, even by supporters.

As for those against affirmative action, advocacy groups and elite actors have also shifted their arguments. Since they could not directly say or provide clear evidence of reverse discrimination against white applicants, these entities preyed more on fears of the audience by using threat frames within abstract liberal arguments, which we labeled *Racialized Framing*. As early as *Bakke*, the rhetoric had already been established to suggest that any affirmative action policy within any public or private setting was an attack on the American foundations of equality and meritocracy. Of course, the overarching problem with this argument, as noted in Chapters 5 and 6, is that conservative actors and groups' briefs seemed to leave out the fact that the US has never functioned as an equal and fair society. Even when these briefs pointed out past racial discrimination, they often attempted to subvert the narrative of the Civil Rights Movement and the words of Dr Martin Luther King Jr to point out the racial injustices faced not just by African Americans but by whites as well. With their quick color-blind tongues, they erased the racist history of the past and present, and inserted their narratives of how racial classification and racism ruined chances for all groups, regardless of the color of their skin.

However, the rhetoric of opponents did not stop there. Advocacy groups and elite actors with more conservative orientations doubled down and vehemently argued that affirmative action threatened the very American fabric that had made white America so privileged. Specifically, these briefs argued that affirmative action had taken away white America's birthright to higher education, and had given it to lesser-qualified and under-prepared non-whites. In brief after brief, these conservative entities pointed out how white applicants would lose out due to their skin color in the name of "diversity," but never once provided any scientific evidence to support this claim. Moreover, they never raised any concern about the persistent racism and discrimination felt by non-whites.

Opponent briefs also repeatedly pointed out that non-whites were mismatched with higher education and would fail out or drop out given that they were underprepared for the rigor of elite college curriculum. Only a handful of opponent briefs (four in total) pointed out that the institution of education had failed non-white students before they reached higher education. Moreover, many argued that even if non-white students could survive the rigors of higher education, they would ultimately struggle psychologically due to stereotypes and fail in the workplace post-graduation. That is to say, these briefs repeatedly described concerns they had for pernicious stereotypes that would psychologically ruin non-whites on college campuses. Many briefs further suggested that the Supreme Court should strike down affirmative action because it would protect non-whites from ultimately failing in the workforce on graduation due to a lack of training and preparation.

Despite all of this rhetoric about protecting non-whites, the message just veiled the true intent of these briefs. They all wanted to see affirmative action end in college admissions policies because they did not want to see their advantages shared with others. The most powerful discourse in all the conservative-leaning briefs analyzed was that affirmative action threatened white access to a resource that has been proven to catapult all Americans into higher incomes and better lifestyles. In short, these briefs wanted to make sure that whites kept this resource to, as Michael Omi and Howard Winant (2015) have argued, continually prop up white privilege.

## Affirmative action and politics

The fight against affirmative action has gained traction on many fronts, including national and local politics and in the legal arena. Politically, however, affirmative action is either dying a slow death or is already dead. Republican and Democratic presidential administrations of the last half of the 20th century and into the beginning of the 21st century have each expressed great disdain for the policy, particularly in higher education admissions, and have installed like-minded individuals in high positions (in their administrations as well as in the justice system). Lee Cokorinos (2003) outlined in detail the damage done in Ronald Reagan's first presidential term, where he loaded the Justice Department with anti-civil rights policy hawks. These core opponents not only set the agenda for the Reagan presidency, but also set in motion the conservative agenda (eg, interest group formation) to fight affirmative action in the future.

This fight has also been apparent in the surprising rise of Donald Trump to the presidency of the US in 2016. Trump's administration has committed to using the Civil Rights Division of the Department of Justice to punish universities that use race in making admissions decisions. This direction was brought to the press's attention via a leaked hiring document that expressed an interest in applicants who litigated "intentional race-based discrimination" in college admissions decisions, particularly focusing on institutions that discriminated against white applicants (Savage, 2017). Moreover, President Trump recently announced that he would abandon the policies of former President Barack Obama's administration, which had supported the use of race as a factor in higher education admissions, and would instead support more color-blind standards (Green et al, 2018). This hiring initiative and ideological stance against the use of race reflects a broader view of Republicans in general, and the state of mind of the current Republican administration under Donald Trump in particular.

State-level politics have also been unkind to affirmative action. Eight states have legislatively put an end to affirmative action in any fashion, including the use of race in admissions to public colleges and universities. In 1996, Proposition 209 in California served as the first state to ban affirmative action, followed by Washington (1998), Florida (1999), Michigan (2006), Nebraska (2008), Arizona (2010), New Hampshire (2011), and Oklahoma (2012). Via Amendment 46, Colorado tried to follow suit and ban affirmative action in 2008 (The Associated Press, 2008). However, the Amendment was not supported by the then Governor Bill Ritter, and nor was it supported by the then Mayor of Denver John Hickenlooper. It was also not supported by three prominent and well-respected men's college basketball coaches. Consequentially, the measure was voted down and never materialized. Florida similarly banned affirmative action in 1999 and implemented a neutral race program. Labeled the "Talented Twenty" program, applicants who graduate in the top 20 percent of their class in the state of Florida, complete the certain required course, and take the SAT or ACT were guaranteed admission to a state college or university. The state of California soon followed with a similar policy, termed the "Eligibility in the Local Context" program in 2001. This policy provides assured applicants who graduate in the top 4 percent of their classes access to the states' universities and colleges. In direct response to the 1996 *Hopwood* decision, Texas moved to a system where the top 10 percent of students in a graduating class would gain acceptance to any public college or university. Like other states, its ban on the use of race has been lauded as a race-neutral alternative putting justice and fairness back into the admissions decision process.

Cokorinos (2007) posed that the courts have served as the primary arena for the fight against affirmative action in higher education. Opponents have poured many resources into defeating the policy in the courts, with four cases reaching the Supreme Court. As suggested earlier, success for the opponents of affirmative action may become much easier in future

Supreme Court cases with the successful blocking of former President Obama's justice nominee Merrick Garland and the surprise election of Donald Trump who successfully nominated conservatives Neil Gorsuch and Brett Kavanaugh to the Supreme Court. The Court continues to be even more conservative-leaning, and thus, civil rights laws in general and affirmative action in particular will be on the proverbial chopping block (Jayakumar et al, 2015). Kavanaugh replaced retiring Supreme Court Justice Anthony Kennedy, and seems to hold an anti-affirmative action perspective. Kavanaugh will also invariably cast a critical vote in the next affirmative action case. While Kennedy was considered a conservative Justice, he supported the use of affirmative action and fell on the side of his more liberal counterparts in the *Fisher II* case.

Clearly, the political and legal winds are turning against affirmative action. And this trend does not seem to be easing up as we get further away from the 1960s Civil Rights Movement. It is also clear that decades of backlash by white conservative elites sufficiently crippled affirmative action as a viable ameliorative policy. Furthermore, and more telling, the anti-affirmative action rhetoric, which will be discussed further below, has turned the policy into a call to arms for conservatives rather than a way to minimize the disadvantage felt by marginalized groups. In terms of legal fights, there is one prominent case against Harvard University currently winding its way through the court circuits that could eventually spell the end for affirmative action in higher education (Jacobs, 2014). Given the increased conservative bent of the Supreme Court and the uptick in negative rhetoric against the policy, this case could very well end the use of affirmative action in higher education for good.

## Harvard University: The surprising argument against affirmative action

While many of the arguments are old, the new case against affirmative action in higher education has a new angle, yet with similar ideas. This could possibly be the perfect way to finally bring the era of affirmative action to an abrupt end. Harvard's admissions policy is quite similar to that of other elite universities in the sense that it takes a more holistic approach, where race is used as a factor in the admissions process. Consequently, because of the overlap with policies from other elite universities, a defeat for Harvard's admissions policy could mean a bigger take-down of these schools and how they implement affirmative action to ensure diversity. Indeed, Yale is currently under investigation for its use of race in admissions from the Department of Justice and the Office of Civil

Rights of the Department of Education. In defending their admissions policy, Yale President Peter Salovey wrote in an email that "I write now to state unequivocally that Yale does not discriminate in admissions against Asian Americans or any other racial or ethnic group ... and to affirm our unwavering commitment to diversity as a pillar of this university" (as cited in Mariwala and Park, 2018).

Interestingly, and quite divergent from the typical strategy, the current argument against Harvard poses that affirmative action is unfair because it discriminates against Asian Americans. By focusing on the plight of Asian Americans, the opponents redirect the argument away from whites as victims to another group that has a history of being discriminated against yet tends to have excellent academic credentials. The tactic may very well work—to take the focus away from whites as they are less sympathetic and place it on Asian Americans who many consider more sympathetic. This may be a dangerous ploy, however, as the inclusion of more Asian Americans, who have superior standardized scores than other groups, including whites, may reduce the number of seats available for everyone. Past social science research supports this idea. While this is a new angle, the Harvard lawsuit rehashes old arguments of justice and fairness that pervade affirmative action debates. It is also not surprising that early arguments surrounding this case bring a threat to these principles into the debate.

The Harvard lawsuit was initially filed in 2014 by Edward Blum. His name should sound familiar as he is the architect of the *Fisher* cases and countless other attacks on affirmative action. As discussed in Chapters 1 and 6, Blum has manufactured several affirmative action battles that typically pit a white candidate against a university. In these cases, the white candidate is typically a good citizen with competitive grades, claiming that the university discriminated against them based on their race, a violation of the Equal Protection Clause of the 14th Amendment. These arguments almost always ignore the evidence that other better qualified white candidates were also not admitted for various reasons. They also invariably take a color-blind approach and omit discussion of the history of racism and discrimination in the US higher education system, and how that continues to hurt minority students today. In this latest case in particular, Blum created an advocacy group interestingly named "Students for Fair Admissions" (SFFA), and solicited several Asian American student applicants who had recently been rejected by Harvard who maintained impressive academic credentials and who felt they may have been discriminated against because of their race (Biskupic, 2018). The lawsuit against Harvard has now reached the US District Court, one step closer to the Supreme Court. This case is noteworthy because research typically shows that Asian Americans score higher than whites and other minority groups on a standardized test, yet are underrepresented at Harvard. Recently released records from the university showed that scores were indeed higher for Asian Americans; however, the holistic approach used to decide entrance led to lower scores elsewhere and thus, lower admissions.

## What we saw: Lobbying, framing and the future of affirmative action

### Lobbying participants

There are three distinct yet quite positive observations for affirmative action and its advocates that we observed in the analyses. First, supporters authored the majority of briefs written to the *Gratz/Grutter* and *Fisher* cases by a considerable amount; opponents were clearly in the minority in lobbying the Supreme Court in these cases. That is to say, more supporters used their resources to fight for the policy than opponents. This is a positive sign for the future fight against affirmative action as supporters are stepping up and fighting the fight for an ameliorative policy. While the manifest function of amicus briefs is to provide novel insights into a case, a latent function is to provide the Justices with ideas of the level of support or opposition among the public for the issue at hand (Entman et al, 2009). If this is indeed true, it is clear that the public is more interested in maintaining affirmative action policies in higher education. This effort is sure to be felt by the Justices ruling on future affirmative action Supreme Court cases, as we doubt this level of interest will wane.

Second, another positive sign for affirmative action advocates is that the supporting authors who wrote briefs for the Court tended to be a heterogeneous blend. They often included coalitions of advocacy groups, universities, social science organizations, universities and colleges, students, civil rights organizations, groups of concerned social scientists or professors, college alumni, and state and federal legislators across the US. It was clear that individuals and groups of varying types and relationships with the policy wanted to see it implemented. A third positive sign relates to the second observation. Individuals and groups directly connected to higher education, including students, professors, colleges universities, and administrators, were well represented in this heterogeneous array of supporters. Thus, those most closely tied to the education system are putting up a strong fight to keep a controversial policy in place. They indeed see the legal fight over affirmative action as a matter of social justice, and the policy as an important mechanism to ensure it for marginalized groups. Such a representation, in our eyes, is quite profound and speaks to the level of support and concern felt by a host of individuals and groups that see value in affirmative action and diversity in higher education. It would be surprising to us if the Justices in future cases did not feel the overall weight of support expressed by a diverse body of individuals and groups lobbying the Court using amicus briefs, and have a stake in the implementation of affirmative action in higher education.

On a related note, while a majority of supporters came from an eclectic group of interested citizens, politicians, schools, and states, only a minority of briefs were authored by advocacy groups (mainly SIGs). This can be viewed positively or negatively. On a positive note, it is abundantly clear that individuals in support of affirmative action were interested citizens representing various domains of academia. On a negative note, to a certain extent advocacy groups reflect an organized attempt to support or oppose various social policies relevant to an ideological perspective, and have gained more and more power over the past few decades in the political process. The lack of input from organized interest groups that receive significant funding from wealthy individuals and foundations may highlight the lack of economic support for proponents, which may prove important in the future fight against affirmative action. James McGann (2007) noted that liberal think tanks are playing catchup in terms of matching the organizational support and strategies issued by conservatives.

Such a wide variety of supporters becomes quite notable once contrasted with opponents who lobbied against affirmative action at this level. The primary observation that calls for a broader explanation is that a clear majority of opponents were advocacy groups. Moreover, the majority of these advocacy groups were think tanks. In Chapter 4, we described the insidious roles these groups play in the war of ideas waged in the social and political worlds. What this means for the broader fight against affirmative action is not exactly clear, but it does not bode well for those who support the democratic process that concerns itself with the role of individuals in making a change. We argue that because think tanks (and, to a certain extent, SIGs) have been characterized as "guns for hire" in the political world, the fight has been waged almost exclusively by elite whites who have access to resources. Indeed, looking back at Chapter 4, advocacy think tanks are headed, or at least supported, by elite conservative whites who are pressing their political agendas using their economic and political resources and connections. Cokorinos (2003) argued that while this movement to defeat civil rights initiatives began almost immediately after the Civil Rights Act was passed in the 1960s, it gained traction during the Reagan presidency, and was only strengthened by the younger Bush administration in the early 2000s. Herbert Blumer (1958) sounded the alarm regarding these groups as they could reach the masses and produce the narratives consumed by the general public. Accordingly, we argue that our data support the notion that the death of affirmative action is being ushered in by only a small number of elite whites rather than some grassroots uprising. We do not see this changing under the Trump administration.

The last point we make concerning the authors of these briefs is not so different than the point just made. Looking at the individuals and groups we label as "other entities" who wrote anti-affirmative action briefs reveals similar findings. While supporters were represented by a wide variety of elite individuals, states, schools, and students, this is not the case for opponents. The individuals (not advocacy groups) who wrote opposing briefs were represented by just a few elite political actors, such as Ward Connerly, Gail Herriott, Richard Sander, and Stuart Taylor Jr, to name a few, who seem to be pressing conservative agendas. This is especially true of Ward Connerly, a conservative political activist associated with the conservative think tank American Civil Rights Institute (ACRI). Connerly was also instrumental in Californian Proposition 209 that prohibited the use of race and gender preferences in state hiring as well as a similar campaign in the state of Michigan. With that being said, these opponents are quite homogeneous (both advocacy groups and individuals), and do not match the rich diversity found in supporters. Such a finding provides support for the above argument, that the battle being waged against affirmative action is being led by elite conservative whites who oppose civil rights initiatives.

## Racialized Framing

The primary purpose of this project was to lay out the primary "frames of communication" used in the fight for and against affirmative action in the 21st century. We focused on the debate occurring in the highest court in the land, the Supreme Court. As described below, and as described in previous chapters, we argue that supporters and opponents use multiple frames to make their arguments. In particular, the arguments made on both sides were dominated by color-blind frames, as described by Eduardo Bonilla-Silva (2018), and threat frames, as discussed by Herbert Blumer (1958). In this sense, we draw from prominent sociological theory to explain how and exactly why these individuals and groups make the arguments they are making. While focusing on opponent arguments in particular, we also provide our theoretical framework to describe how color-blind and threat frames are used concomitantly to minimize race and active racial animosity in the same breath in an attempt to finally kill affirmative action as an ameliorative policy in higher education. We termed this tactic *Racialized Framing*, and pose that such a complicated framing technique is necessary for these groups to racialize the arguments without using racist arguments in a society that is supposed to be post-race. We indeed found this to be the case.

What is the purpose of using both color-blind and threat frames in the same arguments? We argue that this is intentional. Opponents who are viewed by many as social authorities attempt to use a slippery framing technique to both minimize the discussion of persistent racial discrimination faced by non-whites and simultaneously activate notions of group threat for whites. We argue that threat is used to produce an emotional response (eg, fear) among white Americans that another more undeserving and non-white group is attempting to gain resources they believe inherently belongs to them above all others. In this case, it is African Americans who have a unique place in the history of the US. By "slippery," we mean these authors are attempting to feign real concern for justice and fairness using vague abstract liberal language while also attempting to slip in frames that have nothing to do with fairness. These frames have everything to do with the maintenance of group positioning, with whites retaining the dominant position and corresponding resources. In this light, by combining frames that minimize and redirect, the authors attempt to make their arguments seem neutral and even benign. We pose that they are anything but benign.

The role of threat in producing prejudice was described by Blumer's group positioning model (1958). Blumer identified four basic types of feelings developed by members of the dominant group over time. First, dominant group members develop feelings of superiority relative to subordinate groups. Second, these members develop feelings that out-group members are somehow alien or different than themselves. Lawrence Bobo and Mia Tuan (2006) posed that these two feelings are akin to feelings associated with traditional racial prejudiced. Third, the dominant group members develop feelings of proprietary claim over valued resources, including property, jobs, and schools. Finally, the dominant group members develop concerns that out-group members are threatening those very resources they believe are solely theirs. It is the latter two feelings that form the basis of racial prejudice. Accordingly, we argue that threat, as used in these briefs, produces racial prejudice in the audience. In this case, the direct audience is the Justices of the Supreme Court. In so doing, we argue that these authors are intentionally or unintentionally (this doesn't really matter) tapping into key ingredients (eg, group threat) that act to produce and reproduce racial prejudice in the US. And in doing so, they contribute to the racist system that pervades the US by killing off a mechanism used by elite colleges and universities to ensure diversity and improve the chances of social mobility for non-whites.

## The diversity problem

It is not surprising that the authors of support briefs relied heavily on the abstract liberal argument of diversity. As noted above, past Court rulings have inputted the diversity rationale into the debate that persists in the most current cases dealing with affirmative action. Supporters have to take seriously the role and impact of diversity in higher education. Indeed, supporters opined about the various benefits of diversity and the role affirmative action plays into achieving those goals. In line with other scholars, we pose that while the notion of diversity within the academy seems noble, the diversity movement in the courts and higher education is problematic and will ultimately lead to the desolution of affirmative action for a few reasons.

One, the diversity argument moves the debate regarding the need for affirmative action in higher education away from persistent racism and discrimination to diversity (Collins, 2011a, b; Herring and Henderson, 2011; Moore and Bell, 2011). Thus, diversity becomes the soup of the day and the reason for maintaining programs to benefit minorities and other marginalized groups. While diversity may be a good thing, pretending systemic racial inequality and persistent discrimination no longer exists eventually leaves our understanding of race and persistent racial inequality incomplete. This paradox is why several critical race scholars describe the diversity initiative as color-blind and potentially harmful to students of color. Wendy Moore and Joyce Bell (2011, p 602) stated succinctly that, "Nearly the instant that 'diversity' in education became a rationale by the [Supreme] Court as an interest so compelling as to justify the use of race-conscious policies like affirmative action, the concept gets de-racialized; securely fitted into the color-blind sub-frame." They also pointed to a second problem with the diversity rationale. Justice Lewis Powell's diversity rationale made any type of diversity (even diversity of thought) open to consideration in higher education. This line of argument allows opponents to further marginalize the insidious history of racism and discrimination in the US, inherently eroding the necessity to address historic and continued racial discrimination.

Another problem with the diversity rationale is that some scholars argue that administrators in higher education latch on to the notion of diversity without any real commitment to producing real results. Diversity becomes a marketing mechanism to parade to future employees, faculty, and students. While diversity is championed, no real initiatives are put in place to account for the unique experiences of non-white students. And without applying any real genuine attention to persistent issues of racism and discrimination and to improving the lived experiences of these students in higher education, diversity becomes an empty promise and benefits no one except administration, who use it for political gain. With that being said, affirmative action and the diversity rationale are insufficient and highly problematic. Moore (2018, p 54) argues that the diversity rationale turned affirmative action into the "metaphorical equivalent of using a band-aid to stop the bleeding from an enormous, gaping wound."

## Final thoughts

As a productive ameliorative policy that can truly reduce inequality, the policy of affirmative action is no longer viable. The policy is dead. As argued by Moore (2018), affirmative action is relegated to a call to arms for conservative politicians, pundits, and citizens in opposition to a racial issue. By focusing on diversity, affirmative action in higher education has been reduced to a shadow of its former self with no bite and no ability to make lasting change. As we see in debates surrounding the most recent Supreme Court cases, elite conservatives and advocacy groups have fought vigorously to eliminate even the smallest (*a* factor, not *the* factor) attempt by colleges and universities to provide access to groups marginalized in the US. Given the state of race relations and political posturing we see today, there is no reason to believe this will change in the near future. As such, we now face a future of arguments where we have to pretend that systemic racism and discrimination do not pervade our society, and that race no longer predicts lived experiences.

# References

AALF (Asian American Legal Foundation) (2018) 'About Us.' Available from: www.asianamericanlegal.com/about-us/

AERA (American Educational Research Association) (2019) 'About AERA.' Available from: www.aera.net/About-AERA

AJC (American Jewish Committee) (2018) 'Who Are We.' Available from: www.ajc.org/whoweare

Alexander, M. (2012) *The New Jim Crow: Mass Incarceration in the Age of Color-Blindness*, New York: The New Press.

Allport, G. (1954) *The Nature of Prejudice*, New York: Addison-Wesley.

Alon, S. and Tienda, M. (2007) 'Diversity, opportunity, and the shifting meritocracy in higher education', *American Sociological Review*, 72(4): 487–511.

Arnwine, B.R. (2007) 'The Battle over Affirmative Action: Legal Challenges and Outlook', in T.N.U. League (ed) *The State of Black America 2007*, Silver Spring, MD: Beckham Publications Group, Inc, pp 159–72.

Associated Press, The (2008) 'Colorado voters reject affirmative action ban', November 7. Available from: www.denverpost.com/2008/11/07/colorado-voters-reject-affirmative-action-ban/

Backes, B. (2012) 'Do affirmative action bans lower minority college enrollment and attainment? Evidence from statewide bans', *Journal of Human Resources*, 47(2): 435–55.

Belyaeva, N. (2012) 'Analysts: "Consultants" or "independent policy actors"', *Politička Misao: časopis za politologiju*, 48(5): 125–40.

Berrey, E.C. (2011) 'Why diversity became orthodox in higher education, and how it changed the meaning of race on campus', *Critical Sociology*, 37(5), 573–96.

Berry, M.F. (1995) *Black Resistance/White Law: A History of Constitutional Racism in America*, Harmondsworth, UK: Penguin.

Bertrand, M. and Mullainathan, S. (2004) 'Are Emily and Greg more employable than Lakisha and Jamal? A field experiment on labor market discrimination', *American Economic Review*, 94(4): 991–1013.

Biskupic, J. (2018) 'Race case against Harvard moves forward', CNN Politics, April 10. Available from: https://edition.cnn.com/2018/04/10/politics/harvard-asian-american-students/index.html

Blume, G.H. and Long, M.C. (2014) 'Changes in levels of affirmative action in college admissions in response to statewide bans and judicial rulings', *Educational Evaluation and Policy Analysis*, 36(2): 228–52.

Blumer, H. (1958) 'Race prejudices as a sense of group position', *Pacific Sociological Review*, 1(1): 3–7.

Bobo, L. (1983) 'Whites' opposition to busing: Symbolic racism or realistic group conflict?', *Journal of Personality and Social Psychology*, 45(6): 1196–210.

Bobo, L. (1988) 'Group Conflict, Prejudice, and the Paradox of Contemporary Racial Attitudes', in P. Katz and D.A. Taylor (eds) *Eliminating Racism: Profiles in Controversy*, New York: Plenum Press, pp 85–109.

Bobo, L. (1998) 'Race, interests, and beliefs about affirmative action: Unanswered questions and new directions', *Behavioral Scientist*, 41(7): 985–1003.

Bobo, L. (2000) 'Race and Beliefs about Affirmative Action: Assessing the Effects of Interests, Group Threat, Ideology and Racism', in D.O. Sears, J. Sidanius and L. Bobo (eds) *Racialized Politics: The Debate about Racism in America*, Chicago, IL: The University of Chicago Press, pp 137–64.

Bobo, L. and Kluegel, J.R. (1993) 'Opposition to race-targeting: Self-interest, stratification ideology, or racial attitudes?', *American Sociological Review*, 58(4): 443–64.

Bobo, L. and Tuan, M. (2006) *Prejudice in Politics: Group Position, Public Opinion, and the Wisconsin Treaty Rights Dispute*, Cambridge, MA: Harvard University Press.

Bobo, L. and Zubrinsky, C.L. (1996) 'Attitudes on residential integration: Perceived status differences, mere in-group preference, or racial prejudice?', *Social Forces*, 74(3): 883–909.

Boden, A. (2013) 'PLF files amicus brief in Fisher v University of Texas.' Available from: https://pacificlegal.org/plf-files-amicus-brief-in-fisher-v-university-of-texas/

Bolick, C. (1988) *Changing course: Civil rights at the crossroads*, New Brunswick, NJ: Transaction Publishers.

Bonilla-Silva, E. (2018) *Racism without Racists: Color-Blind Racism and the Persistence of Racial Inequality in America* (5th edn), Lanham, MD: Rowman & Littlefield.

Bonilla-Silva, E. and Dietrich, D. (2011) 'The sweet enchantment of color-blind racism in Obamerica', *The ANNALS of the American Academy of Political and Social Science*, 634(1): 190–206.

Brader, T., Valentino, N.A. and Suhay, E. (2008) 'What triggers public opposition to immigration? Anxiety, group cues, and immigration threat', *American Journal of Political Science*, 52(4): 959–78.

Brown, S.K. and Hirschman, C. (2006) 'The end of affirmative action in Washington State and its impact on the transition from high school to college', *Sociology of Education*, 79(2): 106–30.

Burke, M. (2016) 'New frontiers in the study of color-blind racism: A materialist approach', *Social Currents*, 3: 103–9.

Bush, G.W. (2003) 'President Bush discusses Michigan Affirmative Action Case', The White House. Available from: https://georgewbush-whitehouse.archives.gov/news/releases/2003/01/20030115-7.html

Caldeira, G.A. and Wright, J.R. (1990) 'Amici curiae before the Supreme Court: Who participates, when, and how much?', *Journal of Politics*, 52(3): 782–806.

Carnevale, A.P. and Strohl, J. (2013) *Separate & Unequal: How Higher Education Reinforces the Intergenerational Reproduction of White Racial Privilege*, Washington, DC: Georgetown University. Available from: https://cew.georgetown.edu/cew-reports/separate-unequal/

Carter, J.S. (2005) 'Reassessing the effect of urbanism and regionalism: A comparison of different indicators of racial tolerance', *Sociation Today*, 3. Available from: www.ncsociology.org/sociationtoday/v32/urbanism.htm

Carter, J.S. and Carter, S.K. (2014) 'Place matters: The impact of place of residency on racial attitudes among regional and urban migrants', *Social Science Research*, 47: 165–77.

Carter, J.S. and Lippard, C. (2015) 'Group positioning, threat and immigration: The role of elite actors and interest groups in setting the "lines of discussion"', *Sociology of Race and Ethnicity*, 1(3): 394–408.

Carter, J.S., Lippard, C. and Baird, A.F. (2019) 'Veiled threat: Colorblind racism, group threat and affirmative action', *Social Problems*, 66(4): 503–18.

Carter, J.S., Corra, M., Carter, S.K. and McCrosky, R. (2014) 'The impact of place? A reassessment of the importance of the south in affecting beliefs about racial inequality', *Social Science Journal*, 51: 12–20.

Carter, J.S., Steelman, L., Mulkey, L. and Borch, C. (2005) 'When the rubber meets the road: The differential effects of urbanism and region on principle and implementation measures of racial tolerance', *Social Science Research*, 34: 408–425.

Cato Institute (2018) 'About CATO.' Available from: www.cato.org/about

Cellini, S.R. and Chaudhary, L. (2014) 'The labor market returns to a for-profit college education', *Economics of Education Review*, 43: 125–40.

Charmaz, K. (2006) *Constructing Grounded Theory: A Practical Guide through Qualitative Analysis*, London, UK: Sage Publications.

Chavez, L. (2008) *The Latino Threat: Constructing Immigrants, Citizens, and the Nation*, Stanford, CA: Stanford University Press.

Clawson, R.A., Strine IV, H.C.N. and Waltenburg, E.N. (2003) 'Framing Supreme Court decisions: The mainstream versus the Black press', *Journal of Black Studies*, 33(6): 784–800.

Cokorinos, L. (2003) *The Assault on Diversity: An Organized Challenge to Racial and Gender Justice*, Lanham, MD: Rowman & Littlefield.

Colburn, D.R., Young, C.E. and Yellen, V.M. (2008) 'Admissions and public higher education in California, Texas, and Florida: The post-affirmative action era', *InterActions: UCLA Journal of Education and Information Studies*, 4(1): 1–25.

Collins, S.M. (2011a) 'From affirmative action to diversity: Erasing inequality from organizational responsibility', *Critical Sociology*, 37(5): 517–20.

Collins, S.M. (2011b) 'Diversity in the post affirmative action labor market: A proxy for racial progress? ', *Critical Sociology*, 37(5), 521–40.

Collins Jr, P.M., Corley, P.C. and Hamner, J. (2015) 'The influence of amicus curiae briefs on US Supreme Court opinion content', *Law and Society Review*, 49(4): 917–44.

Creason, N. (2018) 'Think tanks: Blurred lines of fact, fiction, interest groups', The (Carlisle) Sentinel, January 20. Available from: www.apnews.com/45b4600efaf642b9b3dd90229e6b1810

Cunningham, T.J., Croft, J.B., Liu, Y., Lu, H., Eke, P.I. and Giles, W.H. (2017) 'Vital signs: Racial disparities in age-specific mortality among Blacks or African Americans—United States, 1999–2015', *MMWR: Morbidity and Mortality Weekly Review*, 66(17): 444–56. Available from: www.ncbi.nlm.nih.gov/pubmed/28472021

d'Souza, D. (1991) *Illiberal Education: The Politics of Race and Sex on Campus*, New York: The Free Press.

Denson, N. and Chang, M.J. (2009) 'Racial diversity matters: The impact of diversity-related student engagement and institutional context', *American Educational Research*, 46(2), 322–53.

de Vogue, A. (2017) 'How Gorsuch can transform the Supreme Court', CNN Politics, April 7. Available from: https://edition.cnn.com/2017/04/07/politics/gorsuch-transform-supreme-court/index.html

Doane, A.W. (2006) 'What is racism? Racial discourse and racial politics', *Critical Sociology*, 32(2–3): 255–74.

Doane, A.W. (2017) 'Beyond color-blindness: (Re)theorizing racial ideology', *Sociological Perspectives*, 60(5): 975–91.

Downey, D.B. and Condron, D.J. (2016) 'Fifty years since the Coleman Report: Rethinking the relationship between schools and inequality', *Sociology of Education*, 89(3): 207–20.

Druckman, J.N. (2001) 'On the limits of framing effects: Who can frame?', *Journal of Politics*, 63(4): 1017–66.

Du Bois, W.E.B. (ed) ([1935] 2017) *Black Reconstruction in America: Toward a History of the Part which Black Folk Played in the Attempt to Reconstruct Democracy in America*, New York: Routledge.

Edwards, G. (2016) 'Abigail Fisher: Affirmative action plaintiff "proud" of academic record', BBC News, July 29. Available from: www.bbc.co.uk/news/world-us-canada-36928990

Embrick, D. and Henricks, K. (2015) 'Two-faced-ism: Racism and how race discourse shapes classtalk and gendertalk', *Language Sciences*, 52: 165–75.

Entman, R.M. (1997) 'Manufacturing discord: Media in the affirmative action debate', *Harvard International Journal of Press/Politics*, 2(4): 39–59.

Entman, R.M., Matthes, J. and Pellicano, L. (2009) 'Nature, Sources, and Effects of News Framing', in K. Wahl-Jorgensen and T. Hanitzsch (eds) *The Handbook of Journalism Studies*, New York: Routledge, pp 175–90.

Epstein, L. and Knight, J. (2000) 'Piercing the beil: William J. Brennan's account of Regents of the University of California v. Bakke', *Yale Law and Policy Review*, 19: 341–79.

Fairclough, N. (1989) *Language and Power*, London, UK: Longman.

Farley, J.E. (2011). *Majority-Minority Relations* (6th edn), London, UK: Pearson.

Feagin, J.R. (2006) *Systemic Racism: A Theory of Oppression*, New York: Routledge.

Feagin, J.R. (2010a) *The White Racial Frame: Centuries of Racial Framing and Counter-Framing*, New York: Routledge.

Feagin, J.R. (2010b) *Racist America: Roots, Current Realities, and Future Reparations*, New York: Routledge.

Foran, C. and Biskupic, J. (2018) 'Where Brett Kavanaugh stands on key issues', CNN Politics, October 6. Available from: https://edition.cnn.com/2018/07/09/politics/kavanaugh-on-the-issues/index.html

Fryberg, S.A., Stephens, N.M., Covarrubias, R., Markus, H.R., et al (2012) 'How the media frames the immigration debate: The critical role of location and politics', *Analyses of Social Issues and Public Policy*, 12: 96–112.

Fuchs, C. (2018) 'Asian-American groups take opposing sides in Harvard affirmative action case.' Available from: www.nbcnews.com/news/asian-america/asian-american-groups-take-opposing-sides-harvard-affirmative-action-case-n897276

Gallagher, C.A. (2013) 'Playing the white ethnic card: Using ethnic identity to deny contemporary racism', in A.W. Doane and E. Bonilla-Silva (eds) *White Out*, London, UK: Routledge, pp 147–60.

Gallup (2018) 'Race relations'. Available from: https://news.gallup.com/poll/1687/race-relations.aspx

Gamson, W.A. and Modigliani, A. (1987) 'The Changing Culture of Affirmative Action', in R.G. Braungart and M.M. Braungart (eds) *Research in Political Sociology*, Vol 3, Greenwich, CT: JAI Press, pp 137–77.

Gangl, M. (2006) 'Scar effects of unemployment: An assessment of institutional complementarities', *American Sociological Review*, 71(6): 986–1013.

Glazer, N. (1987) *Affirmative Discrimination: Ethnic Inequality and Public Policy*, Boston, MA: Harvard University Press.

Goffman, E. (1974) *Frame Analysis: An Essay on the Organization of Experience*, Cambridge, MA: Harvard University Press.

González, B.E. and Sweeney, K.A. (2010) 'The color of affirmative action: Exploring contemporary racial ideologies through public responses to affirmative action policies in Michigan', *The Journal of Race & Policy*, 6(1): 105–21.

Greeley, A.M. and Sheatsley, P.B. (1971) 'Attitudes toward racial integration', *Scientific American*, 225(6): 13–19.

Green, D.O.N. (2004) 'Fighting the battle for racial diversity: A case study of Michigan's institutional responses to Gratz and Grutter', *Educational Policy*, 18(5): 733–51.

Green, E.L., Apuzzo, M. and Benner, K. (2018) 'Trump officials reverse Obama's policy on affirmative action in schools', *The New York Times*, July 3. Available from: www.nytimes.com/2018/07/03/us/politics/trump-affirmative-action-race-schools.html

Grossman, G. and Helpman, E. (2001) *Special Interest Politics*, Boston, MA: Massachusetts Institute of Technology.

Gryphon, M. (2005) *The Affirmative Action Myth*, Policy Analysis No 540, April 6, Washington, DC: Cato Institute.

Guillermo, E. (2018) 'Tuesday's vote, our Asian American racial identity, and the Harvard case.' Asian American Legal Defense and Education Fund. Available from: www.aaldef.org/blog/emil-guillermo-tuesday-s-vote-our-asian-american-racial-identity-and-the-harvard-case/

Gurin, P., Dey, E., Hurtado, S. and Gurin, G. (2002) 'Diversity and higher education: Theory and impact on educational outcomes', *Harvard Educational Review*, 72(3): 330–67.

Haveman, R. and Smeeding, T. (2006) 'The role of higher education in social mobility', *The Future of Children*, 16: 125–50.

Herring, C. and Henderson, L. (2011) 'From affirmative action to diversity: Toward a critical diversity perspective', *Critical Sociology*, 38(5): 629–43.

Herrnson, P.S., Deering, C.J. and Wilcox, C. (2012) *Interest Groups Unleashed*, Washington, DC: Sage.

Ho, C. (2012) 'The Washington duo behind Texas affirmative action case', *The Washington Post*, March 4. Available from: www.washingtonpost.com/business/capitalbusiness/the-washington-duo-behind-texas-affirmative-action-case/2012/02/28/gIQAEfsrqR_story.html?noredirect=on

Hout, M., Levanon, A. and Cumberworth, E. (2011) 'Job Loss and Unemployment', in D.B. Grusky, B. Western and C. Wimer (eds) *The Great Recession*, New York: Sage Publications, pp 59–81.

Hyman, H.H. and Sheatsley, P.B. (1956) 'Attitudes toward desegregation', *Scientific American*, 195: 35–9

Hyman, H.H. and Sheatsley, P.B. (1964) 'Attitudes toward desegregation', *Scientific American*, 211(1): 16–23.

Jackman, M.R. (1994) *The Velvet Glove*, Berkeley, CA: University of California Press.

Jacobs, P. (2014) 'Harvard is being accused of discriminating against Asians', *Business Insider*, November 17. Available from: www.businessinsider.com/harvard-and-unc-chapel-hill-sued-over-affirmative-action-policies-2014-11?r=US&IR=T

Jayakumar, U.M., Garces, L.M. and Fernandez, F. (eds) (2015) *Affirmative Action and Racial Equity: Considering the Fisher Case to Forge the Path Ahead*, New York: Routledge.

Jones, J.M. (2016) 'Americans still say postsecondary education very important', Gallup, April 12. Available from: https://news.gallup.com/poll/190580/americans-say-postsecondary-education-important.aspx

Jones, J.M., Schmitt, J. and Wilson, V. (2018) '50 years after the Kerner Commission: African Americans are better off in many ways but are still disadvantaged by racial inequality', Economic Policy Institute, February 26. Available from: www.epi.org/publication/50-years-after-the-kerner-commission/

Kahlenberg, R.D. (2008) 'Barack Obama and affirmative action', Inside Higher Ed, May 12. Available from: www.insidehighered.com/views/2008/05/12/barack-obama-and-affirmative-action

Kellough, J.E. (2006) *Understanding Affirmative Action: Politics, Discrimination, and the Search for Justice*, Washington, DC: Georgetown University Press.

Kinder, D.R. and Sanders, L.M. (1996) *Divided by Color: Racial Politics and Democratic Ideals*, Chicago, IL: The University of Chicago Press.

Kollman, K. (1998) *Outside Lobbying: Public Opinion and Interest Group Strategies*, Princeton, NJ: Princeton University Press.

Kozol, J. (2005) *The Shame of the Nation: The Restoration of Apartheid Schooling in America*, New York: Broadway Books.

Kozol, J. (2012) *Savage Inequalities: Children in America's Schools*, New York: Broadway Books.

Krysan, M. and Crowder, K. (2017) *Cycle of Segregation: Social Processes and Residential Stratification*, New York: Russell Sage Foundation.

Legal Momentum (2019) 'About Us.' Available from: www.legalmomentum. org/about-us

Levine, M.E. and Crimmins, E.M. (2014) 'Evidence of accelerated aging among African Americans and its implications for mortality', *Social Science & Medicine*, 118: 27–32.

Liptak, A. (2016) 'Supreme Court upholds affirmative action at University of Texas', *The New York Times*, June 23.

Lowery, D. (2007) 'Why do organized interests lobby? A multi-goal, multi-context theory of lobbying', *Polity*, 39(1): 29–54.

Luther, C.A. and Miller, M.M. (2005) 'Framing of the 2003 US–Iraq war demonstrations: An analysis of news and partisan texts', *Journalism & Mass Communication Quarterly*, 82(1): 78–96.

Mariwala, J. and Park, A. (2018) 'Yalies stand by affirmative action as Harvard admissions trial begins', Yale News, October 16. Available from: https://yaledailynews.com/blog/2018/10/16/yalies-stand-by-affirmative-action-as-harvard-admissions-trial-begins/

Mayer, J. (2016) *Dark Money: The Hidden History of the Billionaires Behind the Rise of the Radical Right*, New York: Doubleday.

McGann, J.G. (2007) *Think Tanks and Policy Advice in the United States: Academics, Advisors, and Advocates*, New York: Routledge.

McGuire, K. (1993) *The Supreme Court Bar: Legal Elites in the Washington Community*, Charlottesville, VA: The University of Virginia Press.

Medvetz, T. (2012) *Think Tanks in America*, Chicago, IL: The University of Chicago Press.

Mencimer, S. (2015) 'Justice Scalia suggests Blacks belong at "slower" colleges', Mother Jones, December 9. Available from: www.motherjones. com/politics/2015/12/justice-scalia-suggests-blacks-belong-slower-colleges-fisher-university-texas/

Mills, C.W. (2017) *Black Rights/White Wrongs: The Critique of Racial Liberalism*, Oxford, UK: Oxford University Press.

Moore, W.L. (2018) 'Maintaining White supremacy by blocking affirmative action', *Contexts*, 17(1): 54–9.

Moore, W.L. and Bell, J.M. (2011) 'Maneuvers of whiteness: "Diversity" as a mechanism of retrenchment in the affirmative action discourse', *Critical Sociology*, 37(5): 597–613.

Myrdal, G. (1944) *An American Dilemma: The Negro Problem and Modern Democracy*, Vol 1, New York: Harper & Row.

NAACP (National Association for the Advancement of Colored People) (2018) 'What We Do.' Available from: www.naacp.org/about-us

National Center for Health Statistics (2017) *Health, United States 2016: With Chartbook on Long-Term Trends in Health*, Hyattsville, MD. Available from: www.ncbi.nlm.nih.gov/pubmed/28910066

Neville, H.A., Lilly, R.L., Duran, G., Lee, R. and Browne, L. (2000) 'Construction and initial validation of the color-blind racial attitudes scale (CoBRAS)', *Journal of Counseling Psychology*, 47: 59–70.

Newport, F. (2016) 'Most in US oppose colleges considering race in admissions', Gallup, July 8. Available from: https://news.gallup.com/poll/193508/oppose-colleges-considering-race-admissions.aspx

Norris, P., Kern, M. and Just, M. (eds) (2003) *Framing Terrorism: The News Media, the Government, and the Public*, New York: Routledge.

Omi, M. and Winant, H. (2015) *Racial Formation in the United States* (3rd edn), New York: Routledge.

Orfield, G. (ed) (2001) *Diversity Challenged: Evidence on the Impact of Affirmative Action*, Cambridge, MA: Harvard Education Publishing Group, Harvard Graduate School of Education.

Owens, A. (2018) 'Income segregation between school districts and inequality in students' achievement', *Sociology of Education*, 91(1): 1–27.

Pérez, R. (2017) 'Racism without hatred? Racist humor and the myth of "colorblindness"', *Sociological Perspectives*, 60(5): 956–74.

Pierce, J. (2012) *Racing for Innocence: Whiteness, Gender, and the Backlash against Affirmative Action*, Stanford, CA: Stanford University Press.

PLF (Pacific Legal Foundation) (2014) 'Racial preferences are set for extinction.' Available from: https://pacificlegal.org/racial-preferences-set-extinction/

PLF (2018) 'Cases.' Available from: https://pacificlegal.org/cases/

Renfro, C.L., Duran, A., Stephan, W.G. and Clason, D.L. (2006) 'The role of threat in attitudes toward affirmative action and its beneficiaries', *Journal of Applied Social Psychology*, 36(1): 41–74.

Richardson, J.D. and Lancendorfer, K.M. (2004) 'Framing affirmative action: The influence of race on newspaper editorial responses to the University of Michigan cases', *Harvard International Journal of Press/Politics*, 9(4): 74–94.

Rohlinger, D.A. (2015) *Abortion Politics, Mass Media, and Social Movements in America*, Cambridge: Cambridge University Press.

Roosevelt Thomas Jr, R. (1990) 'From affirmative action to affirming diversity', *Harvard Business Review*, March–April. Available from: https://hbr.org/1990/03/from-affirmative-action-to-affirming-diversity

Sander, R. and Taylor Jr, S. (2012) *Mismatch: How Affirmative Action Hurts Students It's Intended to Help, and Why Universities Won't Admit It*, New York: Basic Books.

Sanders, B. and Adams, F. (2003) *Alienable Rights: The Exclusion of African Americans in a White Man's Land, 1619–2000*, New York: HarperCollins Publishers.

Savage, C. (2017) 'Justice Dept to take on affirmative action in college admissions', *The New York Times*, August 1.

Scanlan, L.C. (1996) 'Hopwood v Texas: A backward look at affirmative action in education', *New York University Law Review*, 71: 1580–1633.

Scheer, J. (2018) 'The American Jewish affirmative action about-bace: Why major Jewish organizations switched sides in the affirmative action debate', Tablet, July 31. Available from: www.tabletmag.com/jewish-news-and-politics/267470/the-american-jewish-affirmative-action-about-face

Schrock, D., Holden, D. and Reid, L. (2004) 'Creating emotional resonance: Interpersonal emotion work and motivational framing in a transgender community', *Social Problems*, 51(1): 61–81.

Schuman, H. and Bobo, L. (1988) 'Survey-based experiments on white racial attitudes toward residential integration', *American Journal of Sociology*, 94(2): 273–99.

Schuman, H., Steeh, C., Bobo, L. and Krysan, M. (1997) *Racial Attitudes in America: Trends and Interpretations*, Cambridge, MA: Harvard University Press.

Sedler, R.A. (1977) 'Racial preference, reality and the constitution: Bakke v. Regents of the University of California', *Santa Clara Law Review*, 17(2): 329–84.

Shapiro, T.M. (2004) *The Hidden Cost of Being African American: How Wealth Perpetuates Inequality*, New York: Oxford University Press.

Shelton, J.E. and Coleman, M.N. (2009) 'After the storm: How race, class, and immigration concerns influenced beliefs about the Katrina evacuees', *Social Science Quarterly*, 90(3): 480–96.

Smith, J.M. (2012) 'The party of exclusion: The Republican Party's race problem and Strom Thurmond's legacy', *Daily Beast*.

Snow, D.A. and Benford, R.D. (1988) 'Ideology, frame resonance, and participant mobilization', *International Social Movement Research*, 1(1): 197–217.

Source Watch (2017) 'Pacific Legal Foundation.' Available from: www.sourcewatch.org/index.php?title=Pacific_Legal_Foundation

Source Watch (2018) 'Cato Institute.' Available from: www.sourcewatch.org/index.php?title=Cato_Institute

Sowell, T. (2003) 'Damaging admissions: Increasing faculty diversity', *Capitalism Magazine*, February 8. Available from: www.capitalismmagazine. com/2003/02/damaging-admissions-increasing-faculty-diversity/

Spriggs, J.F. and Wahlbeck, P.J. (1997) 'Amicus curiae and the role of information at the Supreme Court', *Political Research Quarterly*, 50(2): 365–86.

Steeh, C. and Schuman, H. (1992) 'Young white adults: Did racial attitudes change in the 1980s?', *American Journal of Sociology*, 98(2): 340–67.

Stefoff, R. (2006) *The Bakke Case: Challenge to Affirmative Action*, Tarrytown, NY: Marshall Cavendish Benchmark.

Sumerau, J.E. and Grollman, E.A. (2018) 'Obscuring oppression: Racism, cissexism, and the persistence of social inequality', *Sociology of Race and Ethnicity*, 4(3): 322–37.

Sweeney, K.A. and González, B.E. (2008) 'Affirmative Action Never Helped Me: Public Response to Ending Affirmative Action in Michigan', in C.A. Gallagher (ed) *Racism in Post-Race America: New Theories, New Directions*, Chapel Hill, NC: Social Forces Publishing, pp 135–48.

Synnott, M.G. (2004) 'The evolving diversity rationale in university admissions: From Regents v. Bakke to the University of Michigan cases', *Cornell Law Review*, 90(2): 463–504.

Taylor, D.G., Sheatsley, P.B. and Greeley, A.M. (1978) 'Attitudes toward racial integration', *Scientific American*, 238(6): 42–9.

Thernstrom, S. and Thernstrom, A. (1997) *America in Black and White: One Nation Indivisible*, New York: Simon & Schuster.

Thrall, A.T. (2007) 'A bear in the woods? Threat framing and the marketplace of values', *Security Studies*, 16: 452–88.

Tuch, S.A. and Hughes, M. (2011) 'Whites' racial policy attitudes in the twenty-first century: The continuing significance of racial resentment', *The Annals of the American Academy of Political and Social Science*, 634: 134–52.

van Laar, C., Levin, S., Sinclair, S. and Sidanius, J. (2005) 'The effect of university roommate contact on ethnic attitudes and behavior', *Journal of Experimental Social Psychology*, 41(4): 329–45.

Visser, N. (2015) '"#StayMadAbby" is Black students' perfect response to Justice Scalia', *Huff Post*, October 12. Available from: www. huffingtonpost.co.uk

Walsh, K.R. (2004) 'Color-blind racism in Grutter and Gratz', *Boston College World Law Journal*, 24(2): 443–67.

Watkins, M. (2016) 'US Supreme Court upholds UT-Austin's affirmative action system', *The Texas Tribune*, June 23. Available from: www. texastribune.org/2016/06/23/us-supreme-court-rules-fisher-case-involving-ut-au/

Western, B., Bloome, D. and Percheski, C. (2008) 'Inequality among American families with children, 1975 to 2005', *American Sociological Review*, 73(6): 903–20.

Williams, D.R., Mohammed, S.A., Leavell, J. and Collins, C. (2010) 'Race, socioeconomic status and health: Complexities, ongoing challenges and research opportunities', *The Annals of the New York Academy of Sciences*, 1186(1): 69–101.

Wise, T. (2005) *Affirmative Action: Racial Preference in Black and White*, New York: Routledge.

Zamani-Gallaher, E.M., Green, D.O.N., Brown II, M.C. and Stovall, D.O. (2009) *The Case for Affirmative Action on Campus: Concepts of Equity, Considerations for Practice*, Sterling, VA: Stylus Publishing, LLC.

Zuberi, T. (2001) *Thicker than Blood: How Racial Statistics Lie*, Minneapolis, MN: University of Minnesota Press.

Zuberi, T. and Bonilla-Silva, E. (eds) (2008) *White Logic, White Methods: Racism and Methodology*, Lanham, MD: Rowman & Littlefield.

Zubrinsky, C.L. and Bobo, L. (1996) 'Prismatic metropolis: Race and residential segregation in the city of the angels', *Social Science Research*, 25(4): 335–74.

# Index

References to figures and tables are in *italics*

14th Amendment *see* Equal Protection Clause

## A

abstract liberalism 9, 121, 122
  affirmative action opponents 104,
    128–31, *137*, *152*, *168*, 168–70,
    173, *173*, 179, 184–5, *185*, 191,
    199
  affirmative action supporters 153–4,
    *162*, 163–4, 166–7, *167*, 176,
    177, 190, 200–1
  *see also* diversity rationale; Equal
    Protection Clause
academic freedom 61, *139*, 140, 144
Academic Index (Texas) 157, 158
acceptance, promotion of 49
activating race 9, 10, 14
advocacy groups/actors (general)
    67–113
  affirmative action opponents 70–1,
    98–112, 190, 191–4, 195, 196–8
  affirmative action supporters 70–1,
    80–98, 111, 112, 190–1, 196–7
  amicus curiae briefs 80–111
  amount of support 196–7
  case studies 93–8, 103–11
  coalitions of 111
  funding of 71, 75, 77
  and group positioning theory
    79–80
  leadership of 75, 93–4, 95, 101
  primary actors 69–71

rise of 12, 71–6
and rise of conservative agenda
    76–9
types of 72–4
  *see also individual court cases and
    individual organizations/actors*
affirmative action (general)
  framing of 7–10
  future of 189, 193–7, 201
  and higher education 22–6
  ideological divide 26–34
  and politics 26–30, 192–4
  the study 10–14
affirmative action opponents
  abstract liberalism 104, 128–31,
    *137*, *152*, *168*, 168–70, 173,
    *173*, 179, 184–5, *185*, 191, 199
  advocacy groups/actors 70–1,
    98–112, 190, 191–4, 195, 196–8
  amicus curiae briefs 98–111
  *Bakke* case 56
  case studies of advocacy groups
    103–11
  color-blind frames 47, 77, 78–9,
    128–38, 167–75, 184–5, 190–1,
    198–9
  diversity rationale 32, 62, 108, *128*,
    129, 132–4, 148–9, 153–4, *168*,
    170, 172–3, 189–90
  *Fisher* cases 2–3, 30–3, *99–100*,
    101, *102*, 103, 108, 110, 161–2,
    167–74, 178–86
  future success of 193–4
  *Gratz* and *Grutter* cases *99–100*,
    *102*, 103, 108, 123–4, 128–38,
    142–54

affirmative action opponents (contd.)
Harvard University case 195–6
homogenous nature of 197–8
ideological divide 27, 31–4
minimization of racism *128*, 128–9,
132–4, *137*, *152*, *168*, 170, 173,
*185*
mismatch theory 32–4
neoliberalism 32
past discrimination, remedying 106,
*128*, 150, 191
paternalism 8, *128*, 134–8, *143*,
149–51, *168*, 171–2, 182–3, 186
in public opinion polls 34–9, *35–7*
race-conscious frames 128–38
and racial inequality in US today 47
racialized framing 142–52, 174–5,
178–83, 191, 198–200
reverse discrimination 31–2, 47–8,
49, 147–9, 151–2
threat frames 142–51, 174–5,
178–83, 185–6, 191–2, 198–200
affirmative action supporters
abstract liberalism 153–4, *162*,
163–4, 166–7, *167*, 176, 177,
190, 200–1
advocacy groups 70–1, 80–98, 111,
112, 190–1, 196–7
amicus curiae briefs 80–98
*Bakke* case 56
case studies of advocacy groups 93–8
color-blind frames 124–8, 162–7,
184, 190–1
diversity rationale 30–1, 62–3, 85,
92, 96, 97, 124–8, *139*, 140–1,
162–7, 175–7, 184, 200–1
*Fisher* cases 30, 33, *81–3*, *86–91*,
92, 97, 159–60, 161–7, 175–7,
184
*Gratz* and *Grutter* cases *81–3*,
*86–91*, 92, 96, 123–8, 138–42
heterogeneous nature of 196–7
ideological divide 27, 29–32
level of support 196–8
minimization of racism *125*, 126–7,
*127*, 166–7

past discrimination, remedying 32,
36, 37, *125*, 125–7, *162*, 164–5,
190–1
in public opinion polls 34–9, *35–7*
race-conscious frames 124–8, *125*,
*127*, *162*, 162–7, *167*
and racial inequality in US today
45–6
racialized framing 138–42, 175–7,
198
threat frames 138–42, 175–7
African American Leadership Forum
151
Alito, Justice Samuel 33–4
American Association for Affirmative
Action 163
American Bar Association 126, 177
American Civil Liberties Union
(ACLU) 140
American Civil Rights Institute 68, 78,
101, 198
American Civil Rights Union 169
American Educational Research
Association (AERA) 93–4
American Enterprise Institute 69
American Jewish Committee (AJC)
95–6, 125, 163
American National Election Studies
(ANES) 34, 36
American Sociological Association 93,
126
American values, threat to *143*, 143–5,
151, *151*, *152*, 180–1
Amherst College 126
amicus curiae briefs, function of
12–13, 70
Amicus Curiae Society of American
Law Teachers 164
Asian American Coalition for
Education 107, 108
Asian American Legal Defense and
Education Fund 107, 111
Asian American Legal Foundation
(AALF) 101, 107–9, 129
Asian Americans, and Harvard
University case 195–6

**B**

Backes, B. 50

*Bakke* case (1978) 22–3, 25, 31, 32, 52–6, 67, 96, 115, 120, 127, 130, 133, 190–1

banning of affirmative action (states) 28–9, 49–50, 193

Beckenhaur, Molly Ann 59–60

Bell, J.M. 163, 184, 200

Belyaeva, N. 73–4

Berrey, E.C. 62

Blum, Edward 2, 32, 69, 159, 195

Blume, G.H. 49–50

Blumer, H. 5, 9, 10, 14, 39, 69, 79–80, 116–17, 122, 123, 139, 142, 174, 198–9

Bobo, L. 5, 117, 199

Boden, A. 110

Bogrow, Aimee 59–60

Bolick, C. 78, 106

Bollinger, Lee 61–2

Bonilla-Silva, E. 7, 14, 39, 45, 63, 69–70, 116, 117, 121–2, 128–9, 132, 134, 152, 179

Bradley Foundation 101, 104

Brown, Jerry 29

*Brown v Board of Education* (1954) 130–1, 133, 164–5, 190

Burke, M. 118

Bush, Jeb 29, 133–4, 134–5, 136, 143, 147, 150

Bush, President George H.W. 27, 115–16

Bush, President George W. 27, 47, 93, 116

business owners 92, 124–5, 140

busing initiatives 35, *35*

**C**

Caldeira, G.A. 13

California (state)

    banning of affirmative action 28–9, 50, 193

    color-blind admissions policy 29, 193

    Proposition 209 23, 28–9, 110, 198

    *see also* University of California

Carnevale, A.P. 46

Cato Institute 74, 103–6, 130, 145, 146, 147–8, 161, 169, 180

Center for Constitutional Jurisprudence 170

Center for Equal Opportunity 2, 68, 78, 133, 137, 145–6, 148, 150

Center for Individual Freedom 101, 149

Center for Individual Rights (CIR) 68, 78, 101, 120, 161

Center for New Black Leadership 101, 133, 147, 151

Center for the Advancement of Capitalism 129, 146

Chang, M.J. 63–4

Chavez, Linda 78

Civil Rights Act 1964 21–2, 54

Civil Rights Division of the Department of Justice 26–7, 192–3

Civil Rights Movement 11, 48, 70, 76–7, 97, 115, 130

Claremont Institute 131, 134, 135–6, 144, 147, 150

Classification Act 1940 20

classification system 107, 109, 129–31, 168–9, 170, 180, 183

Clegg, Roger 2

Cokorinos, L. 3, 27, 32, 50–1, 71, 75, 76–7, 111, 112, 192, 193, 197

Colburn, D.R. 50

College Board 164

Collins Jr., P.M 70

color-blind admissions policy 29, 32, 50, 110

color-blind frames 6–7, 8, 9, 10, 14, 29–30, 32, 47, 63, 116–18, 121–3, 198–9

    affirmative action opponents 47, 77, 78–9, 128–38, 167–75, 184–5, 190–1, 198–9

    affirmative action supporters 124–8, 162–7, 184, 190–1

    *Bakke* case 54

color-blind frames (contd.)
    and diversity 31, 56, 62–3, 124–34,
        162–4, 166–7, *168*, 170, 172–3,
        184, 200
    *Fisher* cases 162–75, 184–5
    *Gratz* and *Grutter* cases 116,
        124–38, 151–2
    and threat frames 151–2, *152*,
        *185*
Colorado, banning of affirmative action
    28, 193
Colvin, Reynold H. 67
compelling interest, diversity as 3, 55,
    56, 57–8, 59–60, 119, 120, 156,
    158, 189
competition, affirmative action as 8–9,
    10, 174, 186
Connerly, Ward 29, 101, 129, 131,
    133, 146, 149, 150, 198
Constitutional Accountability Center
    84–5, 165
Constitutional Law Scholars 165
Corley, P.C. 70
Council for Minority Affairs at Texas
    A&M 166
Cox, Archibald 67
Crimmins, E.M 44
critical discourse analysis (CDA)
    154*n*1
Critical Race Studies 9–10
cultural racism 7, 121, *128*, 134–8,
    *152*, *168*, 171–2, 173, *185*
Current and Former Federal Civil
    Rights Officials 183

**D**
Declaration of Independence 131, 144,
    146
*DeFunis v Odegaard* (1974) 51–2, 54
Denson, N. 63–4
Department of Education (US) 137,
    148
desegregation 32, 35, 76
Diamond, Josef 52
disincentive, affirmative action as
    171–2

diversity rationale
    affirmative action opponents 32, 62,
        108, *128*, 129, 132–4, 148–9,
        153–4, *168*, 170, 172–3,
        189–90
    affirmative action supporters 30–1,
        62–3, 85, 92, 96, 97, 124–8,
        *139*, 140–1, 162–7, 175–7, 184,
        200–1
    and color-blind frames 31, 56,
        62–3, 124–34, 162–4, 166–7,
        *168*, 170, 172–3, 184, 200
    earlier court cases 51, 55–6, 57–8,
        59–60
    *Fisher* cases 30–1, 62, 160–1,
        162–7, 175–7, 181, 183, 184
    *Gratz* and *Grutter* cases 61, 119–20,
        124–8, 129, 148–9, 153–4, 158,
        166–7
    ideological divide 30–2
    impact of 49, 60–4, 158, 163–4
    problems with 200–1
    and threat frames *139*, 140–1,
        148–9, 150, 175–7, 181, 183
Doane, A.W. 6, 7, 118
Druckman, J.N. 6
Du Bois, W.E.B. 20, 96

**E**
Eleventh US Circuit Court of Appeals
    60
Eligibility in the Local Context
    (California) 29, 193
elite actors and groups 47, 74, 76, 101,
    112–13, 161–2, 197–8
    frames produced by 69–70, 79–80,
        117, 122, 191
Embrick, D. 6
Empire State Diversity Honors
    Scholarship Program 25
employment 21–2, 43, 150, 151, 164
    hiring preference 35–6, *35*, 37
Entman, R.M. 6, 8–9, 122, 174, 186
Equal Employment Opportunity
    Commission 22, 77–8
Equal Opportunity Center 144

Equal Protection Clause
(14th Amendment)  30, 48,
190–1, 195
*Bakke* case  54, 55
*DeFunis* case  51–2, 54
*Fisher* cases  62, 108, 159, 160, 165,
169
*Gratz* and *Grutter* cases  119, 130,
131, *139*, 140, 143–4
*Hopwood* case  57, 116, 157
eugenics paradigm  *143*, *178*, 181, 186

**F**

Fairclough, N.  154*n*1
fairness and justice  32, 47
Farmer, Rob  60
*Farmer v Ramsay* (1999)  60
Feagin, J.R.  45, 122
fear of loss  8, 122, 174
Fifth US Circuit Court of Appeals
56–8, 157, 159, 160
Fisher, Abigail  1, 31, 68, 158–9
*Fisher* v *University of Texas at Austin*
(2013 and 2016)  *see Fisher I and
II* cases
*Fisher I and II* cases  155–87
abstract liberalism  163–4
affirmative action opponents  2–3,
30–3, *99–100*, 101, *102*, 103,
108, 110, 161–2, 167–74,
178–86
affirmative action supporters  33,
*81–3*, *86–91*, 92, 97, 159–60,
161–7, 175–7, 184
color-blind frames  162–75, 184–5
compared to *Gratz/Grutter*  166–7
concerns about Supreme Court
159–60
context of  156
cultural racism  171–2
diversity rationale  30–1, 62, 160–1,
162–7, 175–7, 181, 183, 184
Equal Protection Clause  62, 108,
159, 160, 165, 169
lawyers  68–9
minimization of racism  170

naturalization  172–4
and Obama, President Barack  27,
30
public opinion  34
race-conscious frames  162–7
racialized framing  175–87
ruling of  1–2, 30–1, 62, 160–1
summary of  1–3, 157–61
threat frames  174–83, 185–6
threat to minorities  182–3
threat to society  179–81
threat to white resources  178–9
Florida  28, 29, 50, 193
*Forbes* magazine  106
*Fordice* case  165
frames/framing (theory)  5–9, 14–15,
79–80, 116–17, 120–3
*see also individual frames*
frames of communication  6, 7–8, 14,
122
frames of thought  6, 122
Frankfurter, Justice Felix  13
Fuchs, C.  107

**G**

Gallagher, C.A.  152
Gallup polls  34, 153
Garland, Judge Merrick  28, 194
Garre, Gregory G.  68
General Social Survey (GSS)  34, 35, 37
genetics  146
Georgia  50, 59–60
Ginsburg, Justice Ruth Bader  58, 160
Goffman, E.  5
Gorsuch, Justice Neil  27–8, 194
*Gratz* v *Bollinger* (2003)  *see Gratz* and
*Grutter* cases
*Gratz* and *Grutter* cases  115–54
abstract liberalism  128–32
affirmative action opponents
*99–100*, *102*, 103, 108, 123–4,
128–38, 142–54
affirmative action supporters  *81–3*,
*86–91*, 92, 96, 123–8, 138–42
and Bush, George W.  27, 47

color-blind frames  116, 124–38,
    151–2
compared to *Fisher* cases  166–7
context of  115–16
cultural racism  134–8
diversity rationale  61, 119–20,
    124–8, 129, 148–9, 153–4, 158,
    166–7
Equal Protection Clause  119, 130,
    131, *139*, 140, 143–4
lawyers  68
minimization of race  132–4
paternalism  134–8, 149–51
race-conscious frames  124–38
racialized framing  138–52
reverse discrimination  *143*, 147–9,
    151–3
ruling of  26, 119–20
summary of  118–20
threat frames  138–52
Gratz, Jennifer  68, 118
Green, D.O.N.  68
Greve, Michael  68
Grollman, E.A.  7
Grossman, G.  72–3
group positioning theory  14, 79–80,
    199–200
*see also* threat frames
Grutter, Barbara  68, 119
*Grutter* v *Bollinger* (2003)  *see Gratz* and
    *Grutter* cases
Gryphon, M.  105
Gurin, P.  63

**H**
Hamacher, Patrick  118
Hamner, J.  70
Harris, David  95
Harvard University  2, 107, 159, 194–6
Hatch Act 1939  20
health disparities  44
Helpman, E.  72–3
Henricks, K.  6
Heriot, Gail  101, 182
*Hernandez* v *Texas* (1954)  26
Hickenlooper, John  193

higher education (general)
    and affirmative action  22–6
    impact of  48–50
    and racial inequality  45–50
hiring preference  35–6, *35*, 37
history of affirmative action  19–40
    beginnings of  20–2
    in the courts  51–61
    and higher education  22–6
    ideological divide  26–34
    public opinion polls  35–8, *35–7*
    role of government  20–2
holistic approach to admissions  25–6,
    62, 157, 160, 194
Hopwood, Cheryl  57, 67–8
*Hopwood* v *University of Texas Law School*
    (1996)  29, 56–8, 67–8, 116,
    157–8, 193
Hout, M.  49

**I**
ideological divide  26–34
    diversity rationale  30–2
    individual states  28–9
    and mismatch theory  32–4
    public opinion  29–30
    in Supreme Court  27–8
income/wealth disparities  43
Independent Women's Forum  68
Indiana University  140
individualism critique  31
industry leaders  92, 124–5, 140
Initiative 200 (Washington)  29, 59
Interactionists  9–10
interracial marriage  *37*, 38

**J**
Jackman, M.R.  135, 182, 186
Jefferson, Thomas  144
Jewish organisations  95–6, 125, 163
Johnson, Derrick  96
Johnson, Jennifer  59–60
Johnson, President Lyndon  22, 46
*Johnson* v *Board of Regents of the
    University of Georgia* (2000)
    59–60

**K**

Kagan, Justice Elena 1, 109, 160
Kavanaugh, Brett 27, 28, 194
Kennedy, Justice Anthony 28, 30–1, 61, 62, 160, 194
Kennedy, President John F. 21
*Keyishian v Board of Regents* (1967) 61
King, Martin Luther 131, 148, 169
Koch brothers 103–4
Kollman, K. 80

**L**

Lawyers Committee for Civil Rights 166
League of Cities 175–6
legal advocacy groups 84, 92, 98, 107–9
Legal Momentum 84
Levine, Felice J. 93–4
Levine, M. E. 44
Liptak, A. 2, 30–1
Long, M.C. 50
Louis D. Brandeis Center for Human Rights Under Law 181, 183

**M**

Mahoney, Maureen E. 68
Mariwala, J. 195
Marshall, Justice Thurgood 27, 55, 116
Maryland 60
Matthes, J. 6
Mayer, J. 104
McCluskey, N. 106
McDonald, Michael 68
McGann, J.G. 71, 73, 77, 111–12, 197
McGuire, K. 67
media, and affirmative action 6, 8–9, 13, 75, 122, 184
Medvetz, T. 72, 74, 112
Meese, Ed 78
Mencimer, S. 33
meritocracy 23–4, 31–2, 34, 47, *128*, 130–2, 145–6, 169, 181, 191
Michalewicz, Rachel 158–9
Michigan *see Gratz* and *Grutter* cases

Mills, C.W. 145
minimization of racism 7, 9, 14, 121
  affirmative action opponents *128*, 128–9, 132–4, *137*, *152*, *168*, 170, 173, *185*
  affirmative action supporters *125*, 126–7, *127*, 166–7
mismatch perspective 32–4, *128*, 137, 150, *168*, 171, 182, 191–2
Moore, W. 31, 70, 153, 163, 184, 189, 200, 201
Mosk, Justice Stanley 55
Mountain States Legal Foundation 78, 98, 168, 180
Myrdal, G. 20

**N**

*narrowly tailored* 2–3, 26, 60, 120, 127, 133, 156, 159, 189–90
National Association for the Advancement of Colored People (NAACP) 30, 84, 96–8, 140
National Association of Scholars 144
National Education Association (NEA) 84
national solidarity *143*, 147, *178*, 180, 181
naturalization 121, *168*, 172–3, *173*, *185*
neoliberalism 32, 45, 47–8, 62, 134, 144
*New York Times, The* 3
Nieli, Russell K. 108
Ninth Circuit Court of Appeals 59
NOW Legal Defense and Education Fund 84

**O**

Obama, President Barack 27, 28, 30, 93, 156, 193
O'Connor, Justice Sandra 61, 120
Omi, M. 45, 130, 144–5, 153, 192
One Florida 29, 50
opinion polls 34–9, *35–7*
Orfield, G. 50
Owns, A. 136

**P**

Pacific Law Foundation 130
Pacific Legal Foundation (PLF) 78,
    101, 109–11, 136, 144, 147, 149,
    180, 183
Park, A. 195
Parker, Jay 77–8
past discrimination, remedying
    affirmative action opponents 106,
        *128*, 150, 191
    affirmative action supporters 32,
        36, 37, *125*, 125–7, *162*, 164–5,
        190–1
    Supreme Court rulings 26, 51, 55,
        60–1
paternalism 8, *128*, 134–8, *143*,
    149–51, *168*, 171–2, 182–3,
    186
Paxton, Ken 31
Payton, John 68
Pellicano, L. 6
Personal Achievement Index 157,
    158
perspective diversity 133
Pierce, J. 8
*Plessy v Ferguson* (1896) 20
points system 25, 118–19, 119–20
politics, and affirmative action 26–30,
    192–4
poverty levels 43
Powell, Justice Lewis 26, 31, 55–6, 61,
    63, 120, 127, 130, 133, 184, 200
professional homogeneity, threat of
    *176*, 177
Project on Fair Representation (POFR)
    2, 3, 69, 159
Proposition 209 (California) 23, 28–9,
    110, 198
public opinion
    ideological divide 29–30
    opinion polls 34–9, *35–7*
    principle–implementation divide
        38–9
    and racial inequality in US today
        45–7
Pyle, Michael 58–9

**Q**

quota system 25, 27, 47, 55, 56, 60

**R**

race-conscious frames
    affirmative action opponents
        128–38
    affirmative action supporters 124–8,
        *125*, *127*, *162*, 162–7, *167*
racial classification 107, 109, 129–31,
    168–9, 170, 180, 183
racial inequality
    current state of 42–5, 189
    in higher education 45–50
racialized framing 9, 14, 117, 120–3,
    198–200
    affirmative action opponents
        142–52, 174–5, 178–83, 191,
        198–200
    affirmative action supporters
        138–42, 175–7, 198
    *Fisher* cases 174–87
    *Gratz* and *Grutter* cases 138–52
racism lite 63, 121
Reagan, President Ronald 27, 77–9,
    192
Reason Foundation 136
*Regents of the University of California v
    Bakke* (1978) *see Bakke* case
Rehnquist, Chief Justice William
    119–20
Rein, Bert 68–9
representation, legal 67–9
resources, threat to 80, 117, 118, 191,
    199
    *Fisher* cases 174–5, *178–9*, 178–9,
        186
    *Gratz* and *Grutter* cases *143*, 145,
        *151*, *152*,
reverse discrimination
    *Bakke* case 54, 55
    and color-blind argument 47–8
    *Fisher* cases 31–2, *178*, 178–9,
        184–6
    *Gratz* and *Grutter* cases *143*, 147–9,
        151–3

*Hopwood* case 57
see also diversity rationale; Equal
    Protection Clause (14th
    Amendment)
Ritter, Bill 193
Rock, Angela 58–9
Roosevelt Thomas Jr, R. 2

**S**

Salovey, Peter 195
Sander, Richard 171
Scalia, Justice Antonin 1, 28, 32–3,
    109, 156, 160
Scanlan, L.C. 58
Scheer, J. 96
Scholars of Economics and Statistics
    172, 180
scholarships 25
School of Law of the University of
    North Carolina 139
*Scientific American* 38
Sedler, R.A. 54
segregation 20–1, 37–8, 126, 165
    desegregation 32, 35, 76
    self-segregation *168*, 172–3
separate but equal doctrine 20
Session, Jeff 106
Shapiro, John 95–6
Shapiro, T. 43–4
Shea Jr., Joseph A. 68
*Shelby County v Holder* (2013) 2, 159
Shorett, Judge Lloyd 52
Sinensky, Jeffrey 96
Smith, J.M. 21
Smith, Katuria 58–9
*Smith v the University of Washington*
    (2004) 58–9
social mobility 22, 23, 30, 39, 45, 46,
    48, 54
society, threat to
    affirmative action opponents *143*,
        145–6, 147, 168, 176–7, *176–9*,
        179–81, 184–6
    affirmative action supporters *139*,
        140–1, *142*, *162*, 163, 164,
        166–7

special interest groups (SIGs) 69, 70,
    71–6
    affirmative action opponents 98
    affirmative action supporters 84,
        92, 95–6
    see also advocacy groups/actors
        (general)
    see also individual organizations and
        legal cases
State Supreme Court of California
    54–5
State University of New York (SUNY)
    25
stereotyping *139*, 141, *143*, 150–1,
    176, *176*, *178*, 181, 183, 192
Strohl, J. 46
structural racism
    in higher education 45–50, 133,
        190
    in society today 6, 42–5, 63, 121,
        134–5, 138, 139
Students for Fair Admissions (SFFA) 2,
    159, 195
Sumerau, J.E. 7
Superior Court of California 54
Superior Court of King County,
    Washington 52
Supreme Court, political balance of
    27–8, 115–16, 194
Symbolic Interactionists 9–10

**T**

Talented Twenty programme (Florida)
    29, 193
Taylor Jr, Stuart 171
Teach for America 176
Texas (state)
    Top 10% Rule 29, 33, 50, 62,
        157–9, 160, 170, 193
    see also Fisher I & II cases
    see also individual universities
        in Texas
Texas A&M 50, 166
Texas Association of Scholars 181
Thernstrom, Abigail 171–2,
    172–3

think tanks  68, 69, 71–6, 92
    affirmative action opponents  98,
        103–6, 111–12, 197
    affirmative action supporters  84–5
    independence of  74, 75, 76, 112
    *see also* advocacy groups/actors
        (general)
    *see also individual organizations and
        legal cases*
Think Tanks and Civil Societies
    Program  71
Thomas, Justice Clarence  27, 78, 116
threat frames
    affirmative action opponents
        142–51, 174–5, 178–83, 185–6,
        191–2, 198–200
    affirmative action supporters
        138–42, 175–7
    and color-blind frames  151–2, *185*
    and diversity rationale  *139*, 140–1,
        148–9, 150, 175–7, 181, 183
    *Fisher* cases  174–83, 185–6
    *Gratz* and *Grutter* cases  138–52, 183
    theoretical framework  8–9, 10, 14,
        80, 116–18, 122–3, 198–9
Thurmond, Strom  21
Top 10% Rule (Texas)  29, 33, 50, 62,
    157–9, 160, 170, 193
Tribe, Lawrence H.  30
Truman, President Harry  20–1
Trump, President Donald  27–8, 192–3,
    194
Tuan, M.  5, 117, 199

**U**
UCLA School of Law Students of
    Color  141
United Negro College Fund  164–5
*United States v Fordice*  165
university goals, threat to  *139*, 140,
    *142*, *176*, *177*
University of California
    affirmative action ban  23, 28–9, 50
    *Bakke* case  22–3, 25, 31, 32, 52–6,
        67, 96, 115, 120, 127, 130, 133,
        190–1

UCLA School of Law Students of
    Color  141
University of California-Davis (UC-
    Davis)  52–6
University of Florida  50, 133–4
University of Georgia  59–60
University of Maryland School of
    Medicine (UMSM)  60
University of Michigan  *see Gratz* and
    *Grutter* cases
University of North Carolina  139
University of Texas at Austin  *see Fisher
    I and II* cases
University of Texas Law School (UT
    Law)  56–8
University of Washington Law School
    (UWLS)  51–2, 58–9
US Commission on Civil Rights  78,
    101
US Constitution, threat to  *139*, 140,
    *143*, 143–5, 180
    *see also* Equal Protection Clause
        (14th Amendment)
US District Court for the Southern
    District of Georgia  59–60
US District Court for the Western
    District of Texas  57
US General Counsel  130

**V**
victimization  *143*, *151*, *152*, 182, *185*
    *see also* paternalism
Voting Rights Act 1965  2, 159

**W**
Washington (state)  28, 29, 52, 59, 193
Washington Supreme Court  52
Watkins, M.  31, 32, 33–4
wealth/income disparities  43
Winant, H.  45, 130, 145, 153, 192
Wright, J.R.  13

**Y**
Yale University  194–5
Yellen, V.M.  50
Young, C.  50